TEACHER'S EDITION

MW00581465

On Location 1

Reading and Writing for Success in the Content Areas

Thomas Bye
with John Chapman

On Location 1 Teacher's Edition, 1st Edition

Published by McGraw-Hill ESL/ELT, a business unit of The McGraw-Hill Companies, Inc., 1221 Avenue of the Americas, New York, NY 10020.

ISBN-13: 978-0-07-288675-7
ISBN-10: 0-07-288675-7

2 3 4 5 6 7 8 9 QPD/QPD 11 10 09 08 07 06

Editorial director: Tina B. Carver
Executive editor: Erik Gundersen
Senior developmental editor: Mari Vargo
Developmental editor: Fredrik Liljeblad
Production manager: Juanita Thompson
Cover designer: Wee Design Group
Interior designer: Wee Design Group

Photo Credits:

Cover Images: From the Getty Images Royalty-Free Collection: Female College Student; Railroad Crossing; Ice Cream Cone; Praying Mantis; Shark; **From the Corbis Royalty-Free Collection:** Male College Student; Lion; Guitar; **Other Images:** Volcano: Jim Sugar/CORBIS; Avalanche Area: Dave Schiefelbein/Getty Images; Outfielder: Getty Images; Goalkeeper: Chris Cole/Getty Images; Akashi Kaikyo Bridge: Kyodo News; Man with Frozen Sunglasses: Patrick Endres/Alaska Stock; Angel Falls: James Marshall/CORBIS; Globe spread: William Westheimer/CORBIS.

www.esl-elt.mcgraw-hill.com

The McGraw·Hill Companies

TABLE OF CONTENTS

Scope and Sequence

Unit	Readings	Genres/ Writing Tasks	Reading Strategies	Word Work/ Spelling and Phonics
1 All about Me! page 2	Frame and name collages from the Internet	Personal information: "Me" collages	Using pictures to understand written information	Adjectives that describe people Pronouncing words with the letter *i*
2 Signs page 20	Selections from the book *Signs*	Environmental print: signs and symbols	Using pictures and images to understand environmental print	Root words Pronouncing words with the letter *a*
3 My Web Page page 38	Personal Web pages on the Internet	Personal Web pages Sentences	Using pictures to predict	Compound words Pronouncing words with the pattern *o* + consonant + *e*
4 Where Are We? page 56	Selections from *Looking at Maps and Globes*	Maps and mapping	Using pictures and visuals to understand written information	Antonyms Spelling the /s/ sound as in *miss* and *city*
5 Mean and Lazy page 74	Selections from *The Meanest: Amazing Facts about Mean Animals* and *The Laziest: Amazing Facts about Lazy Animals*	Informational writing: field guide	Finding details	Word groups: size, length, and weight Pronouncing words with the letter *a*

Grammar	Organization	Style	Writing Conventions	Content Area Connections	Links to Literature
The verb *be*	Organizing information in categories	Expressing meaning with visual images	Capitalization with the names of people	Art Math	Name poem
Imperatives	Organizing information in categories	Expressing meaning with visual images	Capitalization with the names of towns and cities	Civics	Poem "NO" by Shel Silverstein
Complete sentences	Organizing information in categories	Expressing meaning with visual images	End-of-sentence punctuation	Computers Graphing (Column Charts)	Autobiography poem
Plural nouns	Using elements of maps	Using features and conventions of maps	Capitalization with place names on maps and globes	Geography (location, measurement terms, landforms)	Poem "Number Four" by Charlotte Pomerantz
Subject-verb agreement	Using elements of field guides	Using precise adjectives	Using colons to introduce information	Animal life Geography Measurement: size and weight	Alphabet poem

Scope and Sequence

Unit	Readings	Genres/ Writing Tasks	Reading Strategies	Word Work/ Spelling and Phonics
6 You Can Cook! page 92	Recipes from the *Everything® Kids' Cookbook*	How-to instructions: recipes	Visualizing	Compound words Idioms Spelling the /k/ sound as in *king* and *cat*
7 Top Five page 110	Feature articles from *Time for Kids*	Surveys	Comparing Note taking	Word families: related nouns and verbs Words with digraphs
8 Memories page 128	Selections from "My First Sports Memory," from *Sports Illustrated for Kids*	Personal memories	Questioning the author	Synonyms Pronouncing words with silent consonants
9 Tall, Taller, Tallest page 146	Selections from *Hottest, Coldest, Highest, Deepest*	Short reports: our world	Using visuals to understand written information	Ordinal numbers Reading words with *i* + consonant + *e*
10 What Do You Think? page 164	Pro and con opinion columns from *Sports Illustrated for Kids*	Opinion columns	Evaluating ideas	Word families: related nouns and adjectives Spelling the sound /ī/ as in *my* and *high*

Grammar	Organization	Style	Writing Conventions	Content Area Connections	Links to Literature
Prepositions of location	Using elements of how-to instructions; time order	Using snappy names and titles	Numbering: time order	Measurement: amounts Nutrition Home Economics	Recipe poem
Present tense questions	Structuring of a report of information	Writing introductions that grab the reader's attention	Numbering: order of importance	Fractions, decimals, percent Graphing (pie charts)	List poem
Simple past tense	Using elements of personal narrative	Using descriptive adjectives	Capitalization of pronouns	Athletics	Memory poem
Comparatives and superlatives	Organizing an informational paragraph	Combining sentences	Exclamation points	Geography (location, measurement terms, landforms) Graphing (pictographs)	Diamante poem
Making comparisons: *as…as, more…than*	Using elements of opinion columns	Using quoted words in writing	Punctuation with quotation marks	Civics	Poem "Point of View" by Shel Silverstein

Welcome to On Location

How Does the Teacher's Edition Work?

The *On Location* **Teacher's Edition** is organized around each unit in the Student Book. An overview of each unit describes the lessons and identifies the standards that are addressed in each lesson. Each page from the Student Book is reproduced and accompanied by helpful notes and suggestions for use.

Each lesson has three parts—

- A **Warm Up** engages the attention of students and focuses them on the lesson objective.
- **Teaching the Lesson** provides teachers with step-by-step suggestions for actively engaging students in each activity.
- A **Wrap Up** provides lesson closure—enabling the teacher to assess student learning.

In addition to providing procedural notes and suggestions for use, each unit in the Teacher's Edition includes extra teaching tips and ideas for employing best practices, technology tips, culture notes, and tips for using the Practice Book. Opportunities for assessment and recycling are also included. Many of these useful features are accompanied by icons:

Best Practice	✓ Assessment
Access for All	Re-teaching/Recycling
Using Technology	**PB** Practice Book reference

Student Book answer keys are included after the procedural notes for each lesson, and a Practice Book answer key can be found at the back of the Teacher's Edition.

Components at a Glance

The *On Location* program is organized into three levels. Book 1 enables students to meet beginning-level standards for reading, writing, and oral language. By the end of Book 1, students are able to read simple paragraphs and write well-formed, connected sentences. Book 2 enables students to meet early intermediate standards. By the end of Book 2, students are able to read simple multi-paragraph selections and write related paragraphs. Book 3 enables students to meet intermediate-level standards. By the end of Book 3, students are able to read and produce simple essays—writing that informs, explains, analyzes, and persuades.

Each **Student Book** is organized into ten engaging, task-based units, each focusing on a particular nonfiction reading and writing genre. Every reading is authentic—giving students opportunities to read a variety of real-world text selections they will encounter in school and in their lives and to produce writing in the same academic genres.

Along the way, students engage in structured listening and speaking activities that develop academic language functions, promote thinking and discussion, and build motivation.

Each unit also opens doors to academic content. Students explore topics in science, social studies, and geography, and learn essential academic vocabulary and skills to help them tackle grade-level content across the curriculum. In addition, every unit provides literature that extends the content of the readings.

The **Practice Book** provides students with the opportunity to master the reading skills, vocabulary, and grammar introduced in the Student Book while allowing them to evaluate their own writing and practice test-taking skills. Activities allow students to further explore unit topics, respond to literature selections, and discover how much they learned from the activities and writing tasks in the Student Books.

The **Audio Program** includes taped activities that develop social and academic listening skills. Each reading selection in the Student Book is accompanied by audio, providing students with the opportunity to listen to multiple speakers and various genres.

***On Location* Phonics** provides systematic, explicit instruction that helps students who are new to English hear the sound patterns of their new language and use knowledge of sound-letter relationships to read and write high-frequency words and phrases that they hear and see around them. Incorporating a "fast-track" approach, this optional component enables newcomers to learn both language and content from day one. Teaching notes at the bottom of each student page make *On Location* Phonics a self-contained program.

The *On Location* program includes a powerful **Staff Development Video** to support implementation of the program. The video provides strategies for teaching reading and writing from a language arts perspective—focusing on best practices such as pre-teaching vocabulary, use of read aloud/think aloud techniques, interactive reading, modeled writing, shared writing, use of rubrics, and cooperative learning. The training video provides strategies for reading and writing in the content areas and demonstrates how *On Location* can be used effectively.

The *On Location* **Assessment System** includes a placement test, a diagnostic, end-of-unit tests, and an end-of-level test for each book. Task-specific rubrics (or "ChecBrics") help students plan, revise, and evaluate their work.

Due to the *On Location* program's emphasis on academic reading and writing, teachers can be sure that *On Location* will help their school meet Adequate Yearly Progress (AYP) targets. The *On Location* assessment system supports district accountability efforts by providing tools that enable teachers to evaluate mastery of English language development/English language arts standards.

ACADEMIC LITERACY: FIVE "POWER STANDARDS" FOR SUCCESS

If English Learners are to achieve world-class standards in the content areas, they must develop high levels of academic literacy—the language, thinking, and learning tools needed to achieve content standards across the academic curriculum. Five *On Location* Power Standards guarantee that students can compete across the academic curriculum. Organized in three levels, *On Location* benchmarks ramp students up to early advanced proficiency in English.

❶ Use listening and speaking skills and strategies to accomplish academic tasks in the content areas.

Book 1	Book 2	Book 3
▪ Listen for the main idea ▪ Use academic language functions—seeking information, identifying, describing, narrating, sequencing, and classifying ▪ Ask and answer informational questions ▪ Participate in structured whole-class, group activities ▪ Give short oral presentations	▪ Listen for details ▪ Use academic language functions—comparing, analyzing, justifying, persuading, and evaluating ▪ Initiate and answer questions that elicit explanation ▪ Work with peers to complete a task or solve a problem ▪ Give more extended oral presentations	▪ Listen to learn ▪ Use academic language functions—inferring, problem solving, and synthesizing ▪ Initiate and answer questions that involve higher-order thinking ▪ Participate in sustained discussion and debate ▪ Give elaborate oral presentations

❷ Use decoding and word attack skills, knowledge of vocabulary, and knowledge of grammar to read fluently.

Book 1	Book 2	Book 3
▪ Decode familiar words ▪ Read common sight words ▪ Use simple word clues to unlock meaning	▪ Use knowledge of English phonemes, morphemes, and syntax to decode simple text ▪ Use word attack skills to read unfamiliar words ▪ Use context to figure out the meaning of new words	▪ Read aloud with accuracy, correct pacing, and expression ▪ Distinguish words with multiple meanings ▪ Identify members of word families ▪ Recognize idioms and figurative language

❸ Read and understand a range of academic text materials.

Book 1	Book 2	Book 3
■ Read familiar words, phrases, and short sentences ■ Answer simple factual questions ■ Identify sequence and logical order in text ■ Read and respond to literature ■ Use pictures and signpost words to predict ■ Read short connected paragraphs with guidance	■ Read simple narratives and informational texts ■ Identify the main idea and details ■ Identify patterns in text: sequence, compare/contrast, and cause and effect ■ Read and respond to literature ■ Identify the purposes of different texts ■ Use context to predict ■ Restate and summarize information ■ Use basic reading strategies to unlock meaning	■ Read a range of narrative, expository, and persuasive texts (essays) ■ Read text from the content areas ■ Follow the logical sequence of arguments in persuasive text ■ Read and respond to literature ■ Compare and contrast information ■ Use cognitive and metacognitive strategies to unlock meaning

❹ Write effectively across a variety of academic genres.

Book 1	Book 2	Book 3
■ Write three or four related sentences within a guided structure ■ Record information and ideas in categories ■ Use graphic tools to record ideas and information ■ Use the writing process	■ Produce writing that shows a simple awareness of purpose, audience, and style ■ Use graphic tools to organize ideas ■ Write a paragraph with a topic sentence and details or examples ■ Use the writing process	■ Produce writing that shows a more sophisticated awareness of purpose, audience, and style ■ Show personal voice in writing ■ Write an essay with a controlling idea that sheds light on a subject ■ Use graphic tools to show relationships ■ Use the writing process

5 **Apply the conventions of English usage orally and in writing.**

Book 1	Book 2	Book 3
■ Produce subject-verb-object sentences ■ Produce target grammatical forms in structured activities ■ Spell words in sentences with controlled vocabulary ■ Spell familiar short vowel and sight words ■ Use sentence-level punctuation and capitalization ■ Edit writing for correctness	■ Produce sentences with some variation and elaboration ■ Accurately produce target grammatical forms in structured activities ■ Spell words in sentences with controlled vocabulary ■ Edit writing for correctness	■ Use complex sentences in writing with correct coordination and subordination of ideas ■ Use transitions to elaborate ideas ■ Spell frequently misspelled words ■ Use conventions in grade-level written work ■ Edit writing for correctness

Best Practices: Helping Students Develop Academic Literacy

The *On Location* Teacher's Editions are designed for teachers who are working to ensure that their students develop powerful reading and writing skills—teachers just like you! Each lesson in the Teacher's Edition describes an array of research-based teaching practices whose use will ensure that English Learners will master the five *On Location* Power Standards.

***On Location* Power Standard ❶** Use listening and speaking skills and strategies to accomplish academic tasks in the content areas.

Structured Listening—Students listen for a purpose to a taped activity, then respond by sharing with a classmate, writing a sentence, taking a position, or otherwise showing that they understand. Structured listening activities are most effective when the tape or CD is played twice—each time with a different listening prompt.

Structured Interaction—Working in pairs (**Heads Together**), small groups (**Team Talk**), or as a class (**Let's Talk**), students explore a question or topic that results in a written product—a word or sentence, a completed chart or other graphic, or some other work product.

Oral Presentation Rubrics—Before students give an oral presentation, they work together to develop a checklist-type rubric that will help them plan their presentation and that the class will use to evaluate each presentation. The rubric should include from three to five indicators related to effectiveness of the presentation, accuracy of content, and "stage presence."

***On Location* Power Standard ❷** Use decoding and word attack skills, knowledge of vocabulary, and knowledge of grammar to read fluently.

Fluency and expression

Shared Reading—Students share the reading of a text to develop fluency and expression. Typical shared reading activities may include *echo reading* (students echoing the words of the teacher after reading), *choral reading* (students reading at the same time as the teacher), and *partial-completion reading* (teacher reading most of the text, then pausing for students to read words or phrases).

Preteaching vocabulary: alternatives to dictionary use

Word Check—Using finger signals (thumbs up, thumbs down, thumbs sideways), students show whether they think they can define a word, have seen the word but can't define it, or have never seen the word. This strategy is used before and after a vocabulary lesson to help engage students in the study of words and to enable the teacher to assess learning.

Contextual Redefinition—Working in small groups, students attempt to define six to eight words they will encounter in a reading, using prior knowledge. They are then presented with each word used in a sentence that provides clues to the word's meaning. Students revisit and modify their definitions

Word Clues—The teacher presents challenging new vocabulary in short explanations or anecdotes that help students hear the words in context. The teacher takes care to provide examples, to paraphrase the target word, and to make explanations concrete.

Developing word-analysis and vocabulary skills

Word Study—Each unit of *On Location* includes structured word study activities which focus on the development of vocabulary, how words are formed, and spelling and phonics.

Mini-Lesson—Each short lesson focuses on a single skill, strategy, or procedure related to the reading or writing students are doing. For example, as students read, the teacher might stop to show students how knowledge of prefixes can help them understand the meaning of unfamiliar words. Mini-lessons usually include both explanation and demonstration. These lessons are most effective when students help contribute additional examples.

Word Map—A word map is a visual representation of a definition. A word map shows the category to which a word belongs, its features or properties, and examples of the term. For example, a word map might show that a reptile is an animal (category), that it is cold-blooded and covered with scales (properties), and that rattlesnakes, alligators, and crocodiles are examples. The teacher can help students create word maps on the chalkboard, using shared/interactive writing techniques.

Word Family Charts—Students fill in partially-completed charts that include word family members that are related in meaning but are different parts of speech—for example, *educate*, *educated*, and *education.*

Understanding how English grammar works

Grammar Study—Each unit of *On Location* includes a structured grammar study lesson that focuses on a rule of English grammar or on how English sentences work. These lessons include a "Listen Up" activity, which develops metalinguistic awareness.

Structured Language Practice Activities—Structured language practice—including both guided and independent practice activities—helps students produce and practice specific points of grammar or the use of functions. *Completion activities* require students to supply the target form in an oral sentence stem. *Transformation activities* require students to change a particular prompt—for example, changing the subject from singular to plural, then making other changes in the sentence.

On Location Power Standard ❸ Read and understand a range of academic text materials.

Three-Step Passage Reading—For each selection, the Teacher's Edition provides a three-step approach to help students read and understand the passage.

1. **My Turn (Read Aloud/Think Aloud)**—The teacher reads a selection aloud to students, modeling what good readers do, what readers are thinking as they read, and how they use reading strategies to unlock meaning. This step also provides an opportunity for the teacher to—

   - build background knowledge
   - note the author's purpose and audiences
   - focus on the meaning of individual words and how words are strung together to form sentences
   - note a grammar point
   - teach and model a specific reading strategy—for example, predicting what comes next

2. **Our Turn (Interactive Reading)**—Interactive reading is a collaborative reading experience guided by the teacher. Students follow along as the teacher reads, then they join in on the reading. The teacher focuses on aspects of the reading process, again modeling the use of strategies to unlock meaning. During passage reading, the teacher may comment on the selection or pose questions that cause students to engage more deeply in the meaning and language of the selection. The teacher can help students figure out the meaning of unfamiliar vocabulary as they read, using context and specific word-solving skills (e.g., knowledge of roots and affixes, word relationships, etc.) and encourage students to talk about the text. The teacher can also prompt students to notice text structure, identify stylistic features, or comment on the language in the text.

3. **Your Turn (Independent Reading)**—Finally, the student tackles the text on his or her own. The direction line before each reading always provides the student with a task of some sort that will enhance student learning.

Use of graphic organizers: clusters, charts, diagrams—A graphic organizer is a visual that defines relationships among ideas, concepts, or elements of a text. Graphic organizers can be used before, during, and after reading. They can enhance readiness for learning, understanding of materials, and recall.

Graphic organizers are most often used to develop knowledge of vocabulary and key concepts; to help organize pre-reading predictions; to tap prior knowledge and organize thinking; to analyze the structure of various forms of narrative; and to organize information presented in expository text. A variety of graphic organizers is always provided in the student materials.

Checks for Understanding—Frequent checking for understanding is essential for monitoring student learning and adjusting teaching. A variety of strategies for checking for understanding is embedded throughout each unit.

- **Summarizing**—After reading a paragraph or passage, have students summarize what they have read or respond to the text.
- **Question All-Write**—The teacher interrupts students as they read to pose a written question about the passage. The teacher uses student responses to enhance discussion of the reading or reteach an important concept. The strategy also builds "wait time" into question-answer routines.
- **Outcome Sentence**—Students respond to a written sentence stem at the end of a lesson. Typical sentence stems include "I learned that ____________" or "I still wonder about ____________." Students then share their responses with classmates, enabling the teacher to audit student learning and to build on student responses.
- **Sentence Synthesis**—The teacher writes three or four key terms from the reading or lesson on the board. Students use these words to write a meaningful sentence (or two) that summarizes the main idea of the reading or lesson.

On Location Power Standard ❹ Write effectively across a variety of academic genres.

Use of the Writing Process—Students move through a structured process that results in a polished written product in a particular genre and shares it with an audience. Steps in the writing process include "Getting It Out," during which students select a writing topic and organize their ideas, typically using a graphic organizer of some sort; "Getting It Down," during which students develop a first draft, typically using an outline;

"Getting it Right," during which students revise and edit their writing, usually relying on the supportive feedback of peers (**Group Share**); and "Presenting It"—when students share a final draft with classmates.

Shared Writing—The teacher and students discuss, then share in the writing of a common text related to a topic under discussion, something the class has been studying, or a common class experience. The teacher is the scribe, using the board, chart paper, or an overhead transparency. The teacher can use the shared writing to model both reading and writing strategies as text is created—facilitating discussion and providing instruction in text organization, style, grammar, and conventions of print. The students are seen as writing "apprentices."

Interactive Writing—Like shared writing, interactive writing is a collaborative activity in which the teacher and students create text. Students typically share the decision about what they are going to write and also "share the pen." As in shared writing, the students are seen as writing "apprentices."

Language Experience Approach—The language experience approach (LEA) promotes reading and writing—usually some form of narrative—through the use of personal experiences and oral language. The underlying premise is that students will learn to read material that stems from their own experiences. Students generate their own reading material from their own oral language and begin to read the words they already know.

The most basic form of LEA involves the transcription of an individual student's personal experience. The experience is transcribed as the learner dictates it, without transcriber corrections to grammar or vocabulary. This technique keeps the focus on the content rather than the form of what is written. Errors are corrected later, during revising and editing stages of the writing process. With beginning students, the writing may only be several sentences long.

Modeled Writing—Modeled writing enables students to see how the teacher thinks as s/he writes. In a modeled writing episode, the teacher chooses the genre, particular focus, content, and structure. The product is the teacher's—not a product that is the result of collaboration among students. It is a well-formed piece of writing that helps students develop insights into the writing process.

Writing Frames—Writing frames provide a scaffold for students as they produce writing that follows a particular organizational pattern. The frame provides words and phrases that help guide the student's writing.

Graphic Organizers—Graphic organizers—timelines, T-charts, Venn diagrams, or concept charts—help students organize their ideas and generate support to make their writing come alive. Every unit in the Student Book provides a graphic organizer to help students "get it out." The Practice Book includes blank graphic organizers to help students move through prewriting activities.

Use of Rubrics—Students are encouraged to use task-anchored "ChecBrics," which are included at the end of the Student Book and at the end of the Practice Book to plan and polish their writing. Organized around four major facets of writing—organization, content, style, and grammar/mechanics—students "check" to make sure that they have addressed each indicator, then give themselves an overall rating. They attach the ChecBric to their writing before they put it in their portfolios.

Guided Revision—Every Writer's Workshop provides step-by-step guidance that helps students revise their writing. Focusing on key traits related to the writing task, students systematically examine their first drafts and are provided with structured guidance for additions or modifications.

Group Share—Students produce their best writing when they have a chance to "audition" their writing and receive feedback from peers before they develop a final draft.

Portfolios—Portfolios enable students to keep their best writing in one place and help the teacher conference with students. The teacher might consider creating a tabbed hanging folder for each student, kept in a colorful plastic bin in the classroom.

Notebooks—Notebooks allow students to create their own reference lists of important ideas, useful vocabulary, word formations, grammar rules, etc. Students can include definitions and sample sentences to enrich their personal reference materials.

***On Location* Power Standard ❺** Apply the conventions of English usage orally and in writing.

Mini-Lesson—As with word analysis and vocabulary skills, mini-lessons on oral or written conventions can be embedded in reading or writing activities that students are doing. For example, as students read, the teacher might stop to point out the use of punctuation with quotation marks. Or, as students talk, the teacher might address the appropriate use of a particular academic language function.

Interactive Editing—The teacher either dictates or presents several sentences that include problems related to capitalization, punctuation, grammar, spelling, or word choice. Students write or copy the sentences, then edit them individually or with a partner. The class then discusses the particular convention and its use.

Developing Academic Literacy: A Research-Based Approach

Thomas Bye, Ph.D.

If English Learners are to achieve rigorous *academic standards*, they must develop high levels of *academic literacy*—that is, the language, thinking, and learning tools needed to achieve content standards across the curriculum. Related to the construct of cognitive academic language proficiency (Cummins, 1981), the concept of academic literacy is broad, encompassing the listening and speaking skills students need to read and write in the content areas; strategies for comprehending, processing, and producing texts in academic disciplines and contexts; the formal rules and patterns of language; readers' and writers' purposes and roles; and knowledge of language use in a social context. *On Location* incorporates key elements of traditional literacy approaches, student-centered frameworks such as the Cognitive Academic Language Learning Approach (Chamot & O'Malley, 1994, 1999), and a socioliterate view of academic literacies (Johns, 1997), providing a genre-based approach that—

- enables students to explore the purposes, structures, and stylistic ground rules of various forms of text—within a social context;
- helps students gain insight into their own reading and writing processes as a means of taking responsibility for their own learning;
- helps students develop a toolkit of strategies for comprehending text and producing academic writing;
- helps students master the patterns, rules, and conventions of written language.

Best teaching approaches and practices, confirmed by research, provide the underpinnings for the innovative *On Location* approach.

Skills for Beginning Readers

❶ **Explicit, systematic phonemic awareness and phonics instruction helps students learn to read—provided that it helps make text comprehensible.**

On Location recognizes that many students who are new to English need to develop phonemic awareness and decoding skills if they are to read fluently. The National Reading Panel (2000) reports that teaching phonemic awareness provided value-added results for students across a range of grade levels and that systematic phonics instruction improves older students' decoding, spelling, and oral reading skills. *On Location* enables teachers to incorporate phonics instruction into a comprehensive reading program that allows for the differentiated use of phonics instruction, based on individual need—especially students who do not know how an alphabetic language like English works. Because *On Location* Phonics activities are always linked to meaningful text rather than presented as isolated rules or patterns, the direct teaching of phonics helps make selections more comprehensible—and thus helps students learn to read (Krashen, 2004; Smith, 1994). And each unit in Books 1–3 provides instruction that enables students to explore relationships between common sound/spelling patterns—promoting fluent reading and comprehension.

❷ **Reading fluency contributes to comprehension of text.**

The ability to read orally with ease, accuracy, and expression is one of several critical factors necessary for reading comprehension. According to National Reading Panel findings, structured practice in oral reading has a significant and positive impact on word recognition, fluency, and comprehension. *On Location* Phonics includes structured oral reading activities that build fluency. The Teacher's Editions for Books 1–3 provide suggestions for interactive passage reading activities that promote reading with accuracy and expression.

Reading Comprehension

On Location adopts the definition outlined by the RAND Reading Study Group (RRSG) that reading comprehension is a process of both extracting and constructing meaning involving the interaction of three elements: the reader, the text, and the activity or purpose for reading (RRSG, 2002)—within a social context. *On Location* helps teachers orchestrate these elements to ensure that English Learners develop powerful reading comprehension skills.

❶ Effective comprehension instruction is driven by clear student outcomes.

Effective teachers identify clear learning outcomes for their students, and they provide highly-scaffolded instruction to help students meet these goals. Scaffolded instruction includes explanation and modeling of the reading process and coaching in how to use the process to understand novel text (Dole et al, 1991; Hogan & Pressley, 1997; Roehler & Duffy, 1991; National Reading Panel, 2000). Every *On Location* unit incorporates a predictable, "backwards buildup" approach that enables students to produce academic writing based on models of authentic, high-quality text. Carefully designed learning activities address standards for academic literacy. Standards are identified for every lesson in the Teacher's Edition, and step-by-step suggestions show the teacher how to scaffold each activity in the Student Book.

❷ Effective reading comprehension instruction relies on the use of challenging but manageable text materials.

Effective teachers use text selections that students can read with guidance from the teacher. They consider the linguistic and cognitive demands of reading selections and scaffold reading experiences to provide all students with access to high-level text (Hiebert, 1999). *On Location* provides students with high-interest, instructional-level text that helps them read in the content areas. The Teacher's Edition provides passage reading techniques for ensuring that all students can access reading selections.

❸ Effective teachers have a repertoire of techniques for enhancing students understanding of different types of text.

Effective teachers have a repertoire of techniques for enhancing students' comprehenion of specific texts—including use of quick writes and other evidence checks; techniques for structured engagement, including cooperative learning; use of questioning strategies; and summarization (National Reading Panel, 2000; Duke & Pearson, 2002). *On Location* provides an array of interactive activities—including accountable talk—that promote comprehension and provides frequent checks for understanding throughout every lesson.

❹ Effective reading comprehension instruction activates prior knowledge and builds background.

Accomplished teachers recognize that background knowledge is a critical factor in reading for meaning, and they help activate prior knowledge before students read so that topics and concepts in reading selections are more accessible (Keene & Zimmermann, 1997). Teachers also help build background knowledge during the reading process. Every unit of *On Location* includes interactive activities that connect students to prior experiences, introduce the topic of the readings, and develop key concepts and vocabulary they will need as they tackle the readings.

❺ Effective reading comprehension instruction teaches students the processes and strategies used by expert readers.

Expert readers use an array of strategies to construct meaning before, during, and after reading. Research confirms that comprehension can be improved when students learn to use specific cognitive and metacognitive strategies and to reason strategically when they encounter difficult text (Baker & Brown, 1984; Rinehart et al., 1986; Pearson et al., 1990). English Learners, in particular, benefit from instruction that focuses on the use of cognitive and metacognitive strategies (Padron, 1992; Chamot & O'Malley, 1994).

On Location helps students use key reading strategies that researchers have identified as critical to comprehension and vary the use of strategies according to the purpose and characteristics of the genre (Cooper, 1993; Kintch, 1998; National Reading Panel, 2000). Students learn to *identify important information*, including critical facts and details; use *prediction* and *inferencing* skills; *monitor their own understanding* of text and adjust their use of strategies; practice *generating questions* as they read; and *summarize* what they have read to show understanding. And, on nearly every page, students use *graphic organizers* to organize their thinking.

❻ Vocabulary instruction increases text comprehension.

The larger the student's oral and reading vocabulary, the easier it is to make sense of text (National Reading Panel,

2000). Both direct and indirect vocabulary instruction predicts gains in reading comprehension. Researchers have also established that vocabulary and word analysis skills instruction increases the reading vocabulary of English Learners (Jimenez, 1997; Klinger & Vaughn, 2000).

On Location provides students with a variety of engaging activities for learning new vocabulary—before, during, and after reading. Students use context to define words, use new words in meaningful sentences, and engage in activities that extend content-area vocabulary.

❼ Effective reading comprehension instruction engages students in reading across the curriculum.

If students are to succeed, they must be able to read across a wide variety of academic genres—including narrative, descriptive, expository, persuasive, and simple literary texts. They do this through a well-planned curriculum that includes reading in the content areas (Chamot & O'Malley, 1994). *On Location* units are organized by genre, providing students with content-based reading selections across the academic curriculum.

❽ Instruction in a variety of genres, text structures, and coherence relations improves comprehension.

Research shows a strong relationship between text comprehension and how expository text is organized (Pearson & Fielding, 1991). Students' ability to understand the complex material in textbooks is increased when they are able to identify coherence relations in text—using words, phrases, sentences, and other markers to understand the organization and flow of ideas (Graesser et al., 2002). Every *On Location* lesson helps students explore and analyze the organizational features of the reading selections they have read, focusing on strategies the writer uses to create coherence—that is, reader-friendly text.

Developing Powerful Writers

❶ Students learn to write by writing.

As with reading, students learn to write through frequent in-class and out-of-class opportunities that involve writing for a variety of purposes and audiences (NCTE, 2004). *On Location* provides students with a variety of writing scenarios and tasks that enable them to explore a range of purposes, audiences, and social contexts for producing written discourse. The Practice Book provides students with extension activities that reinforce the use of new writing skills.

❷ Reading and writing are inter-related meaning making processes.

Students who are good readers are more likely to develop as effective writers. In order for students to write a particular type of text, it is helpful if they read the same type of text. Writing also helps students become better readers (NCTE, 2004). Further, when reading and writing occur together, evaluative thinking and taking other perspectives occurs (Tierney, 1990). In every unit, students read two or more exemplars of the type of writing they will produce. Activities cause students to engage in oral communication that uses the same academic language functions they will use in writing.

❸ Writing in the content areas improves both academic literacy and content learning.

When students write about topics in the content areas, they examine concepts and ideas in a subject area and develop and practice key literacy skills related to reading comprehension, vocabulary, and word attack skills. Writing across the curriculum helps students explore new concepts and take the time to process what they are learning. Writing also helps students thoughtfully explore issues, in the context of various content areas (Barr et al., 1991). Writing in the content areas also helps students move beyond the textbook, inquiring into topics as they write (Fredricks et al, 1997). *On Location* provides students with writing tasks that link to the social sciences, sciences, and, through response, to literature.

❹ Instruction in the writing process develops effective writers.

Researchers have explored how accomplished writers write, examining how students plan, draft, and revise their work (Emig, 1971; Graves, 1983; Calkins, 1986, 1991). Writers move back and forth among the stages of the writing process as they shape and polish their work. As students become more experienced, making the writing process their own, they become more skillful at producing academic writing. Whatever the content area or the type of writing, students can use the writing process to produce writing across the content areas. Every unit of *On Location* includes a culminating writer's workshop, which provides practice, within an interactive setting, in use of the writing process.

5 Grammar and conventions are most effectively taught within the context of writing.

Because writing occurs in a social context, students need to learn to control the conventions established for public texts (NCTE, 2004). Experts argue for the teaching of grammar and mechanics in context (Weaver, 1996). *On Location* provides both lessons in grammar—focusing on grammar points that commonly occur in student writing—and mini-lessons that focus on written conventions.

All about Me!

Unit Overview

Section	At a Glance	Standards
Before You Begin	Students explore a collage of photos, drawings, and words that describe a young girl.	■ Derive meaning from visual information ■ Name people and objects
A. Connecting to Your Life	Students do a "People Search," finding classmates who fit various descriptions.	■ Listen for details ■ Ask questions ■ Describe people
B. Getting Ready to Read	Students talk about what makes them and others special. They also learn useful vocabulary.	■ Use context to understand the meaning of new words ■ Describe people and share information about yourself
C. Reading to Learn	Students read a collage, then talk about things they are good at. PRACTICE BOOK: Students write sentences about someone based on his collage.	■ Read and understand words and phrases ■ Share information about yourself
D. Word Work	Students learn positive and negative adjectives that describe people. PRACTICE BOOK: Students match words with pictures.	■ Describe others ■ Identify sound/spelling relationships
E. Grammar	Students make sentences using the simple present tense of the verb *be*. PRACTICE BOOK: Students complete sentences using *am/'m*, *is/'s*, and *are/'re*.	■ Recognize and use complete sentences
F. Bridge to Writing	Students read a second collage. PRACTICE BOOK: Students practice taking Reading Vocabulary and Reading Comprehension tests. PRACTICE BOOK: Students use a Venn diagram to compare what different people like and dislike.	■ Describe and compare likes and dislikes ■ Use a graphic organizer to organize and express information

Section	At a Glance	Standards
G. Writing Clinic	Students organize information about what people are like, what they like, and what they like to do. PRACTICE BOOK: Students use information in a short paragraph to complete a chart describing Stefan. PRACTICE BOOK: Students explore what images can tell about people.	■ Categorize information ■ Use visuals to express information
H1. Writer's Workshop: Getting It Out	Students plan a "me" collage, thinking of words and collecting images that tell about themselves. PRACTICE BOOK: Students use a chart to brainstorm information about themselves.	■ Use the writing process: prewriting ■ Write words and phrases ■ Identify images that have meaning
H2. Writer's Workshop: Getting It Down	Students organize words and images in their collages.	■ Use the writing process: drafting
H3. Writer's Workshop: Getting It Right	Students revise their collages.	■ Use the writing process: revising and editing
H4. Writer's Workshop: Presenting It	Students present their collages to their classmates and give each other positive feedback.	■ Give a short oral presentation
I. Beyond the Unit	Students stage an art show for their collages. Students read and respond to name poems, then write their own. PRACTICE BOOK: Students use a form to complete their own name poems.	■ Read and understand simple written instructions ■ Label information ■ Write a short invitation ■ Read and respond to poetry ■ Write a simple poem

BEFORE YOU BEGIN

Standards
- Derive meaning from visual information
- Name people and objects

- Have students look at the collage on page 3. Ask: *How is this different from most pictures?* (It's a combination of a lot of different words and pictures.) Ask: *Who made the collage? What does this collage tell us?* (It tells us something about Connie, the person who made it.)

Shared Writing Ask students to name things they see in the collage. List their responses on the board.

- Have students read the title of the unit. Ask: *What do you think you are going to do in this unit?* (Make a collage, describe myself.)

Unit 1 All about Me!

Read...
- "Me" collages. Learn about what other students are like.

Link to Literature
- Name poems written by students.

Objectives:

Reading:
- Understanding words and phrases
- Strategy: Connecting visuals with text
- Literature: Reading poetry

Writing:
- Personal information: Making a "me" collage
- Organizing information into categories
- Choosing images and words to describe yourself

Vocabulary:
- Learning adjectives that describe people
- Learning names of things students like (foods, school subjects, sports)

Listening/Speaking:
- Finding out more about others
- Talking about things that you like and are good at

Grammar:
- Using the verb *be* correctly

Spelling and Phonics:
- Pronouncing words with the letter *i*

Collage by Connie, Grade 9

[B]EFORE YOU BEGIN

[Tal]k with your classmates.

1. Look at the collage. What do you see?
   ☐ photographs ☐ drawings ☐ words
2. Read the caption. Who made the collage?
3. Help your teacher make a list of the things you see in the collage.

A CONNECTING TO YOUR LIFE

Standards
- Listen for details
- Ask questions
- Describe people

WARM UP

- Ask students to take turns naming themselves and then telling one thing they like. Model possible responses. For example: *My name is Jaime. I like pizza.* Record on the chalkboard as students share.

TEACHING THE LESSON

1. Tuning In

- Tell students they are going to hear a boy talk about things he likes. Explain and model the task, using several prompts: *I like pizza. What about you? I like burritos. What about you?*
- Play the tape or CD, or read the script as students listen. Then play it a second time, having students use thumb signals to show agreement or disagreement.

2. Talking It Over

- Have students do a "people search." Begin by having them tell what they see in each picture. Repeat each response, showing and explaining unfamiliar words.
- Model simple questions as students repeat and answer you. For example: *1. Do you like to read? 2. Are you good at sports?* Have students move around the room, asking other students questions and writing names of students under the appropriate pictures. Then have them share.
- Have a volunteer read the title of the unit aloud. Have students use finger signals to show what they think the unit is about.

READING

A CONNECTING TO YOUR LIFE

1. Tuning In Listen to a boy talk about what he likes. Point your thumb up if you like the same thing. Point your thumb down if yo do not.

2. Talking It Over Look at the pictures and descriptions below. Wa around your classroom and find one person for each description. Write the person's name on the line.

Find someone who...

...likes to read.

1. ______________

...is good at sports.

2. ______________

...likes pizza.

3. ______________

...speaks three languages.

4. ______________

...likes math.

5. ______________

...plays basketball.

6. ______________

...likes to watch TV.

7. ______________

...is a nice person.

8. ______________

...likes music.

9. ______________

Read the title of this unit. What do you think the unit is probably abou Check (✓) the correct answer.

_____ 1. It's all about sports.

_____ 2. It's all about animals.

_____ 3. It's all about you.

4 Unit 1

✓ WRAP UP

- **Outcome Sentence** Have students complete these sentence stems in writing and then share:

  My name is _______. *I like* _______.

- Ask students to bring a picture of themselves to the next class. The picture can show them with a relative, playing a game, etc. Ask them to be prepared to say something about the picture.

TEACHING TIP Encourage students to talk about themselves, but don't pressure them. Allow reluctant students to watch and listen to others, and join in when they are ready.

ANSWER KEY

Talking It Over: 3.

3 GETTING READY TO READ

Learning New Words Read the sentences below. Try to figure t the meanings of the underlined words.

1. I speak *five* languages. I am <u>special</u>!
2. I like being with other kids. I have a lot of <u>friends</u>!
3. I like <u>sports</u>. I like baseball, basketball, and football.
4. A lot of people like me. I am <u>popular</u>.
5. I always get an A+ in every class. I am the <u>best</u> student in school.
6. My friend Tran is a very nice person. He is <u>loveable</u>.

atch each word on the left with the correct definition on the right.

1. special	a. games people or teams play against each other
2. friend	b. having a lot of friends
3. sports	c. different from most other people and things
4. popular	d. easy for other people to love
5. best	e. someone you like and who likes you
6. loveable (*also spelled* lovable)	f. better than anyone or anything else

Talking It Over Talk with a partner. Share three or four things at make you special.

I speak two languages.

I play the violin.

I'm a really good soccer player.

B GETTING READY TO READ

Standards

- Use context to understand the meaning of new words
- Describe people and share information about yourself

WARM UP

Heads Together Ask students to work in pairs, sharing the pictures they have brought to class. Then invite volunteers to tell the class about their pictures.

TEACHING THE LESSON

1. Learning New Words

- Ask volunteers to read the numbered list of words and expressions and the lettered list of definitions aloud.
- Write the sentence, *I am <u>special</u>*, on the chalkboard. Then ask yourself aloud: *What does the word special mean?* Pause. Now write additional sentences as you think aloud:

  I speak five languages. (*Five languages! Most people speak only one language!*) *I have ten brothers.* (*Ten brothers! Most people have only one or two brothers!*)
- Do the same with the other new words.
- Have students complete the activity. Review the correct responses, reteaching as necessary.

2. Talking It Over

- Ask: *What makes you special?* Referring to the speech bubbles, elicit and record responses.

Heads Together Have students work in pairs to share three or four things that make them special.

✓ WRAP UP

Outcome Sentence Have students complete these sentence stems about their partners orally:

______________________ *is special.*
He/she ______________________.

ANSWER KEY

Learning New Words: 1. c; 2. e; 3. a; 4. b; 5. f; 6. d.

C READING TO LEARN

Standards
- Read and understand words and phrases
- Share information about yourself

WARM UP

- Ask students to close their eyes and think about one thing they like about themselves. Provide an example or two: *I am a good teacher ... I have many friends*. Have them share.

TEACHING THE LESSON

1. Before You Read

Heads Together Ask students to write a word that says something about themselves and then share with a partner. Have volunteers share with the class.

2. Let's Read

- Ask students to look at the collage. Have a volunteer point to the frame.

My Turn: Read Aloud/Think Aloud Read each word and phrase aloud. As you read, define or comment on key words. Begin with words students already know. For example: *Here's the word "best." What does it mean?*

- Talk with students about the image in the collage. For example: *Juan is smiling. He is a happy guy.*
- Now play the tape or CD, or read the words and phrases twice.

Our Turn: Interactive Reading Have individual students help you read some of the words and phrases. As they read, focus on the glossed words, ask questions, and make comments. For example: *When do we use the word "wow"?*

READING

C READING TO LEARN "Me" Collage

READING STRATEGY
Using Pictures:
When you see pictures and words together, the pictures can help you understand the meaning of the words.

1. Before You Read Write down a word that says something about you. Share what you wrote with a partner. Word: ______

2. Let's Read Look at Juan's "me collage." Read the words and sentences that make the frame.

hip-hop—a type of music that lots of kids like
Wow!—what you say when something surprises you

6 Unit 1

Have a different student read each word or phrase after you. Encourage students to copy your pronunciation and intonation.

- **Build Fluency** Have students repeat as you read each word or phrase.

Your Turn: Independent Reading Have students read the collage on their own and then write down words or phrases that describe themselves. Have them share out.

CULTURE NOTE

In some cultures, people don't like it when you say good things about yourself. Only other people can say good things about you. Ask students if it's OK for them to say good things about themselves in their home culture. Do they see people do it in the U.S.? Do they think it is OK?

Unlocking Meaning

Identifying the Main Idea Who are the words in the collage about? Check (✓) the correct answer.

______ 1. the boy in the picture

______ 2. the boy's best friend

______ 3. the boy's family

Finding Details Look at the collage again. Some of the words have letters next to them. Match the words to the sentences below. Write the letters on the lines.

__*b*__ 1. The boy in the picture is named Juan.

______ 2. Juan is a happy person. He smiles a lot.

______ 3. Juan always works hard.

______ 4. Juan has many friends.

______ 5. Juan likes football and basketball.

______ 6. Juan is one of a kind.

______ 7. Juan likes himself.

Think about It List three things you are good at. Choose from the activities below, or think of different ones. Share your list with a partner.

1. __________ 2. __________ 3. __________

math

2.

baseball

3.

cooking

dancing

5.

drawing

6.

basketball

Before You Move On Make a sign for your desk with a frame. Write words about you on the frame. Then tape the sign to your desk.

3. Unlocking Meaning

IDENTIFYING THE MAIN IDEA

- With a show of fingers, have students indicate which choice is correct.

✓ FINDING DETAILS

- Help students match each sentence with a lettered word, phrase, or image in the collage. Model the first sentence as an example.
- Review the correct answers. Referring to sentence 7, explain that we use words with "-self" on the end such as "myself," and "himself" when the subject of the sentence is the same as the object of the sentence. Instead of saying, "He saw *him* in the mirror" we say "He saw *himself* in the mirror." Instead of saying, "I like me," we usually say "I like myself."

THINK ABOUT IT

- Make a simple statement about each picture and ask students to point to the one you are talking about. For example: *Some people are good at sports.* (Picture 6) *I'm good at math* (Picture 1.)
- **Heads Together** Ask students to write three things they are good at. Tell them they can use ideas from the six pictures to get started. Have them share their lists with a partner. Ask volunteers to share out.

BEFORE YOU MOVE ON

- **Modeled Writing** Make a sign with your name on it for your desk as students watch. Include a frame around your name. Write five words that tell about you around the frame.
- Now have students make their own signs. Have them brainstorm words they might use and then give them time to make their signs.
- If you wish, have students take a "gallery walk," looking at each student's sign.

✓ WRAP UP

- **Outcome Sentence** Have students complete these sentence stems in writing and then share:

  Juan is __________.

  He likes __________.

PB PRACTICE BOOK ACTIVITY

See Activity A, Revisit and Retell, on Practice Book page 1.

ANSWER KEY

Identifying the Main Idea: 1.

Finding Details: 1. b; 2. a; 3. g; 4. e; 5. c; 6. d; 7. f.

D WORD WORK

Standards
- Describe others
- Identify sound/spelling relationships

WARM UP

Quick Write Ask students to write a positive or good word about themselves. Have them share as you record. Save for the next activity.

TEACHING THE LESSON

1. Word Detective

- Have students look at the words on the board. Which ones are important in a friend?
- Tell students they are going to listen to Juan and Lori describing their friends. Ask them to listen for words that describe what each person is like.
- Play the tape or CD, or read the script. Have students follow the directions as they listen.

2. Word Study

- Read each sentence aloud and ask a volunteer to name the noun and the adjective. Explain the meaning of each adjective or invite volunteers to do this.
- Encourage students to start lists of positive and negative adjectives in their notebooks.

3. Word Play

Heads Together Ask students to work with partners to complete the activity. Have volunteers share answers, then write sentences. Inform students that many people might be offended by the word "stupid."

Spelling and Phonics

- Have students listen to how the *i* sounds in each word. Then have them complete the chart and share out.

D WORD WORK

Matt

1. Word Detective Listen to Juan and Lori talk about their friends. Point your thumb up 👍 if you would like the person as a friend. Point your thumb down 👎 if you would not.

1. Maria is funny.
2. Stefan is quiet.
3. Zaida is friendly.
4. Matt is athletic.
5. Wen-Ying is nice.
6. Sau-Lim is shy.

2. Word Study Adjectives are words that describe nouns. They can sometimes be positive ☺ or negative ☹.

☺	☹
Maria is a **nice** girl.	Stefan is a **lazy** kid.
Lori is always **polite**.	Zaida is sometimes **rude**.

3. Word Play Work with a partner. Decide if each of the following adjectives is positive ☺ or negative ☹. Color in your choices. Then write two sentences with positive adjectives and two sentences with negative adjectives. You can use your dictionary.

smart ☺ ☹	lazy ☺ ☹	friendly ☺ ☹	mean ☺ ☹
beautiful ☺ ☹	popular ☺ ☹	loud ☺ ☹	stupid ☺ ☹

Positive:
1. ______________________
2. ______________________

Negative:
1. ______________________
2. ______________________

SPELLING AND PHONICS: To do this activity, go to page 182.

✓ WRAP UP

Outcome Sentence Invite volunteers to use the adjectives in this lesson to describe themselves. Have them complete these sentence stems, then share:

I'm ____________. *I'm not* ____________.

PB PRACTICE BOOK ACTIVITY

See Activity B, Word Work, on Practice Book page 2.

ANSWER KEY

Word Play: Positive smart, beautiful, popular, friendly; **Negative** lazy, loud, mean, stupid.

Spelling and Phonics: pride: like, wild, I'm, nice, (live); **winner**: stupid, in, picture, (live).

GRAMMAR — The Verb *Be*

Listen Up Listen to each sentence. Point your thumb up if it ınds correct. Point your thumb down if it sounds wrong.

1. I am a student.
2. You is a very nice person.
3. Juan and Maria is in the ninth grade.
4. They are good friends.
5. We are both in the ninth grade.
6. Juan and Maria is good students.

Learn the Rule Now read the following rules for the verb *be*, then ›eat Activity 1.

THE VERB *BE*		
1. The verb *be* must agree with the subject of the sentence. Sometimes the subject is a noun (*Juan, bicycle*), and sometimes it is a pronoun (*he, it*).		
am *a student.*	*You* ***are*** *a student.*	*Juan* ***is*** *a student. He* ***is*** *in ninth grade.*
2. When you talk, you usually use the subject pronoun + the short form of the verb *be*. This is called a contraction.		
I'm *a student.*	***You're*** *a student.* (1 person)	***He's*** *a student.*
We're *students.*	***You're*** *students.* (2+ people)	***They're*** *students.*

Practice the Rule Work with a partner. Complete each sentence ow with the correct full form of the verb *be*. Then say each sentence ›ud, using the short form when it is possible.

1. I ______ in the ninth grade.
2. Tran ______ from Vietnam.
3. Juan and Maria ______ friends.
4. They ______ the same age.
5. You ______ a very nice person.
6. She ______ from Mexico.
7. We ______ both ninth graders.
8. Ms. Lee said, "You ______ all good students."

All about Me! 9

E GRAMMAR

Standard

- Recognize and use complete sentences

WARM UP

- Write the following pair of sentences on the board: *I fifteen years old. I am fifteen years old.* Ask students which sentence is correct.

TEACHING THE LESSON

1. Listen Up

- Ask students to listen carefully. Then play the tape or CD, or read the sentences twice. Have students point their thumbs up if the sentence sounds correct, and down if it sounds wrong.

2. Learn the Rule

- Use the chart to present the present tense of *be* (am, is, and are). Point out the boldface words. Help students identify all the subjects (I, you, he, you, we, they). Then ask a volunteer to say which verb goes with each subject. (I am, you are, he is, we are, they are)
- Explain that a pronoun is a word that takes the place of the name of a person or thing. Ask: *Can I say, "(your name) is a teacher?"* (No) *What do I have to say?* (I am a teacher.) Ask students to make up similar sentences about themselves and their classmates using the pronouns *I, you, he,* and *she.*
- Repeat the Listen Up activity.

3. Practice the Rule

Heads Together Have students complete the activity with a partner. Review the correct answers.

✓ WRAP UP

- Repeat the Listen Up activity. This time ask students to write the correct form of each incorrect sentence.

PB PRACTICE BOOK ACTIVITY

See Activity C, Grammar, on Practice Book page 3.

ANSWER KEY

Listen Up: Correct sentences: 1, 4, 5

Practice the Rule: 1. am 2. is 3. are 4. are 5. are 6. is 7. are 8. are.

F BRIDGE TO WRITING

Standards

- Describe and compare likes and dislikes
- Use a graphic organizer to organize and express information

WARM UP

- Have students look at Lori's collage. Without reading any words, what can they tell about her by looking at the pictures and images? Record students' ideas on the board.

TEACHING THE LESSON

1. Before You Read

Heads Together Ask students to write down three things they love and then share the list with a partner. Have them share out, round robin, each student adding something that no one else has mentioned.

2. Let's Read

Explain that pictures and images can help you figure out what something is about (Reading Strategy box).

My Turn: Read Aloud/Think Aloud Read the words and phrases in the collage aloud. As you read, stop to comment on words and images:

Talk with students about the images in the collage. For example: *Which activity looks like the most fun to you?*

Point out the Valentine's Day card. Ask: *Who do you think sent this card to Lori?*

Define words and phrases that are unusual. For example, *"Hotmail" is an Internet company that gives you a free email account. A "Tropical Sno Cone" is a special kind of flavored ice.*

WRITING

F BRIDGE TO WRITING "Me" Collage

READING STRATEGY
Using Pictures:
When you see pictures and words together, the pictures can help you understand the meaning of the words.

1. Before You Read Write down three things you love. Share your list with a partner.

1. ______ 2. ______ 3. ______

2. Let's Read Look at Lori's collage. Make a list of the words that you see. Circle the words that describe you too.

Hotmail—an Internet e-mail service

10 Unit 1

- Play the tape or CD, or read the words and phrases twice. As students listen, ask them to circle words that describe themselves. Have them share out.

Our Turn: Interactive Reading Have individual students help you read the words and phrases in the collage. As they read, focus on the new words, ask questions, and make comments:

How many people are in Lori's family?

How old do you think Lori is? How do you know?

- **Build Fluency** Have pairs of students take turns reading alternate words and phrases to each other.

Your Turn: Independent Reading Have students read the words in the collage on their own. Ask them to write three words or phrases that do not apply to themselves, then share.

Making Content Connections On a separate piece of paper, draw a Venn diagram like this one. Compare yourself with Lori.

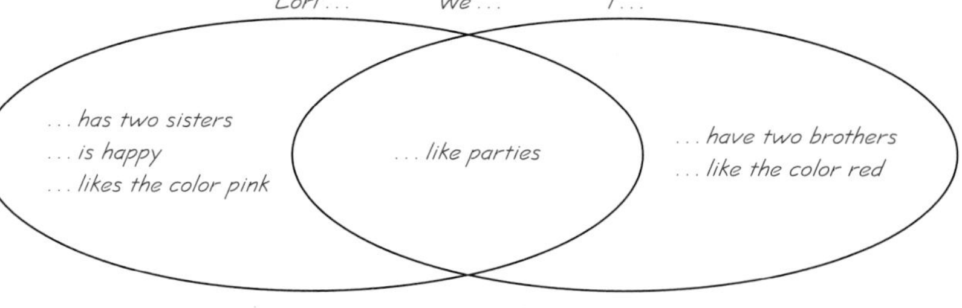

Expanding Your Vocabulary What are some things that you like? Tell a partner.

Foods

pizza

hot dog

fruit

ice cream cone

salad

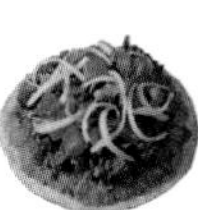
tostada

School Subjects

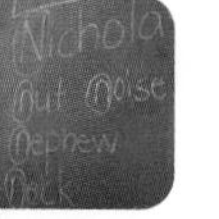
English

math

science

PE

art

computers

Sports

football

baseball

volleyball

basketball

soccer

tennis

3. Making Content Connections

- Draw an empty Venn diagram on the board. As you point to parts of the diagram, explain: *A Venn diagram looks like two overlapping ovals. The parts of the ovals that don't overlap belong to two different people.* Point to the left oval. *This part belongs to Lori.* Write "Lori" above the oval. Then point to the right oval and write "I" above the oval. *This part belongs to me.* Then shade in the shared portion and say: *This part in the middle that overlaps is shared by both people.* Write "We" above the overlap.
- Copy the information about Lori. Then write some true information about yourself and true information about yourself and Lori.
- Point out the items in Lori's portion of the diagram. Explain that these items belong only to Lori. Then call attention to the items in the overlapping part at the center of the diagram. Remind people that these items belong to both people.
- Have students draw a blank Venn diagram on a piece of paper. Ask them to write Lori's name above one circle and *I* above the other. Then have them enter the information about Lori and themselves in the correct ovals or in the overlap. Invite several students to share their Venn diagrams with the class.

4. Expanding Your Vocabulary

Heads Together Say the names of the foods, subjects, and sports as students follow along. Then have students work in pairs, telling each other which of these things they like. Invite volunteers to report what they learn about their partners to the class.

- With a show of hands, have boys "vote for" their favorite food, school subject, and sport. Tally the votes. Then do the same for girls. Are there differences between how boys and girls vote?

Team Talk Form a large circle and play a memory game. The first student names a thing he or she likes. (I like pizza.) The next student in the circle repeats the first item and adds one. (Gail likes pizza and I like black cats.) When someone makes a mistake, the game starts over.

✓ WRAP UP

Outcome Sentence Have students complete this sentence stem, then share:

Hi! My name is _______. I like _______.

PB PRACTICE BOOK ACTIVITIES

See Activity D, Test-Taking Practice, on Practice Book pages 4 and 5.

See Activity E, Using New Vocabulary, on Practice Book page 6.

G WRITING CLINIC

Standards
- Categorize information
- Use visuals to express information

WARM UP

- Ask students to look once again at Juan's and Lori's collages. How are they the same? How are they different?

TEACHING THE LESSON

1. Think about It

- Ask: *Why would someone make a "me" collage?* Have students choose an answer from the choices.

2. Focus on Organization

- Tell students that the information in a "me" collage usually tells

  what the person *is like*
  what the person *likes*
  what the person *likes to do*

- Help students understand the difference between *is like*, *likes*, and *likes to*. Model several examples of each and write them on the board: *I am happy most of the time. I like ice cream. I like to ride my bike on weekends.*
- Discuss the lettered explanations as they relate to Lori's collage (Part 1).

G WRITING CLINIC "Me" Collages

1. Think about It Why would you make a "me" collage?

☐ to tell people who you are and what you like ☐ to make people laugh ☐ to tell a story about a friend

2. Focus on Organization

❶ Study the collage. Look at the lettered explanations below the collage for an explanation of each word or picture.

ⓐ This picture shows Lori.
ⓑ This picture shows Lori's family.
ⓒ This picture shows Lori with her friends.
ⓓ This word explains what Lori is like.
ⓔ This word explains what Lori likes.
ⓕ This word explains what Lori likes to do.

Work with a partner. Look at Lori's collage again. Complete the chart below.

Words that explain what Lori is like	Words that explain what Lori likes	Words that explain what Lori likes to do
Loveable		

Focus on Style

le" collages often use photographs, drawings, and other images to strate what a person is like. Match each of the following images to the rect sentences below.

b.

c.

e.

f.

c 1. I like to go to amusement parks.

____ 2. I like purple.

____ 3. I like to go to the beach.

____ 4. I like baseball.

____ 5. I like fast food hamburgers.

____ 6. My family and I are from Mexico.

Heads Together Now have students complete the chart in Part 2 in pairs and then share out.

Access for All Have preproduction students make collages using different shapes, colors, and pictures with no words.

PB PRACTICE BOOK ACTIVITY

See Activity F, Focus on Organization , on Practice Book page 7.

3. Focus on Style

- Explain that people often use visual images in their collages not just to make them prettier or more interesting, but to help communicate ideas. Point to the images in the book and invite students to guess what each one might mean about the person who used it in their collage. For example, the Mexican flag might mean the person wants to visit Mexico or is from Mexico. Ask students to write the letter of each picture next to the correct sentence.

✓ WRAP UP

Outcome Sentence Have students complete these sentence stems, then share:

I am ________________.
I like ________________.
I like to ________________.

Have students bring pictures of themselves, friends, family, and things they like to do to the next class.

PB PRACTICE BOOK ACTIVITY

See Activity G, Focus on Style, on Practice Book page 8.

ANSWER KEY

Think about It: to tell people who you are and what you like.

Focus on Organization: Possible answers: **What Lori is like**: loveable, happy, smart; **What Lori likes**: music, her family, movies, pink, orange, Hotmail, friends, sports, Tropical Sno Cones; **What Lori likes to do**: take pictures, draw, drive, dance.

Focus on Style: 1. c; 2. e; 3. f; 4. d; 5. a; 6. b.

H WRITER'S WORKSHOP

Standards

- Use the writing process: prewriting and drafting
- Write words and phrases
- Identify images that have meaning

1. Getting It Out

WARM UP

- Have students look back at Connie's collage on page 3. Ask them what they learn about Connie from looking at the collage.
- Brainstorm with the class possible *kinds of materials* you might use in a collage as well as various *sources*. Students will probably start out with fairly traditional ideas such as words cut from newspapers, magazine photos, and personal snapshots. Encourage them to come up with more unusual types of materials such as movie tickets, candy wrappers, and post cards.

TEACHING THE LESSON

- Review the contents of the chart in Part 1.
- Have students use the chart on Practice Book page 9 to complete this activity. After five or ten minutes, have volunteers share out. Give students more time as needed.
- Ask students to suggest types of things they might include in their collages in addition to the ones suggested in Part 2. If you have magazines and newspapers available, students can start the gathering process in the classroom. Students should have brought some items from home.
- Ask students to complete Part 2 individually. Have them display the pictures and words they have chosen and/or brought from home and think about what each one tells the reader

WRITING

H WRITER'S WORKSHOP "Me" Collag

Make a collage that tells your classmates what you are like and what yo like to do.

1. Getting It Out

❶ Think about *what you are like, the things you like,* and *what you lik to do.* Make an idea chart about yourself like the one below.

Words about me	What I like	What I like to do
funny	pizza	play sports
cute	funny movies	go to Eliza's house
smart	books about animals	listen to music
...	...	...

❷ Collect images—words and pictures—that describe you and your lif Look at these examples for help.

1. Pictures of you

2. 

Pictures of your family (and pets!)

3. 

Pictures of you and your frier

4. 

Pictures of things you like or things you like to do

5. 

Words and pictures from magazines

6. 

Words from food wrappers

14 Unit 1

about them. Encourage them to think about important parts of their lives that aren't represented in these words and pictures. Suggest that they make drawings or cut out more words to fill in any gaps.

Using Technology Remind students that millions of images are available free on the Internet. Suggest that they explore Web sites that represent their special interests (cooking, music, sports) and print out pictures to use in their collages.

✓ WRAP UP

- Ask volunteers to share the favorite word or picture they have discovered so far and tell the class why it tells others something about them.

PB PRACTICE BOOK ACTIVITY

See Activity H, Writer's Workshop, on Practice Book page 9.

Getting It Down

Select the images you like best from those that you have collected.

Place your images on a piece of paper. Do not paste them!

re is Carlos's "me" collage. What do you think?

MINI-LESSON

Capitalizing Names: Always capitalize the names of people. Names are proper nouns.

Juan
Lori

2. Getting It Down

WARM UP

- Ask: *What things are the same about making a collage and writing a story? In what ways is making a collage different from writing a story?*

TEACHING THE LESSON

TEACHING TIP Read over the suggestions for both Getting it Down and Getting it Right. Consider doing *both steps* in the *same class period*. You will need to have on hand a sheet of poster paper for each student, scissors, paper and magic markers for last-minute word additions, glue, sealant spray, and hooks to use when hanging the pictures.

- Have students spread out the materials they have gathered and think about which pieces most clearly represent who they are (Part 1). Suggest that they choose no more than fifteen items to include in their collages.
- Have students arrange their words and pictures on a large piece of paper (Part 2). Remind them not to paste anything down yet.
- Have students look at Carlos's collage and then consider the comments in the speech bubbles. Invite students to add their own comments about the collage.

Mini-Lesson on Conventions

Point out the Mini-Lesson box at the top of the page. List some of the students' names on the board. Circle the capital letter at the beginning of each. Explain the meaning of *capitalize* and use the words *capital letters* and *capitalize* in several sentences. For example: *John begins with a capital J. When you capitalize a letter, you use a big letter, not a small letter.*

- Explain that a proper noun is a name that describes one and only one person, place, or thing. Give examples such as *Justin Timberlake, Chicago,* and *The Empire State Building.* Help students identify other examples of proper nouns in each category.

WRAP UP

- Tell students that the next step will be to show their collages to others before they paste down the words and pictures. Have them save their draft collages between two sheets of cardboard or paper.
- Tell students that they will have a chance to revise their work during the next session. Have them locate the ChecBric for this unit in the Student Book or Practice Book. Have them prepare for Getting it Right by reviewing the ChecBric on their own, underlining indicators they're not sure about.

H WRITER'S WORKSHOP

Standards

- Use the writing process: revising and editing
- Give a short oral presentation

3. Getting It Right

WARM UP

- Guide students through the ChecBric for this unit in the Student Book or Practice Book. Explain that they will use the ChecBric to prepare a final draft of their writing.
- Have volunteers explain, in their own words, what each indicator in the ChecBric means.

TEACHING THE LESSON

- Have students use the information in the chart and the ChecBric to revise their work (Part 1).

Group Share Model how students will share their collages and give feedback (Part 2). Have several volunteers practice giving feedback on a classmate's collage.

- Now have students share their collages with two classmates. Have students tell one thing they like about their classmates' collages.

TEACHING TIP Move around the class as students share, guiding how they give feedback. Have an instructional aide or adult volunteer help with this step.

- Using words and images from magazines, demonstrate the steps for finalizing collages (Part 3). Have students finish their collages.

3. Getting It Right

❶ Take a careful look at your collage. Use this guide to help you revise your work.

Question to Ask	How to Check	How to Revise
1. Do I use both words and images?	Count the number of words and images in your collage.	Add more words or images.
2. Does my collage tell all about me?	Look again at your idea chart. Does your collage have words and pictures that say everything about you?	Add words or images that help tell more about you.
3. Is my collage nice to look at?	Make sure all parts of your collage go together.	Try moving words and images around to make them more attractive.

❷ Share your collage with two classmates. Talk about it. Ask them what they think.

❸ Finish your collage.

1. 

Add words or pictures.

2. 

Take away words or pictures.

3. 
Put words or pictures in a different place.

4. 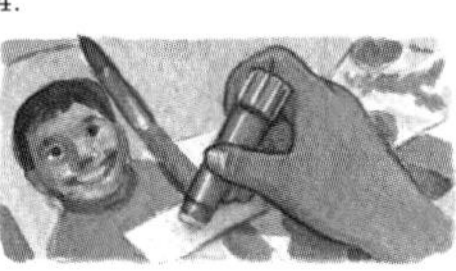
Glue each word or picture on a sheet of paper.

5. 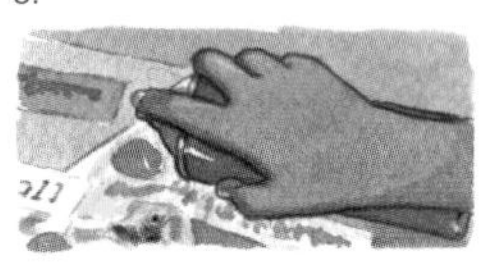
Spray your work with sealant.

6. 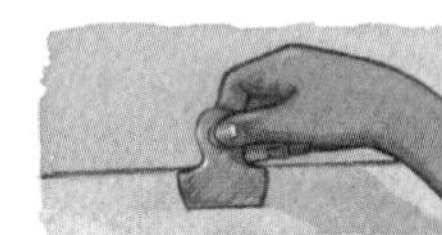
Attach a hook to the back.

WRAP UP

- Tell students that they are now ready to share their collages with the class. Suggest that they think about what they are going to say about various parts of their collages and practice saying it aloud several times before the next class.

 Help students complete the ChecBric on page 101 of the Practice Book. Ask them to attach it to their collages before putting them in their portfolios.

4. Presenting It

- Share your collage with your classmates. Explain to the class three things your collage says about you.

- After each collage presentation by your classmates, say something nice about the work they have done.

4. Presenting It

WARM UP

- It's time for students to present their collages! Remind students to listen politely as others present.
- As a class, develop a simple presentation checklist. Focus on content, organization, speaking skills (posture, volume, eye contact), enthusiasm, use of visuals, creativity, and length of presentation.

TEACHING TIP Students may be reluctant to present before the entire class. Consider having them present in small groups based on their general level of oral proficiency.

Access for All Have preproduction students point to pictured objects and words in their collages as you name them. Have early production students use one or two words to identify words or pictures in their collages.

TEACHING THE LESSON

- Have students display their collages and tell their classmates the meaning of at least three of the images or words on the collage.
- Tell students that you want them to pay attention to these things as they present their work:
  1. Use a loud and clear voice.
  2. Read slowly.
  3. Show your audience your work as you present.
  4. Ask for feedback.
- Review with students the kinds of feedback they might give—referring to the speech bubbles.
- Remind students to clap politely after each presentation. Invite one or two students to say something nice about each collage.

✓ WRAP UP

Outcome Sentence Ask students to complete one of these sentence frames based on something they learned about a classmate from his or her collage.

__________ *is* __________.

__________ *likes* __________.

I BEYOND THE UNIT

Standards
- Read and understand simple written instructions
- Label information
- Write a short invitation
- Read and respond to poetry
- Write a simple poem

1. On Assignment

WARM UP

- Ask how many students have ever visited an art museum or seen an art show. Ask them to describe what it was like. Explain that the students will use their collages to put on their own art show for friends and family members.

TEACHING THE LESSON

Let's Talk Discuss with students where and when you will have your class art show (Part 1).

- Have students make name cards for their collages, mounting and folding them so that they can be opened (Parts 2 and 3).

Interactive Writing As a class, write an invitation to the art teacher (Part 4). Have a student copy the invitation so that it is ready to send. Ask a volunteer to deliver the invitation.

- Have students invite family members to the show (Part 5). At the show, students can show their guests around and have them guess which collage they made.

I BEYOND THE UNIT

1. On Assignment Display your collages. Have a class art show.

❶ Where will you display your collages? When? Talk it over as a class.

❷ Write your name and grade on the bottom half of an index card.

❸ Fold the index card in half. Make sure your name is on the inside. Paste the card to the bottom of your collage.

❹ Invite the art teacher at your school to be a judge of the Collage Art Show.

Dear Ms. Painter:

Please judge our Collage Art Show. It will take place on September 30. Thank you.

Sincerely, ELD I Class

❺ Invite other students or your family to come to the art show when you have it. Can friends and family guess who made each collage?

❻ Award prizes for "most colorful," "most descriptive," "funniest," "most beautiful," and "best" collages.

18 Unit 1

WRAP UP

As a class, award prizes in different categories (Part 6). Or create a ballot with a list of categories and have students vote. Award prizes according to students' votes.

Link to Literature

SHARED READING Read these name poems written by students.

LET'S TALK Answer the following questions.

1. Why are these poems called "name poems"?
2. How is each poem different from the others?
3. Which poem do you like best? Why?

JUST FOR FUN Write your own name poem.

1. Begin each line with the letters, in order, of your first name.
2. Think of a word, phrase, or sentence for each letter that says something about you.
3. Write your poem on a separate piece of paper. Use color, if you wish. Share your name poem with your classmates.

My Name Poem

B is for Butterflies.
E is for Enjoy.
N is for Nature.

Brianna

Brat
Real
Innocent
Awesome
Naughty
Nice
Athletic

John

John is an athlete.
On Saturdays he likes to sleep in.
His favorite food is pizza.
Never call him Johnny.

Sources: diskovery.ltsc.org
saintmarysschools.com
abcteach.com

brat—a bad, difficult child
innocent—sweet or nice
awesome—really, really great
athletic—good at sports
sleep in—to get up later than you usually do

All about Me! 19

2. Link to Literature

WARM UP

- Ask students to share one or two words from their collages that they would definitely include if they were going to write a poem about themselves.

TEACHING THE LESSON

Shared Reading Ask a volunteer to read each poem aloud. Pause after each one to answer any questions students may have about unfamiliar vocabulary.

Let's Talk Use the questions to lead a discussion of the poem. Ask students to point out the "name" in each name poem. Have them point out the differences among the three poems. Ask them to choose a favorite poem and explain why they like it.

- Now play the tape or CD, or read the poems aloud twice. Ask students to think about which person is the most like them. Have them share out.

JUST FOR FUN

Have students write their own name poems, using Activity I, Responding to Literature, on Practice Book page 10.

WRAP UP

- Invite volunteers to write their names on the board and read their name poems to the class.

PB PRACTICE BOOK ACTIVITY

See Activity I, Responding to Literature, on Practice Book page 10.

✓ UNIT WRAP UP

Outcome Sentence Have students complete this sentence stem:

In Unit 1, I learned ________________.

Signs

Unit Overview

Section	At a Glance	Standards
Before You Begin	Students talk about signs that they see every day.	■ Derive meaning from visual information ■ Read environmental print
A. Connecting to Your Life	Students talk about where they see different types of signs.	■ Listen for details ■ Read environmental print
B. Getting Ready to Read	Students consider signs they see at school and in the community. They also learn useful vocabulary.	■ Use context to understand the meaning of new words ■ Read and write words and phrases
C. Reading to Learn	Students learn the meanings of everyday signs in the community. PRACTICE BOOK: Students match pictures with signs.	■ Read environmental print ■ Use visual clues to unlock meaning ■ Match words to visuals
D. Word Work	Students learn to how to make nouns out of verbs by adding *–ing* to the verb form. PRACTICE BOOK: Students match pictures with problems. Then they create some school rules.	■ Use knowledge of words and parts of words to derive meaning ■ Identify sound/spelling relationships
E. Grammar	Students learn to give affirmative and negative commands. PRACTICE BOOK: Students match pictures with commands.	■ Give commands
F. Bridge to Writing	Students learn the meanings of more everyday signs in the community. PRACTICE BOOK: Students practice taking Reading Vocabulary and Reading Comprehension tests. PRACTICE BOOK: Students practice new vocabulary.	■ Read environmental print

Section	At a Glance	Standards
G. Writing Clinic	Students discuss where various types of signs are found, then examine the meanings of various logos. PRACTICE BOOK: Students sort signs by category. PRACTICE BOOK: Students study logos and then fill in the name of the business or office that might go with each one.	■ Use graphic organizers to organize and categorize information ■ Use visual information to express meaning
H1. Writer's Workshop: Getting It Out	Students collect examples of signs to include in a class picture dictionary of signs. PRACTICE BOOK: Students sort signs by function.	■ Use the writing process: prewriting
H2. Writer's Workshop: Getting It Down	Students organize their picture dictionary pages.	■ Use the writing process: drafting
H3. Writer's Workshop: Getting It Right	Students revise and edit their own work.	■ Use the writing process: revising and editing
H4. Writer's Workshop: Presenting It	Students share their picture dictionaries in groups and get feedback from their classmates.	■ Give a short oral presentation
I. Beyond the Unit	Students explore common symbols that are used with, or instead of, words on signs. They also read the poem "NO" by Shel Silverstein. PRACTICE BOOK: Students write their own "NO" poem and draw a picture to accompany it.	■ Understand everyday symbols in school and the community ■ Read and respond to poetry

BEFORE YOU BEGIN

Standards

- Derive meaning from visual information
- Read environmental print

- Have students look at the picture on page 21. Say: *Tell me about the picture. What do you see?* A student might say: *A sign...a boy...he likes to skateboard.* Record student responses on the chalkboard or an overhead transparency. Encourage other students to add their own sentences. For example: *The sign says "No Skateboarding." The boy is thinking about skateboarding in the hall.* As they respond, repeat what they say and add it to the story. At the end, have a student read through all the sentences.
- Ask students to explain the sign in their own words. Invite volunteers to explain what is funny about the picture.
- Have students name signs they see every day. Record students' responses on the board. Ask volunteers to tell what each sign means.

Unit 2 Signs

Read...

- Selections from the book *Signs* by Susan Canizares and Pamela Chanko. Learn how signs tell us important messages in just a few words.

Link to Literature

- "NO," a poem by Shel Silverstein.

Objectives:

Reading:
- Understanding signs all around us
- Understanding the jobs different types of signs have
- Strategy: Using photos and visuals to understand meaning
- Recognizing logos and symbols
- Literature: Reading poetry

Writing:
- Making signs
- Organizing information into categories
- Writing simple captions

Vocabulary:
- Recognizing root words
- Learning words on common signs in different places at school and in the community

Listening/Speaking:
- Understanding simple conversations
- Following commands
- Listening to/giving feedback

Grammar:
- Understanding imperatives

Spelling and Phonics:
- Pronouncing words with the letter *a*

EFORE YOU BEGIN

k with your classmates.

1. Look at the picture. What do you see?
2. What does the sign mean? What is the boy thinking about?
3. Help your teacher make a list of signs you see around you every day.

A CONNECTING TO YOUR LIFE

Standards
- Listen for details
- Read environmental print

WARM UP

- Have students look again at the signs they have named. Ask: *Where do we see signs?* (at school, on the freeway, at the mall, at the supermarket, etc.)

TEACHING THE LESSON

1. Tuning In

- Tell students they will hear people talking. Play the first conversation, then stop. Ask: *Where do you think the girl and boy are?* Help them understand that they are at school.
- Continue to work with one conversation at a time. Play each one twice. After the second time through, guide students to understand where the people are.
- Explain that we use the idiom "The sign says…" to indicate the words on a sign, even though the sign doesn't actually speak out loud.

2. Talking It Over

- Have volunteers read each sign aloud. Help students understand what each one means. Then ask students to figure out the sign that doesn't go with the others. Call on a volunteer to give the correct answer and explain his or her reasons for that answer.

Heads Together Have pairs of students create their own new sign for Kennedy High School. Have volunteers share their signs with the class.

- Have students look at the title, then the pictures to determine what the unit is about. Have students use finger signals to indicate the correct answer.

A CONNECTING TO YOUR LIFE

1. Tuning In Listen to the conversations. People are talking in different places. Where do you think the people are? Write your answers on the lines below.

1. *at a school*
2. ______
3. ______
4. ______
5. ______

2. Talking It Over Look at these signs. Which one does not belong with the others? How do you know? Talk with a partner. Then make a sign that you might see at Kennedy High School.

1.

2.

3.

4.

5.

6.

Read the title of this unit. What do you think the unit is probably about? Check (✓) the correct answer.

_____ 1. It's about learning the letters of the alphabet.

_____ 2. It's about learning what signs mean.

_____ 3. It's about learning school rules.

WRAP UP

- Have students look around the classroom, finding an example of a sign.

ANSWER KEY

Tuning In: Possible answers: 1. at a school; 2. in a car, on the freeway; 3. at a shopping mall; 4. in a food store; 5. on a street corner.

Talking It Over: 5. Reason: Sign 5 is a highway sign. The rest are school signs.

Talking It Over: 2.

GETTING READY TO READ

Learning New Words Read the sentences below. Try to figure : the meanings of the underlined words.

1. There is a large pile of snow and ice on the road. There was an avalanche yesterday!
2. Highway 80 is closed. We have to take a detour on another road.
3. Be careful! That sign says danger—we could get hurt.
4. A traffic guard helps kids cross the street. She stands at the school crossing.
5. Our school has a small lunch area. There is very little space during lunch.
6. People deposit their mail in a mailbox.

tch each word on the left with the correct definition on the right.

1. avalanche	a. to put something into something else
2. detour	b. a part of a building, park, office, etc., for doing something
3. danger	c. snow, ice, and rocks that fall off a mountain side
4. crossing	d. a harmful situation
5. area	e. a place where you can go from one side of the street to the other
6. deposit	f. a different way of going from one place to another

Talking It Over A sign is a board or poster in a public place with ɔrmation on it. Work in small groups. Make a list of signs you see at ool and in the community.

At School	In the Community
NO TALKING	TWO TACOS FOR 99¢

ıat does each sign mean? Tell your classmates about the signs on your list.

B GETTING READY TO READ

Standards

- Use context to understand the meaning of new words
- Read and write words and phrases

WARM UP

- Invite students to take turns telling about signs they can remember seeing on the way to school today. As they speak, make a list of the signs on the chalkboard. Ask other students to explain new words or phrases to each other.

TEACHING THE LESSON

1. Learning New Words

- Describe a situation that will help students understand each sentence or pair of sentences.

Sentence 1: Say: *It is snowing. I am driving in the mountains. Oh, no!...Look out...!* Now read the pair of sentences. Ask: *What does avalanche mean?*

- Repeat this procedure with the rest of the new words.
- Now have students match each word to its definition and then share out. Confirm the correct answers.

2. Talking It Over

- Explain that the new words in Activity 1 are often found on signs. Point out the sample answers on the chart and elicit information about each. Ask: *What does "No Talking" mean?* (Be quiet. Don't talk.) *Where do you see No Talking signs?* (In the library.)
- Ask two or three students to give examples of things they might list in the first column. Repeat for the second column.

Team Talk Have students work in small groups to write at least three more examples of signs. Have them share out as you record.

✓ WRAP UP

- Write three to five signs on the board: NO TALKING, NO RUNNING, etc. Using non-verbal actions or pantomime, have students guess the sign you have in mind.

Technology Tip If you have access to a digital camera, take pictures of signs you see in the community. Invite students who have access to digital cameras to do the same. Copy all of the images onto a CD. Create a collage of community signs to display in the classroom.

ANSWER KEY

Learning New Words: 1. c; 2. f; 3. d; 4. e; 5. b; 6. a.

C READING TO LEARN

Standards

- Read environmental print
- Use visual clues to unlock meaning
- Match words to visuals

WARM UP

- Ask: *How can you understand what a sign says if you don't know the words?* (Look at any pictures or symbols on the sign.)

TEACHING THE LESSON

1. Before You Read

- Give students a few minutes to study the signs. Then point to and read each sign. Ask which sign students see most in everyday life.

2. Let's Read

Remind students that using pictures can help them understand words (Reading Strategy box). Point to the crocodile on the Crocodile Crossing sign and ask: *What is this? The picture tells you what this sign is warning you about—crocodiles.*

My Turn: Read Aloud/Think Aloud Read the text under each pictured sign and then read each sign. Comment on each sign, explaining how you can use pictures to help you understand the sign. Comment on anything you think students may not understand.

- Now play the tape or CD, or read the script twice. As students listen, ask them to point thumbs up for signs that give danger warnings (Crocodile Crossing, Railroad Crossing, Danger! Thin Ice, Avalanche Area).

READING

READING STRATEGY
Using Pictures:
When you see pictures and words together, the pictures can help you understand the meaning of the words.

C READING TO LEARN

1. Before You Read Look at the signs in these pictures. Which sign do you see most often in everyday life?

2. Let's Read You are going to read a book about signs. As you read, use the pictures to help you understand what each sign means.

Signs can tell you...

a.

...where you are.

b.

...where things go.

c.

...when to stop.

d.

...too much snow.

Source: *Signs* by Susan Canizares and Pamela Cha

recycle—to use things again that people throw away

Our Turn: Interactive Reading Have students help you read the sentences and the signs. As they read, focus on the glossed words, ask questions, and make comments:

For example: *Why are the letters on the stop sign all big capital letters?* (To get people's attention.)

- **Build Fluency** Have students practice reading signs with two words (such as railroad crossing), encouraging them to read the words as a pair, rather than individually.

Your Turn: Independent Reading Have students read the signs to themselves. Ask them to write down the sign that is the most important one. Then have them share their ideas about why the signs they chose are important.

Unlocking Meaning

Finding the Main Idea Look at the signs on page 24. What do they do? Check (✓) the correct answer.

_____ 1. They scare us.

_____ 2. They help us.

_____ 3. They make us laugh.

Finding Details Match each of the following sign phrases to the correct picture below.

__e__ 1. STOP

_____ 2. AVALANCHE AREA

_____ 3. RAILROAD CROSSING

_____ 4. CROCODILE CROSSING

_____ 5. DANGER! THIN ICE

_____ 6. RECYCLE AREA

b. c.

d. f.

Think about It What kinds of signs are helpful? Check (✓) the correct answers.

_____ 1. Signs that are easy to read.

_____ 2. Signs that are colorful.

_____ 3. Signs that are red.

_____ 4. Signs that use many pictures.

_____ 5. Signs that have special shapes.

_____ 6. Signs that use just a few words.

Before You Move On Work with a partner. Make up a funny sign for your classroom.

Signs 25

3. Unlocking Meaning

✓ FINDING THE MAIN IDEA

- Read the question and the three numbered choices aloud. Have students hold up one, two, or three fingers to indicate their answers.
- As you review the incorrect answers, point out that sometimes certain signs may make us laugh or may scare us, but that signs *always* help us in some way.

FINDING DETAILS

- Have students match the words and pictures. Have volunteers explain their answers.

THINK ABOUT IT

- Read the directions aloud and have students complete the activity. After they do the task, ask them to point out specific examples of signs pictured in this unit that illustrate each option.

BEFORE YOU MOVE ON

Heads Together Have pairs of students work together to make up a funny sign to post in the classroom. It could concern something that wouldn't make sense to do in a classroom setting. For example: *No Pets Allowed* or *Go Slowly*.

✓ WRAP UP

- Give students clues about various signs, then have students write the words they would find on that sign. For example: *This sign has eight sides. It is red. It tells you not to do something. What are the words on the sign?* (Stop)

PB PRACTICE BOOK ACTIVITY

See Activity A, Revisit and Retell, on Practice Book page 11.

ANSWER KEY

Finding the Main Idea: 2.

Finding Details: 1. e; 2. c; 3. f; 4. b; 5. a; 6. d.

Think about It: Answers will vary.

D WORD WORK

1. Word Detective Sometimes you can figure out what a new word means by looking for a smaller word inside of it. Circle the smaller word inside each of the following underlined words.

1. NO SWIMMING.
2. NO FISHING.
3. NO EATING.
4. NO NAME-CALLING.
5. NO PUSHING.
6. NO CHEWING GUM.

2. Word Study Many verbs in English can be made into *-ing* nouns. Think of a sign at your school that uses an *-ing* noun. What is the verb?

VERB	NOUN
to **skateboard**	NO **SKATEBOARDING** ON CAMPUS
to **run**	NO **RUNNING** IN THE HALLS

3. Word Play Work with a partner. Make at least five signs using the verbs in the following table. Turn the verbs into *-ing* nouns.

EXAMPLE: NO SHOUTING INSIDE THE BUILDING

shout	sleep	fight
fight	wear	eat
talk	play	laugh

SPELLING AND PHONICS: To do this activity, go to page 182.

D WORD WORK

Standards

- Use knowledge of words and parts of words to derive meaning
- Identify sound/spelling relationships

WARM UP

✓Write this sign on the chalkboard: NO SWIMMING. Have students show what they think this might mean by completing this sentence stem:

Do not ____________________

TEACHING THE LESSON

1. Word Detective

- Have students read each sign. Explain that signs often begin with *no* and a word that ends in *–ing*.
- Ask students to locate the small words inside the bigger ones. As they respond, have a student write the list of small words on the chalkboard.

2. Word Study

- Present the information in the chart. Elicit examples of school signs with *–ing* words in them.
- You may wish to introduce simple spelling rules. When a word ends in *e*, drop the *e*, and add *–ing*. (skate, skating) When a word ends in a single vowel plus a consonant, double the consonant and add *–ing*. (swim, swimming)

3. Word Play

Heads Together Have students complete the activity in pairs.

Spelling and Phonics

- Have students listen to the words, then tell you what they notice about the sound of the letter *a*. Pronounce the words and ask students to repeat.
- Have students complete the activity. Review the answers.

✓ WRAP UP

- Ask students to think of signs people might post around the school. Write their examples on the board. For example: *No sitting on steps. No eating in class. Walk Don't Run.*

PB PRACTICE BOOK ACTIVITY

See Activity B, Word Work, on Practice Book page 12.

ANSWER KEY

Word Detective: 1. swim; 2. fish; 3. eat; 4. call; 5. push; 6. chew.

Spelling and Phonics: candy: glass, hat, avalanche; **walk:** draw, wall, paw, swan, eyeball, talk.

GRAMMAR — Commands

Listen Up Listen to these commands. Do what the person tells you do.

1. Take out a piece of paper.
2. Pick up a pencil.
3. Write your name in the upper right-hand corner.
4. Draw a square on the paper.
5. Print "DO NOT TALK" on the paper.
6. Show your sign to a partner.

Learn the Rule Read the following rules to understand when to e commands. Then write two commands on the lines beneath the chart.

To be polite, add "Please..."

COMMANDS	
When you want someone to do something, use a command.	
***Take out** a sheet of paper.*	*Please **take out** a sheet of paper.*
When you want someone not to do something, or to stop doing something, use "Do not..." or "Don't..."	
***Don't talk**!*	

Commands:
1. ____________________
2. ____________________

Practice the Rule Work in pairs. Complete items 11 and 12 with ur own ideas. Tell your partner to do each of the following things.

EXAMPLES: Touch your head. Don't look at me.

1. to touch his or her head
2. to touch his or her shoulder
3. to shut his or her eyes
4. to open his or her eyes
5. to look at the ceiling
6. not to laugh at you
7. not to look at you
8. not to talk to you
9. not to bother you
10. not to sit next to you
11. to look at __________
12. not to __________

Signs 

E GRAMMAR

Standard
- Give commands

WARM UP

- Ask students to stand up. Then ask them to sit down. Explain that "sit down" and "stand up" are examples of commands.

TEACHING THE LESSON

1. Listen Up

- Play the tape or CD, or give the commands in the script. Model each command.
- Play the tape or CD, or give commands a second time. Have students follow each command.

2. Learn the Rule

- Read the rules and examples aloud. Point out that the affirmative command uses just the verb without any endings like *–s* or *–ed* or *–ing*. Elicit that the negative command uses the word *don't* plus the verb.
- Have students write at least two commands in their Student Books.

3. Practice the Rule

- Have students complete the activity in pairs. Then have them take turns giving the commands to their partners.

WRAP UP

- Ask volunteers to tell about a command that someone once gave them and why they are glad they followed it. For example, *Don't move. There's a bee on your neck.*

TEACHING TIP Ask students to add the word *please* to all commands during some or all of the oral exercises. This provides an opportunity for students to practice making polite commands.

PB PRACTICE BOOK ACTIVITY

See Activity C, Grammar, on Practice Book page 13.

ANSWER KEY

Practice the Rule: 1. Touch your head. 2. Touch your shoulder. 3. Shut your eyes. 4. Open your eyes. 5. Look at the ceiling. 6. Don't laugh at me. 7. Don't look at me. 8. Don't talk to me. 9. Don't bother me. 10. Don't sit next to me.

F BRIDGE TO WRITING

Standard

- Read environmental print

WARM UP

- Write these words on the board: *sit, walk, run, talk, push.* Invite volunteers to make up commands using each verb.

TEACHING THE LESSON

1. Before You Read

- Ask students to think of signs they have seen at school that start with *No* or *Don't.* List students' examples. As you record, ask what each means. For example: *There is a "No Talking" sign in the library. What does that mean?* (That means you're not supposed to talk in the library.) Have students point out and explain any similar signs in the classroom.

2. Let's Read

My Turn: Read Aloud/Think Aloud Read the caption under each sign starting with the words *Signs can also tell us…* and then read the sign. Comment on each one, pointing out how the pictures help us understand what the sign says (Reading Strategy box).

- Now play the tape or CD twice, or read the script. As students listen, ask them to point thumbs down for signs that tell us not to do something (No Fishing, Don't Walk, No Swimming, Quiet Please).

Our Turn: Interactive Reading Have students help you read the captions and the signs. As they read, focus on the glossed words, ask questions, and make comments:

Call attention to *e* and *f* and say: *What are the two words we use to give negative commands?* (No, Don't)

WRITING

READING STRATEGY
Using Pictures: When you see pictures and words together, the pictures can help you understand the meaning of the words.

F BRIDGE TO WRITING

Signs

1. Before You Read Look around your classroom for a sign that begins with "NO" or "DON'T." What does the sign tell you?

2. Let's Read Read the rest of the book on signs. Think of one more example of a "NO" sign.

Signs can also tell us…

e.

…not to fish.

f.

…not to walk.

g.

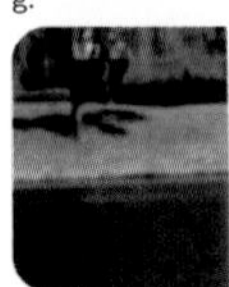

…not to swim.

h.

…not to talk

i.

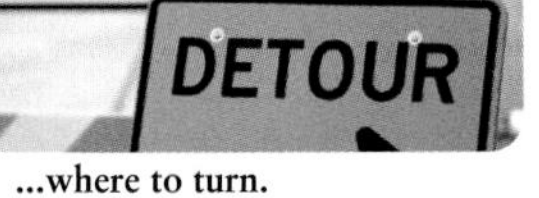

…where to turn.

j.

…where to eat.

k.

…where to find a special treat!

Source: *Signs* by Susan Canizares and Pamela Chan

diner—a restaurant with simple food and low prices

special treat—something good to eat

In *h* ask: *What is another way to say "Quiet please"?*

In *i* ask: *Where do you see signs like these?*

In *j* say: *The word "dinner" is spelled almost the same as the word "diner." What is different about the words "diner" and "dinner"?*

In *k* ask: *What is your favorite "special treat"?*

- **Build Fluency** Point out that when you read two-word signs like NO SWIMMING, you stress both words. Model the pronunciation of the signs. Then have students practice reading signs to each other. Invite volunteers to read signs to the class.

Your Turn: Independent Reading Have students read the signs to themselves. Ask them to write down real-world examples of advertising signs like *j* and *k*.

Access for All If some students are reluctant to read aloud, pair them with a more fluent partner and have that partner read the signs aloud as the less fluent partner repeats.

. **Making Content Connections** Signs are important—especially : school. What can happen if you don't pay attention to signs? Talk it ver with a partner. Then complete the chart below.

Signs can tell you...	Examples	If you don't pay attention to the sign...
...to be careful of something.	CAUTION! Wet floor	...you may slip and fall down
...to do something.		
...not to do something.		

. **Expanding Your Vocabulary** Almost all places have signs to elp you find things. For each place below, circle the sign that you would robably **not** see in that place.

1. A hospital:	EMERGENCY	WAITING ROOM	PRINCIPAL'S OFFICE
2. A restaurant:	PLEASE WAIT TO BE SEATED	PLEASE CLEAN UP AFTER YOUR DOG	DAILY SPECIALS
3. A mall:	DIRECTORY	INFORMATION	NO HUNTING
4. An airport:	NO RUNNING IN THE HALLS	CUSTOMS	BAGGAGE CLAIM AREA
5. A park:	CASHIER	PICNIC AREA	DO NOT FEED THE DUCKS
6. A grocery store:	PRODUCE	ARRIVALS	EXPRESS LINE

3. Making Content Connections

- Point out the chart in the book. Then read aloud and explain the meanings of the phrases in the first column. Give specific examples of the kinds of things signs can tell you. For example: *Signs can tell you to be careful of something.* (There's a hole in the sidewalk. A dangerous dog lives here.); *Signs can tell you to do something.* (Use this container to recycle plastic. Come in this door.); *Signs can tell you not to do something.* (Don't park your car here. Don't cross the street right now.) Invite students to add to the list.
- Then read the second column heading aloud and help students come up with specific examples of signs for the messages you discussed for column 1: *Signs can tell you to be careful of something.* (Walk Carefully. Beware of Dog); *Signs can tell you to do something.* (Recycle Plastic Here. Enter Here.) *Signs can tell you not to do something.* (No Parking. Don't Walk.) Introduce the third column heading and discuss with students what might happen if they don't do what the signs say. (The dog might bite you. You might get a parking ticket.)

Heads Together Ask pairs of students to work together to complete the chart. Copy the chart on the board. Invite volunteers to fill in their responses in the second and third columns. Discuss each new addition and answer any questions students may have.

4. Expanding Your Vocabulary

- Remind students that signs are everywhere. Read the instructions aloud and ask a volunteer to explain them in his or her own words. Read across the first row of items and point out that you would find two of the signs (WAITING ROOM and EMERGENCY) in a hospital. However, you would not find a PRINCIPAL'S OFFICE there. Have students complete the activity on their own, circling the correct answers in their books.

PB PRACTICE BOOK ACTIVITY

See Activity D, Test-Taking Practice, on Practice Book pages 14 and 15.

See Activity E, Using New Vocabulary, on Practice Book page 16.

WRAP UP

- Ask students to help you make up useful signs for use in the classroom. For example: *No talking during tests* or *Don't forget to study.* Have them illustrate their signs if they wish. Post them on the classroom bulletin board.

G WRITING CLINIC

Standards

- Use graphic organizers to organize and categorize information
- Use visual information to express meaning

WARM UP

- Have students imagine that they are on their way home from school. Have them list the signs they might see, then share out. Ask them to save their lists.

TEACHING THE LESSON

1. Think about It

- Point out that we see signs nearly everywhere these days. Ask which of these places we usually do *not* see signs.

2. Focus on Organization

- For Part 1, ask students to give specific examples of each area listed. Have them name nearby towns and cities. Ask them to list some outdoor areas they enjoy visiting. Elicit the names of some local streets and highways. Ask them what schools and libraries they have been in recently. Then point out the sample sign for each of these areas. Elicit other examples of signs they might see in each area.

Heads Together Have students complete the chart (Part 2).

Interactive Writing Copy the chart on the board. Have volunteers help you complete the chart.

G WRITING CLINIC Sign

1. Think about It Where is one place you would probably not see a sign?

☐ at the market ☐ at school ☐ at the beach
☐ in an airplane ☐ in the sky ☐ along a road

2. Focus on Organization

❶ We see signs everywhere.

In towns and cities

Outdoors

Along streets and highways

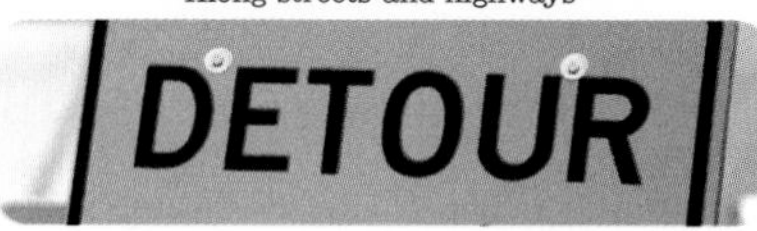

In schools and libraries

"X-ing" is short for "crossing"

❷ Where would you probably find each of the following signs? Comple the chart below. Put each sign in the correct column.

Speed Limit 55	U-Turn OK	~~Sam's Market~~	School X-ing
Watch for Bears	Main Office	U.S. Post Office	No Running
Room 222	Elevation 5,000 Feet	Danger! Falling Rocks	Bijou Theatre

In the City	In the Outdoors	On Streets and Highways	At School
Sam's Market			

Signs have many different jobs to do.

They tell you what to do...or what NOT to do.

They warn you of possible problems.

They help you know where you are.

They tell you where to go.

And, sometimes they make you want to eat, buy, or do something fun.

Work with a partner. Create signs that do each of the following jobs:

- tell you what to do (or *not* to do)
- warn you
- help you
- make you want to do something

. Focus On Style Signs often have logos. Logos are small designs that help you notice or remember a name or idea. Match each logo with the correct type of business below.

b. 

c. 

e. 

f. 

d	1. a clothing store	____	4. a nut supply company
____	2. a music and electronics store	____	5. a restaurant
____	3. a Web site	____	6. a bank

- For Part 3, explain that different signs have different jobs. Review the five general types of signs shown by reading each heading and asking volunteers to explain what it means in their own words. For example: *Signs that tell you "what to do or what not to do" give commands. Signs that "warn you of possible problems" tell you things you should be careful of or stay away from.*
- After discussing the five categories of signs, go back to the signs in Part 1. Ask students to explain how each sign does its job.

Heads Together Read over the four categories for which students will be making signs in Part 4. Have students work in pairs. Ask the pairs to make the signs large enough to display to their classmates.

PB PRACTICE BOOK ACTIVITY

See Activity F, Focus on Organization, on Practice Book page 17.

3. Focus on Style

- Ask students to point out logos on their clothing, backpacks, shoes, or other possessions. Ask students to take turns drawing the logos on the board. Elicit what company or brand name the logo represents and what, if anything, the logo shows about the product. For example the *swoosh* represents Nike athletic products. The shape of the swoosh symbolizes the swift movement of a runner or other athlete.

Team Talk Have students complete the matching activity in small groups. Review the correct answers with the whole class.

PB PRACTICE BOOK ACTIVITY

See Activity G, Focus on Style, on Practice Book page 18.

WRAP UP

- Ask students to revisit the list they made of signs they might see on the way home from school. Have them add one more sign to the list.

ANSWER KEY

Think about It: in the sky.

Focus on Organization 2 : Possible answers: **In the City**: Sam's Market, U.S. Post Office, Bijou Theatre; **In the Outdoors**: Watch for Bears, Elevation 5,000 Feet; **On Streets and Highways**: Speed Limit 55, U-Turn OK, Danger! Falling Rocks; **At School**: Room 222, Main Office, No Running, School X-ing.

Focus on Style: 1. d; 2. f; 3. c; 4. a; 5. b; 6. e.

H WRITER'S WORKSHOP

Standard
- Use the writing process: prewriting

1. Getting It Out

WARM UP

- Display a picture dictionary and pass it around so that students can examine it. Ask students what is special about a picture dictionary (pictures are used to label objects and explain ideas). Tell students that they are going to make their own picture dictionaries of signs.

TEACHING THE LESSON

- Review the sample picture dictionary page. Call attention to what each page is to include: at least three signs that have the same job, a picture for each sign, and a caption for each page.

TEACHING TIP This lesson is designed to enable students to make their own pages. However, you may wish to involve the entire class in contributing to the same four pages—using large sheets of chart paper. Or, you might divide students into teams.

WRITING

H WRITER'S WORKSHOP

Sign

Your class is writing a "picture dictionary" of signs. Each page will be about signs that have the same job.

Job: Telling you what to do

Job: Telling you where you are

Job: Telling you about danger

Job: Making you war something

Each page should have three parts:

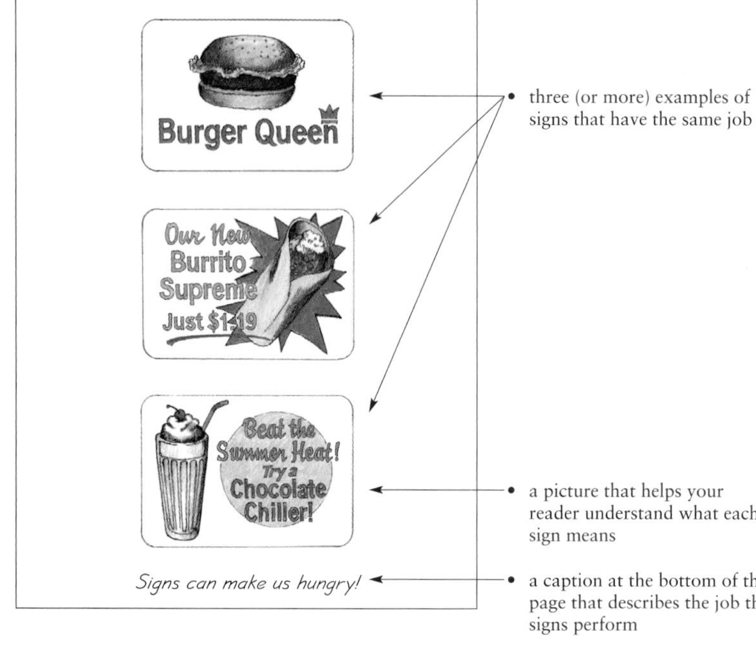

32 Unit 2

Getting It Out Take a field trip. Look for signs!

First, develop a plan. Decide where you will look for signs.

- □ at school
- □ in your community
- □ on the road

Before you begin looking for signs, you will need to get supplies for your field trip.

- notebook or clipboard
- pencil or pen
- colored markers or pencils

Copy each sign you see. Draw the sign in your notebook *exactly* as you see it.

- Use the same words.
- Use the same shape.
- Use the same colors.

After your field trip, sort your signs into groups by the job that they do.

Tell what...

California
US 99

Tell where...

Now entering
Los Angeles

Warn...

Make you want something

Burger Queen
Next Offramp

- Tell students that they are to begin by taking a field trip, or walking tour of an area or neighborhood, looking for interesting signs.

TEACHING TIP For safety, have students walk with a friend or two, each person recording his or her observations.

- Ask students where they might get ideas for their signs—perhaps at school, in the community, or along the highway (Part 1). Encourage students to think of other places where they might find interesting signs.
- Point out the materials students will need (Part 2). Ask different students where they plan to go on their tours. Some of them may end up walking around the inside of the school or around the immediate neighborhood. Others may be able to arrange for a visit to a commercial area where a wider variety of signs can be found. Remind students to copy each sign as exactly as possible, keeping in mind the wording, the shape of the sign, and the colors used (Part 3).
- When students finish their tours, ask them to write the names of the four categories of signs illustrated in the Student Book, then list each sign they found in the appropriate category (Part 4). Invite volunteers to share their findings with the class.

Technology Tip If you have access to a video camera, let selected students check it out as they take their tours. Play back tapes during class, pausing at key points to discuss the functions of various signs (to warn, to tell where something is, etc.) and to discuss words and phrases students may not understand.

✓ WRAP UP

- Ask volunteers to describe a sign that they saw for the very first time on their field trips. Have them tell what the sign looks like and what its function is.

PB PRACTICE BOOK ACTIVITY

See Activity H, Writer's Workshop, on Practice Book page 19.

H WRITER'S WORKSHOP

Standards

- Use the writing process: drafting, revising, editing
- Give a short oral presentation

2. Getting It Down

WARM UP

- Ask volunteers to tell the class about their favorite sign from the field trip and tell how they plan to illustrate it.

TEACHING THE LESSON

- Point out the caption on Carlos's picture dictionary page, *Signs can tell you where you are,* and have a student read the speech bubble comment next to the caption aloud. Then ask students to explain what each sign shows.
- Have volunteers read the other speech bubbles aloud and ask other students if they agree or not. Invite them to add their own comments about Carlos's picture dictionary page.

Let's Talk List the four categories of signs from Getting It Out on the chalkboard as column headings. Explain that each category represents one page of their picture dictionary of signs. Ask two volunteers to come to the front of the room, describe the signs they found, and tell which column each sign belongs in. Then have them write the words from the sign in the appropriate column. Give students time to choose three or more signs for their own picture dictionary pages (Part 1).

- Next, have students illustrate each sign (Part 2). Tell them that if they can't figure out a way to illustrate a sign, they should replace it with another.
- Now have them complete the captions and write a caption at the bottom of each page (Part 3). Have students finish their pages in class or at home.

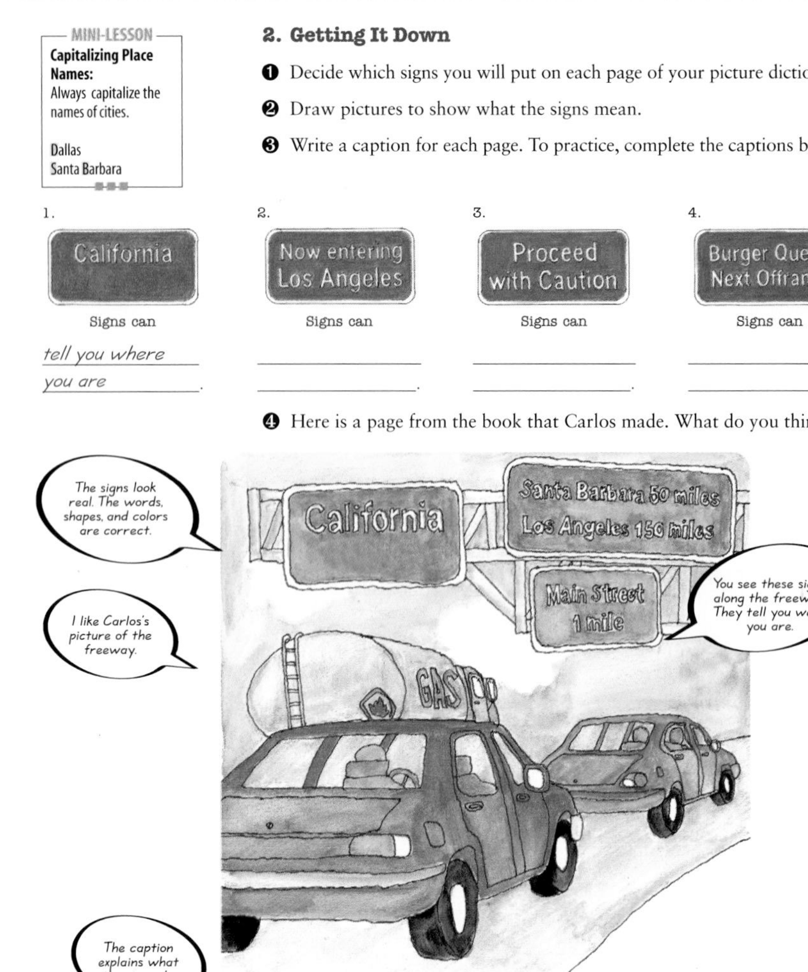

WRITING

MINI-LESSON
Capitalizing Place Names:
Always capitalize the names of cities.

Dallas
Santa Barbara

2. Getting It Down

1. Decide which signs you will put on each page of your picture dictiona
2. Draw pictures to show what the signs mean.
3. Write a caption for each page. To practice, complete the captions belo

4. Here is a page from the book that Carlos made. What do you think?

The signs look real. The words, shapes, and colors are correct.
I like Carlos's picture of the freeway.
The caption explains what the signs do.
You see these signs along the freeway. They tell you where you are.
California
Santa Barbara 50 miles
Los Angeles 156 miles
Main Street 1 mile
GAS
SIGNS CAN TELL YOU WHERE YOU ARE.

34 Unit 2

Mini-Lesson on Conventions Point out the Mini-Lesson box. Explain that we use a capital letter at the beginning of each word in the name of a city. Invite students to take turns writing other two- or three-word city names on the board using correct capitalization.

WRAP UP

- Tell students that they will have a chance to revise their work during the next session. Have them locate the ChecBric for this unit in the Student Book or Practice Book. Have them prepare for Getting it Right by reviewing the CheckBric on their own, underlining indicators they're not sure about.

Getting It Right Take a careful look at each page in your picture tionary. Use this guide to revise the pages you are not happy with.

Question to Ask	How to Check	How to Revise
1. Do the signs on each page have the same job?	Read one sign, then check to make sure the other signs have the same job.	Replace a sign if it doesn't go with the other signs.
2. Does the picture help others understand what each sign means?	Have a partner tell you what each sign means.	Add a drawing or photo to your page that will help others understand.
3. Does each sign look real?	Compare each sign to your field trip notes.	Change the wording of your sign. Change the shape or color.
4. Does your caption explain the signs?	Check that the caption describes all of the signs.	Reword the caption.

Presenting It Share your work with your classmates.

Form a group with classmates that visited different places.

I visited the mall!
I took the bus around town.
I took a walk around school!
My older brother took me on the freeway.

Show each page in your book to the group. Read the signs and captions aloud.

Be sure that each person in your group understands what each sign means.

Ask for feedback from your classmates.

Your English was perfect.

3. Getting It Right

WARM UP

- Guide students through the ChecBric for this unit in the Student Book or Practice Book. Explain that they will use the ChecBric to prepare a final draft of their writing.
- Have volunteers explain, in their own words, what each indicator in the ChecBric means.

TEACHING THE LESSON

- Have students use the chart and the ChecBric to revise their picture dictionary pages.

Group Share Model how students will share their picture dictionary pages and give feedback. Have several volunteers practice giving feedback on a classmate's page.

WRAP UP

- Tell students that they are now ready to share their picture dictionary pages with the class. Suggest that they think about what they are going to say about their pages and practice saying it aloud several times before the next class.

Help students complete the ChecBric on page 103 of the Practice Book. Ask them to attach it to their picture dictionary pages before putting them in their portfolios.

4. Presenting It

WARM UP

- Have students tell you which places they visited. Form presentation groups to ensure balance.
- As a class, develop a simple presentation checklist. Focus on content, organization, speaking skills, visuals, etc.

TEACHING THE LESSON

- Tell students that you want them to pay attention to these things as they present their work:
  1. Use a loud and clear voice.
  2. Read slowly.
  3. Show your audience your work as you present.
  4. Ask for feedback.
- Have students begin by telling their group where they went on their field trip and describe the signs they saw.
- Have each student present his or her pages to the group, then ask for questions and feedback.

WRAP UP

- Ask students in each group to share one page with the whole class.

I BEYOND THE UNIT

Standards

- Understand everyday symbols in school and the community
- Read and respond to poetry

1. On Assignment

WARM UP

- Write the word *symbol* on the board. Help students understand that a symbol is a shape or a picture that represents an idea or word. Give examples such as the + sign (plus) and the $ sign (dollars).

TEACHING THE LESSON

- Have students match the words and symbols on their own, then share and discuss (Part 1).
- Have students look for more symbols as they explore the community on their own (Part 2). Suggest that they keep an illustrated list of the symbols they see and bring it to the next class.
- Have students take turns drawing the symbols they saw on the board or on an overhead transparency, noting which symbols are most common (Part 3).
- Have students copy the symbols in rows on a separate piece of paper (Part 4).

Heads Together Ask students to write a caption under each symbol to explain it (Part 5). Then have them share their work with a partner and comment on each other's work.

TEACHING TIP If some students' families don't allow them the freedom to explore their communities on their own, try to arrange for groups of students, accompanied by a parent or other responsible adult, to go out together looking for symbols.

I BEYOND THE UNIT

1. On Assignment Symbols are often used instead of words on sig
Work with your classmates. Make a poster that shows common symbo
used in the community and explain what each symbol means.

❶ Begin by matching each of the following symbols from school with
correct word below.

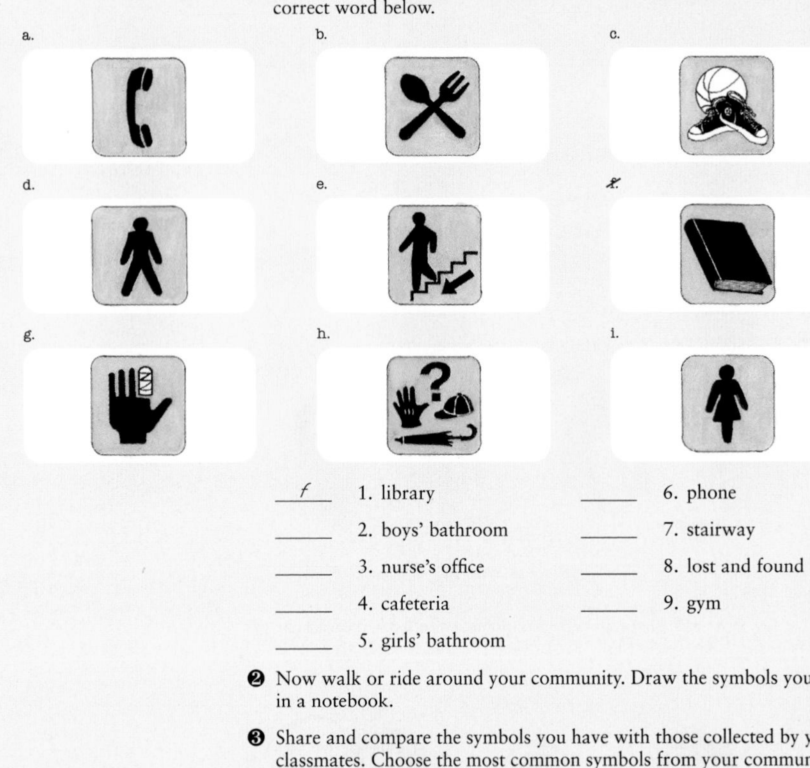

f	1. library	____	6. phone
____	2. boys' bathroom	____	7. stairway
____	3. nurse's office	____	8. lost and found
____	4. cafeteria	____	9. gym
____	5. girls' bathroom		

❷ Now walk or ride around your community. Draw the symbols you
in a notebook.

❸ Share and compare the symbols you have with those collected by y
classmates. Choose the most common symbols from your commun

❹ Place the symbols neatly in rows on a separate piece of paper.

❺ Write a caption that explains each symbol. Your caption should be
short and easy to read quickly.

36 Unit 2

ANSWER KEY

On Assignment: 1. f; 2. d; 3. g; 4. b; 5. i; 6. a; 7. e; 8. h; 9. c.

Link to Literature

SHARED READING Listen to the poem "NO," by Shel Silverstein. Read along as you listen. Then, as a class, practice reading the poem aloud.

LET'S TALK Answer the following questions.

1. Name one "No" sign that you've seen before.
2. Name one "No" sign that you've never seen before.
3. Why is the poem funny?

ABOUT THE AUTHOR

Shel Silverstein was born in Chicago and died in 1999. He wrote nearly twenty-five books, published in 30 different languages. *Where the Sidewalk Ends*, *A Light in the Attic*, and *Falling Up* are three of his most famous collections of poetry and drawings.

Source: *Falling Up* by Shel Silverstein

a spray can sprayer

a fly rod caster

a frisbee heaver

Signs  37

2. Link to Literature

WARM UP

- Write the word *No* on the chalkboard. Ask students to recall commands from this lesson that start with this word. Explain that they will be reading a poem that is made up entirely of commands like these.

TEACHING THE LESSON

Shared Reading Read the poem aloud in chunks of four or five lines. Have students underline any words they don't understand as they listen. After each chunk, go back and clarify the meaning of any words students underlined. Use a combination of paraphrasing (Speeding means going very fast.), pantomime (skipping, fly rod casters) and simple explanations (Loitering means standing around doing nothing.).

- Next go through the poem line by line having volunteers explain in their own words what each line means. Then read the whole poem without stopping.
- **Echo Reading** Read the lines of the poem fluently and with expression. After each line, pause and have students repeat it after you. Keep up the rhythm from beginning to end.
- Then have students chant the poem together all the way through. Consider chunking the lines into groups of five.

Let's Talk Use the questions to lead a discussion of the poem. Ask students to name a "No" sign they were familiar with before they read the poem. Then ask volunteers to describe a "No" sign in the poem that is new to them. Ask students to explain the humor in the poem.

✓ WRAP UP

Have students complete the Practice Book activity and read their poems to the class.

PB PRACTICE BOOK ACTIVITY

See Activity I, Responding to Literature, on Practice Book page 20.

✓ UNIT WRAP UP

Sentence Synthesis Write these words on the board: *signs, school, community*. Have students write a sentence using each word, then share.

This Is My Web Page Unit Overview

Section	At a Glance	Standards
Before You Begin	Students explore a Web page created by a student.	■ Derive meaning from visual information ■ Find details in simple text
A. Connecting to Your Life	Students interview classmates to find out information such as where they come from, what they like and dislike, and what their future plans are.	■ Listen for meaning ■ Ask and answer questions ■ Participate with classmates in classroom discussion
B. Getting Ready to Read	Students talk about their everyday life and their future goals and learn useful vocabulary.	■ Use context to figure out the meaning of new words ■ Share personal information
C. Reading to Learn	Students read another student's actual Web page. PRACTICE BOOK: Students answer questions about the Web page in the Student Book.	■ Read words and phrases ■ Find details in text
D. Word Work	Students learn one-word and two-word compounds. PRACTICE BOOK: Students label pictures using compound words.	■ Use knowledge of compound words to derive meaning ■ Identify sound/spelling relationships
E. Grammar	Students describe themselves using complete sentences. PRACTICE BOOK: Students answer questions about themselves using complete sentences.	■ Use complete sentences to express ideas
F. Bridge to Writing	Students read a Web page created by a class. PRACTICE BOOK: Students practice taking Reading Vocabulary and Reading Comprehension tests. PRACTICE BOOK: Students practice new vocabulary.	■ Read complete sentences

Section	At a Glance	Standards
G. Writing Clinic	Students examine the organization of a Web page. PRACTICE BOOK: Students use a chart to categorize information from a Web page. PRACTICE BOOK: Students write five sentences about a person based on images of things she likes.	■ Organize information into categories ■ Use visual images to express meaning
H1. Writer's Workshop: Getting It Out	Students organize information to use in their own personal Web pages. PRACTICE BOOK: Students list information about themselves and rate it for interest level.	■ Use the writing process: prewriting
H2. Writer's Workshop: Getting It Down	Students outline their personal Web pages and then practice writing the outlined information in the form of complete sentences.	■ Use the writing process: drafting ■ Use a simple outline to organize information ■ Write complete sentences
H3. Writer's Workshop: Getting It Right	Students revise and edit their own work.	■ Use the writing process: revising and editing
H4. Writer's Workshop: Presenting It	Students read each other's Web pages and list one interesting fact they discover about each person.	■ Give a short oral presentation
I. Beyond the Unit	Students make bar graphs illustrating some of the information they learned from classmates. They also read and write autobiographical poems. PRACTICE BOOK: Students write their own autobiography poems.	■ Make a bar graph to express information visually ■ Read and respond to poetry ■ Write a simple poem based on a model

BEFORE YOU BEGIN

Standards
- Derive meaning from visual information
- Find details in simple text

- Have students look at page 39. Ask: What do you see? (a Web page)
- Read the Web page as students follow along. Ask: *Who created, or made, this Web page?* (Timothy Davis) Explain that "Timo" is Timothy's nickname. Tell students that a nickname is a short, sometimes humorous name that friends and family members call you. Invite volunteers to share their own nicknames.
- Ask what the Web page tells them about Timo and list student responses on the board. Define and discuss any new words that students don't understand.
- Ask: *Where do we find Web pages?* (on the Internet)
- Have students imagine that they have a Web page. Have them write a word or short phrase that would be part of their Web page.

Unit 3

This Is My Web Page

Read...
- Web pages written by students your age. Find out what other students are like and what they like to do.

Link to Literature
- An autobiography poem written by a student.

Objectives:

Reading:
- Understanding sentences expressing personal information
- Understanding personal Web pages
- Strategy: Using pictures to predict
- Literature: Responding to poetry

Writing:
- Creating a personal Web page
- Putting information into categories
- Using art and fonts to make writing interesting

Vocabulary:
- Recognizing compound words
- Learning words related to sports, recreation, and hobbies

Listening/Speaking:
- Understanding a simple conversation
- Listening to definitions and descriptions of things
- Asking and answering questions
- Giving personal information

Grammar:
- Using complete sentences

Spelling and Phonics:
- Pronouncing words with the pattern *o* + consonant + *e*

38 Unit 3

FORE YOU BEGIN

: with your classmates.

1. Whose Web page is this? Who created this Web page?
2. What do you know about Timo? Help your teacher make a list.
3. Where do you find Web pages?

A CONNECTING TO YOUR LIFE

Standards
- Listen for meaning
- Ask and answer questions
- Participate with classmates in classroom discussion

WARM UP

- Have students write another word or phrase that tells something about themselves and share it.

TEACHING THE LESSON

1. Tuning In

- Tell students that they will hear two girls talking. Explain that Maria is making something.
- Play the tape or CD, or read the script. Have students listen for, then tell you, what Maria is making.
- Play the tape or CD a second time. Have students tell you what the girls are mostly talking about.

2. Talking It Over

- It's time for a "people hunt!" Explain the task to students. Model questions students might ask, writing each on the board: 1. *Were you born in January?* 2. *Do you come from Asia?* 3. *Do you like hip-hop music?* 4. *Do you like pink?* 5. *Do you plan to go to college?* 6. *Do you like to swim?* 7. *Are you good at soccer?* 8. *Do you get good grades?*
- Now have students move around the room, asking questions related to each item. As students find someone who fits each category, have them write the student's name on the corresponding line.
- Review the responses orally by asking a question about each item. For example: *Who was born in January?*

READING

A CONNECTING TO YOUR LIFE

1. Tuning In Listen to two girls having a conversation. What are th girls talking about?

☐ people in their family ☐ both of their boyfriends ☐ things one of them likes to do

2. Talking It Over

Look at the pictures and descriptions below. Walk around your classro and find one person for each description. Write the person's name on the line.

Find someone who...

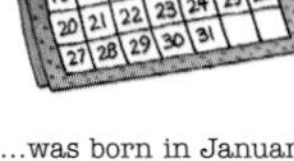

...was born in January.

1. ______________

...comes from Asia.

2. ______________

...likes hip-hop music.

3. ______________

...likes the color pi

4. ______________

...plans to go to college.

5. ______________

...likes to swim.

6. ______________

...is good at soccer.

7. ______________

...gets good grade

8. ______________

Read the title of this unit. What do you think the unit is probably abou Check (✓) the correct answer.

_____ 1. It's about learning how to write about ourselves for a Web page.

_____ 2. It's about learning to use the Internet.

_____ 3. It's about learning how to write e-mail messages.

40 Unit 3

- Have students look at the title of the unit. Have them use finger signals to indicate their answers.

WRAP UP

- Have students revisit what they wrote about themselves. Have them add one new fact, using a word, phrase, or sentence.

ANSWER KEY

Tuning In: things one of them likes to do

Talking It Over: 1.

B GETTING READY TO READ

. Learning New Words Read the sentences below. Try to figure ut the meanings of the underlined words.

1. "Come in! It's nice to see you. Welcome to my home!"
2. *The Simpsons* makes me laugh. I enjoy watching that show.
3. Zaida watches *The Simpsons* every week. It's her favorite TV show.
4. Juan builds model cars every day after school. It's his hobby.
5. Stefan wants to help sick people. His goal is to be a doctor one day.
6. We know what happened yesterday, but nobody knows what will happen in the future.
7. Tran will graduate from high school in June. Then he will go to college.
8. Lori always gets A's and B's. She is a successful student.

latch each word on the left with the correct definition on the right.

1. welcome	a. good at what you do
2. enjoy	b. any time after right now
3. favorite	c. something you hope to do one day
4. hobby	d. a friendly greeting when someone comes to visit
5. goal	e. liked better than anything else
6. future	f. to finish high school, college, or some other educational program
7. graduate	g. to like doing something
8. successful	h. an activity you do for fun, usually by yourself

. Talking It Over Complete the chart below. Then work in a small oup. Talk about your life today and what you hope your life will be like the future.

	Today	Ten Years from Now
Where I live		
What I do every day		
My favorite things		

B GETTING READY TO READ

Standards

- Use context to figure out the meaning of new words
- Share personal information

WARM UP

- Ask students to recall information they learned about their classmates.

TEACHING THE LESSON

1. Learning New Words

- Describe a situation that will help students understand each set of sentences. Tell them to listen as you expand on each situation and read the sentences. Ask them to think about what each person is doing or what they are like.
- Item 1: Say: *You meet a new friend at school. You invite your friend to your house. What do you say when she comes over?* Now have students follow along as you read the sentences in item 1. Have them say the underlined word. Ask: *What does "welcome" mean?* Ask volunteers to share their ideas as you record.
- Repeat this procedure for the rest of the new words, helping to create context for each.
- Now have groups match each word to its definition and then share out. Confirm the correct answers.

2. Talking It Over

Modeled Writing Copy the chart on the board. Explain that you are going to write down information about yourself. Write a phrase or simple sentence about yourself in each cell, as students follow along. Use the simple present tense, even in the second column. Tell students that they will make their own charts.

- Save your own chart for the next lesson.

Team Talk Have students complete the chart. Then have them form small groups to discuss the information in their charts.

- Have volunteers in each group share highlights from their charts.

✓ WRAP UP

Outcome Sentence Have students complete this sentence stem about a classmate, then share:

I learned that ______________.

ANSWER KEY

Learning New Words: 1. d; 2. g; 3. e; 4. h; 5. c; 6. b; 7. f; 8. a.

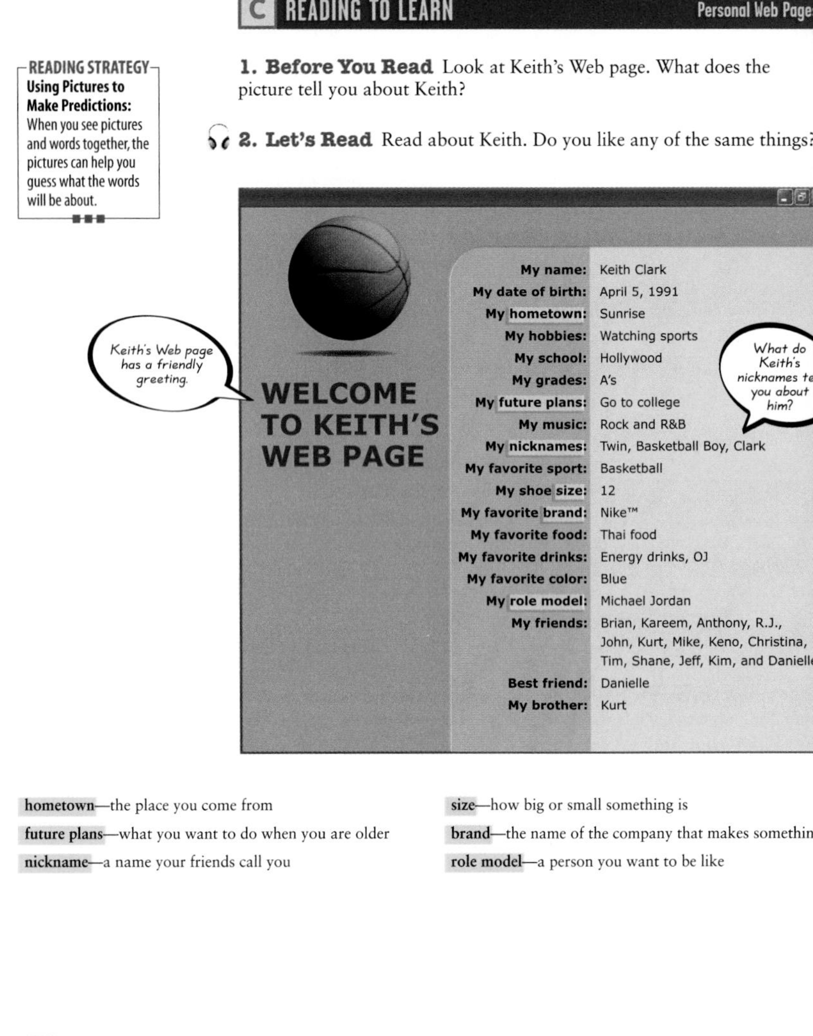

READING

C READING TO LEARN

Personal Web Pages

READING STRATEGY
Using Pictures to Make Predictions: When you see pictures and words together, the pictures can help you guess what the words will be about.

1. Before You Read Look at Keith's Web page. What does the picture tell you about Keith?

2. Let's Read Read about Keith. Do you like any of the same things?

Keith's Web page has a friendly greeting.
What do Keith's nicknames tell you about him?
WELCOME TO KEITH'S WEB PAGE

My name:	Keith Clark
My date of birth:	April 5, 1991
My hometown:	Sunrise
My hobbies:	Watching sports
My school:	Hollywood
My grades:	A's
My future plans:	Go to college
My music:	Rock and R&B
My nicknames:	Twin, Basketball Boy, Clark
My favorite sport:	Basketball
My shoe size:	12
My favorite brand:	Nike™
My favorite food:	Thai food
My favorite drinks:	Energy drinks, OJ
My favorite color:	Blue
My role model:	Michael Jordan
My friends:	Brian, Kareem, Anthony, R.J., John, Kurt, Mike, Keno, Christina, Tim, Shane, Jeff, Kim, and Danielle
Best friend:	Danielle
My brother:	Kurt

hometown—the place you come from
future plans—what you want to do when you are older
nickname—a name your friends call you
size—how big or small something is
brand—the name of the company that makes something
role model—a person you want to be like

42 Unit 3

C READING TO LEARN

Standards

- Read words and phrases
- Find details in text

WARM UP

- Revisit the chart you made about yourself. Explain that if you were creating a *personal* Web page, you might include some of the information in your chart on your Web page.

TEACHING THE LESSON

1. Before You Read

- Ask students to study Keith's Web page. Then point out the picture and ask students what it shows about Keith.

2. Let's Read

- Tell students that pictures can help you predict what you will read or learn (Reading Strategy box). Explain that the word *predict* means to know what's coming in the future, to guess what's going to happen.

My Turn: Read Aloud/Think Aloud Read selected information, commenting as you read and defining unfamiliar words:

Keith is a good student. He plans to go to college.

A role model is someone you want to be like.

- Play the tape or CD, or read the information. As students listen, ask them to listen for things that describe them too.

Our Turn: Interactive Reading Have individual students read information from Keith's Web page aloud. As they read, focus on the glossed words, ask questions, and make comments.

What is the name of Keith's hometown?

What are some examples of brand names?

Question All-Write Have students write the answer to this question: *Keith has a lot of friends, but who is his best friend?*

- **Build Fluency** Have students take turns reading lines of the Web page aloud to each other.

Your Turn: Independent Reading Now have students read on their own. Have them list the things that Keith likes that they also like, then share with a partner. Have volunteers share out.

Heads Together Ask students to compare Keith's activities and interests with their own. When they finish, have students share their thoughts with a partner.

. Unlocking Meaning

Finding the Main Idea Choose the sentence that best describes Keith. Check (✓) the correct answer.

_____ 1. He is a college student who likes computers.

_____ 2. He is an unhappy person.

_____ 3. He is a high school student with many interests.

Finding Details Read the sentences about Keith. Write *T* for True or *F* for False.

_____ 1. He is a good student.

_____ 2. He likes country music.

_____ 3. His favorite sport is football.

_____ 4. He has very small feet.

_____ 5. He loves Thai food.

_____ 6. He has a lot of friends.

_____ 7. He has a younger sister.

Think about It Work with a partner. Complete the chart below. There is a sentence about Keith in each part. Use information on Keith's Web page to support each sentence.

He's good at sports. *His favorite sport is basketball.*	*He's popular.*
He's a good student.	*He's like many other teenagers.*

Before You Move On What do you know about your own name? Find out. Be ready to share with your classmates.

1. Who gave you your name?
2. Why did they choose your name?
3. Does your name mean anything special?
4. Do you have nicknames at home?
5. Do you like your name?
6. If you could choose another name, what would it be? Why?

3. Unlocking Meaning

✓ FINDING THE MAIN IDEA

- Have students use finger signals to choose the sentence that best describes Keith. Have a volunteer or two explain why.

✓ FINDING DETAILS

- Have students complete the activity, then share and discuss.

THINK ABOUT IT

Heads Together Read each of the sentences in the chart aloud and ask students to look back at Keith's Web page and find information to support the sentence. Have them write that information under the appropriate heading. Then ask the pairs to complete their charts together.

Shared Writing Copy the chart on the board. When students finish their own charts, invite volunteers to fill in information on the board. Review the completed chart with the whole class.

BEFORE YOU MOVE ON

- Tell students that names often have an interesting story. Talk about your own name as you answer each question.
- Ask students to find out how their parents chose their names. Have them be prepared to share this information in class.

✓ WRAP UP

Outcome Sentence Have students complete this sentence stem, then share:

I like Keith's Web page because _____________.

PB PRACTICE BOOK ACTIVITY

See Activity A, Revisit and Retell, on Practice Book page 21.

ANSWER KEY

Before You Read: He's interested in basketball.

Finding the Main Idea: 3.
Finding Details: 1. T; 2. F; 3. F; 4. F; 5. T; 6. T; 7. F.
Think about It: Sports: His favorite sport is basketball. His hobby is watching sports. His favorite brand is Nike. His role model is Michael Jordan. **Popular:** He has 14 friends. **Good student:** His grades are A's. He plans to go to college. **Like many other teenagers:** He likes Rock and R&B. His favorite drinks are energy drinks and OJ.

D WORD WORK

Standards

- Use knowledge of compound words to derive meaning
- Identify sound/spelling relationships

WARM UP

- Write the words *baseball, eyeball,* and *football* on the board. Ask students what is special about this set of words. After they note that all three have the word *ball* in them, ask: *What else is special about them?* Guide students to understand that they are all made up of two smaller words.

TEACHING THE LESSON

1. Word Detective

- Have students circle the smaller words in each compound. Have them share out.

2. Word Study

- Explain that there are two kinds of compound words: one-word and two-word compounds. Brainstorm lists of both types and write them on the board. Encourage students to copy the lists in their **notebooks**.

3. Word Play

- Ask volunteers to read the starburst notes and give examples of sports and hobbies.

Heads Together Have pairs of students complete the chart together. Review the completed charts with the class.

Spelling and Phonics

- Say or play the words *role* and *come* several times. Ask students what they notice about the two words. (Both have the vowel *o* but the sound is different.) Read the words in the box aloud.

READING

D WORD WORK

1. Word Detective Two words can sometimes be put together to form a new word. The new word is called a *compound word*. It has its own meaning: **home + town = hometown**

Look at these names for sports and activities. Find the smaller words in each compound word. What does each small word mean?

basketball	skydiving	weightlifting
football	softball	horseback riding

2. Word Study Some compound words are one word. Some are two words. Match each example in this chart with the correct type of compound word.

b	1. roller skates	a. One word
____	2. handball	b. Two words
____	3. baseball	
____	4. running shorts	
____	5. eyeball	

SPELLING AND PHONICS: To do this activity, go to page 183.

3. Word Play Work with a partner. Think about the words in the box. Is each word a sport or a hobby? Complete the chart below. You can use your dictionary.

stamp collecting	windsurfing	bird watching
scuba diving	needlepoint	water-skiing
snowboarding	model building	woodworking

Sports	Hobbies

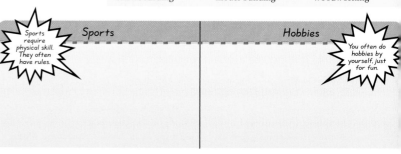

Sports require physical skill. They often have rules.

You often do hobbies by yourself, just for fun.

- Have students complete the chart. Review the correct answers.

✓ WRAP UP

Outcome Sentence Have students complete this sentence stem, then share:

My favorite hobby is ______________.

PB PRACTICE BOOK ACTIVITY

See Activity B, Word Work, on Practice Book page 22.

ANSWER KEY

Word Study: 1. b; 2. a; 3. a; 4. b; 5. a.

Word Play: Sports: scuba diving, snowboarding, windsurfing, water-skiing;

Hobbies: stamp collecting, needlepoint, model building, bird watching, woodworking.

Spelling and Phonics: role: home, Coke, close, go, stove, rope; **come**: shove, done, love, some, none, one.

GRAMMAR — Complete Sentences

Listen Up Listen to each sentence. Point your thumb up if it unds correct. Point your thumb down if it sounds wrong.

1. I student.	4. I am learning English.
2. My name Stefan.	5. Born in Poland.
3. I am in the ninth grade.	6. Am sixteen years old.

Learn the Rule A sentence has to have certain things to be mplete. Read the following rules for complete sentences. Then repeat tivity 1.

COMPLETE SENTENCES

1. A complete sentence has a subject and a complement. The subject is the person or thing that is doing or experiencing something. The **complement** finishes the idea. It identifies what the subject is doing or experiencing.

*Maria **is sixteen years old.*** *Juan **comes from Mexico.***

2. Every complement has a verb.

*Maria **is sixteen years old.*** *Juan **comes from Mexico.***

Practice the Rule Work with a partner. Tell a classmate about urself using the following questions. Speak in complete sentences.

1. What is your name?
2. How old are you?
3. Where do you go to school?
4. Who is your best friend?
5. What grade are you in?
6. What is your favorite hobby?

E GRAMMAR

Standard

- Use complete sentences to express ideas

WARM UP

- Write these two sentences on the board: *I happy. I am happy.* Ask students which one is correct. Have a volunteer tell you why.

TEACHING THE LESSON

1. Listen Up

- Ask students to listen carefully as you play the tape or CD, or read the words aloud. Have students point their thumbs up if the sentence sounds correct, and point them down if it sounds wrong.

2. Learn the Rule

- Write these sentences on the board:

  Maria is sixteen years old.

  Juan comes from Mexico.

  Read the rules for complements aloud and ask a volunteer to circle the subject and underline the complement in each sentence.

- Paraphrase the rules as you point to the sentence parts on the board. For example: *Every sentence has at least two parts. The first part is the subject. It tells who or what you are talking about. Here you are talking about Maria. Here you are talking about Juan. Maria and Juan are the subjects of these two sentences. The second part of a sentence is the complement. It tells something about the subject. This sentence tells how old Maria is. This sentence tells where Juan comes from.*

- Repeat the Listen Up activity, reteaching as necessary.

3. Practice the Rule

Heads Together Read each question aloud and call on a different student to answer. Guide students to answer in complete sentences. Then have students practice the questions and answers in pairs. Invite several pairs to present their questions and answers to the class.

✓ WRAP UP

- Have students look again at the sentences in the Listen Up activity, then rewrite sentences that are not correct.

PB PRACTICE BOOK ACTIVITY

See Activity C, Grammar, on Practice Book page 23.

F BRIDGE TO WRITING — Personal Web Page

READING STRATEGY
Using Pictures to Make Predictions: When you see pictures and words together, the pictures can help you guess what the words will be about.

1. Before You Read Personal Web pages often include personal profiles. Look at the picture below. Who do you think wrote the profiles at the bottom of the page for a Web site?

- ☐ a teacher
- ☐ a student
- ☐ a special class or club

2. Let's Read Read what these students say about themselves. Which person is most like you?

1 Darryl

I enjoy singing and am currently in the chorus.

I enjoy sports such as basketball and football.

My goals for the future are to graduate high school and attend a good college.

2 Rachel

I am on the honor roll.

My favorite subjects are world history and personal living.

My favorite hobbies are doing hair, exercising, listening to music, and playing basketball.

My goal for the future is to live a happy life and to be successful in the job I have.

3 Steven

My favorite subject in school is math because I will need math in the future.

My hobbies are fishing and riding bikes.

My goal for the future is to become an auto wholesaler.

chorus—a group of people who sing together

attend—to go to a class or school regularly

honor roll—a list recognizing students who get all A's and B's

personal living—a class that teaches you skills for everyday life

exercising—doing activities that make you strong and healthy

auto wholesaler—someone who sells cars

F BRIDGE TO WRITING

Standard
- Read complete sentences

WARM UP

- Ask students if they have ever visited a celebrity's Web site. What do they look for when they visit these sites?

TEACHING THE LESSON

1. Before You Read

- Ask students to look at the picture, then identify who wrote the profiles for a Web site.

2. Let's Read

- Tell students they are going to read three student profiles.

My Turn: Read Aloud/Think Aloud Read the profiles, commenting as you read and defining unfamiliar words:

"Currently" means right now.

Only the students with the best grades get on the honor roll.

Rachel has a lot of different types of hobbies.

Steven thinks about the future a lot.

- Read the profiles. Ask students to identify who is probably the best student, explaining why. (Answers may vary.)

Our Turn: Interactive Reading Have individual students read each sentence. As they read, focus on the glossed words, ask questions, and make comments:

Darryl's goal is to attend college. What are some of your goals?

What is the "honor roll" called in our school? Does it have a different name?

What are some things you might learn in a "personal living" class?

Why would someone need math if he or she plans on being an auto wholesaler?

- **Build Fluency** Have different students read each sentence after you. Encourage them to read fluently and with expression.

Your Turn: Independent Reading Have students take turns reading the descriptions to themselves. Ask them to think about which person is the most like them, sharing why.

3. **Making Content Connections** Look at the students' profiles again. Complete the columns for Darryl, Rachel, and Steven in the chart below. Then, write your name at the top of the fourth column and add information about yourself.

	Darryl	Rachel	Steven	________
What does this student like about school?	chorus			
What are this person's favorite hobbies or sports?				
What is this person's goal for the future?				

4. **Expanding Your Vocabulary** Work with a partner. Complete the chart below. Put each word in the box in the correct column.

Favorite Activities Word Bank

skateboarding	sailing	swimming	sewing
hiking	tennis	playing checkers	surfing
stamp collecting	jogging	biking	painting
camping	fishing	golf	bowling

	By Myself	With a Friend
Indoors		
Outdoors		

3. Making Content Connections

- Read aloud and explain the questions in the chart.

Heads Together Have students complete the charts, looking back at the profiles as they do this. Have them fill in the fourth column with information about themselves.

Interactive Writing Copy the chart on the board. Invite volunteers to complete the chart.

4. Expanding Your Vocabulary

- Review the meaning of the terms in the word bank by having volunteers explain what each one is in their own words. Then explain the chart. Say: *In the top left, put words that describe things you do indoors by yourself.*

Heads Together Have pairs of students complete the chart. Review the correct answers orally with the class. Some answers may fit in more than one section. For example, sewing could be done by yourself or with a friend.

JUST FOR FUN

Play Lingo Bingo. Have students work in groups of three or four. Have one member of each group fold a sheet of paper into sixteen squares. Ask each group to write one of the favorite activities from the Word Bank in each square. Then say several sentences about each activity but do not name it—for example: *You ride on something that has four wheels.* Each group circles the word. The first group to complete a row whispers, "Lingo Bingo!"

✓ WRAP UP

Outcome Sentence Have students complete this sentence stem, then share:

My goal for the future is to _________.

PB PRACTICE BOOK ACTIVITY

See Activity D, Test-Taking Practice, on Practice Book pages 24 and 25.

See Activity E, Using New Vocabulary, on Practice Book page 26.

ANSWER KEY

Before You Read: a special class or club

Making Content Connections: **Darryl—School:** chorus; **Sports:** football; **Future:** attend college. **Rachel—School:** world history and personal living; **Sports:** basketball; **Future:** live a happy life, be successful in her job. **Steven—School:** math; **Sports:** fishing and riding bikes; **Future:** become an auto wholesaler.

Expanding Your Vocabulary: Possible answers: **Indoors, By Myself:** stamp collecting, sewing, painting, bowling; **Indoors, With a Friend:** playing checkers; **Outdoors, By Myself:** jogging, fishing, skateboarding; **Outdoors, With a Friend:** skateboarding, hiking, camping, sailing, tennis, swimming, biking, golf, surfing.

G WRITING CLINIC

Standards
- Organize information into categories
- Use visual images to express meaning

WARM UP

- Ask students why they think some people create Web pages. Accept all reasonable answers. (To make new friends. To find other people who are interested in the same things. To advertise a business.)

TEACHING THE LESSON

1. Think about It

- Ask students to think about the question for a few moments and then ask for the correct answer. Point out that the two incorrect answers both involve information that is not true and factual.

2. Focus on Organization

- Ask students to divide a piece of paper into four sections by folding it in quarters (Part 1). Then have them copy the numbered headings in the chart into the sections of their papers.
- Give students time to complete their charts with information from Keith's Web page (Part 2). Have them share out.

G WRITING CLINIC Personal Web Pages

1. Think about It What is a personal Web page like? Explain.

☐ an imaginary story ☐ a true life story ☐ a movie or play

2. Focus on Organization

❶ Fold a sheet of paper in half lengthwise and then fold it again to creat a chart with four parts. Label each part like the following example.

1. Information about Keith	2. Friends and Family
3. School	4. Favorite Things

❷ Look at Keith's Web page again. Put the information from Keith's Web page into the chart you've created. Make sure you include everything.

1. Information about Keith *Name: Keith Clark* *Date of birth: April 5, 1991*	2. Friends and Family *Brother: Kurt*
3. School	4. Favorite Things

Rewrite Keith's Web page on a separate piece of paper. Use complete sentences with bullets. Use the model as an example.

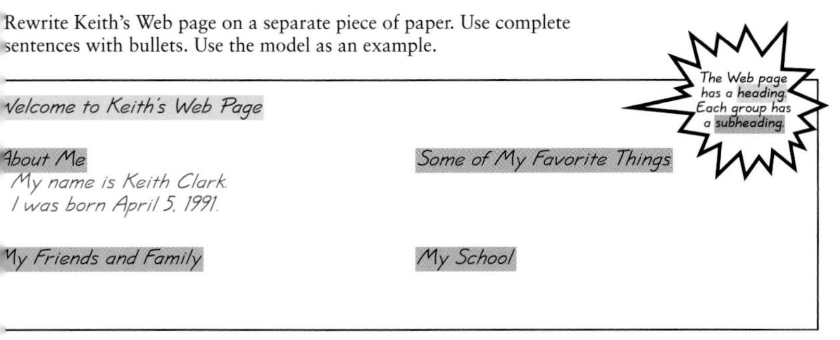

The Web page has a heading. Each group has a subheading.
Welcome to Keith's Web Page
About Me
My name is Keith Clark.
I was born April 5, 1991.
Some of My Favorite Things
My Friends and Family
My School

Focus on Style Web pages often use photos or art to describe a son. Which of these pictures would *you* add to Keith's Web page? y? Circle your answers.

2.

3.

5.

6.

8.

9.

- Now have students work with a partner, recreating Keith's Web page (Part 3). Point out the note about the need for a heading and subheadings.

Access for All Invite students with strong spatial intelligence to add interesting design features to their Web pages. They may enjoy researching Web sites on the Internet and making use of some of the ideas they find there.

PB PRACTICE BOOK ACTIVITY

See Activity F, Focus on Organization, on Practice Book page 27.

3. Focus on Style

- Heads together. Have students discuss which art they might add to Keith's Web page, then share. Have students discuss why each photo or illustration is relevant or not relevant.
- Have students think about their own interests. Which piece of art would they use on their own Web pages?

WRAP UP

- Ask students to suggest other information Keith might *not* want to add to his Web page. (His girlfriend's name. His phone number.) Discuss why he should or shouldn't add each type of information.

PB PRACTICE BOOK ACTIVITY

See Activity G, Focus on Style, on Practice Book page 28.

ANSWER KEY

Think about It: a true life story

Focus on Organization 2: Possible answers: **1. Information about Keith:** My name: Keith Clark; My date of birth: April 5, 1991; My hometown: Sunrise; My Hobbies: Watching sports; My future plans: Go to college; My nicknames: Twin, White Boy, Clark. **2. Friends and Family:** My friends: Brian, Kareem, Anthony, R.J., John, Kurt, Mike, Keno, Christina, Tim, Shane, Jeff, Kim, and Danielle; My best friend: Danielle; My brother: Kurt. **3. School:** My school: Hollywood; My grades: A's. **4. Favorite Things:** My music: Rock and R&B; My favorite brand: Nike; My favorite food: Thai food; My favorite drinks: Energy drinks, OJ; My favorite color: Blue.

Focus on Organization 3: Answers will vary but all information should be in complete sentence form.

Focus on Style: Possible answers: 2. Michael Jordan is Keith's role model.; 3. Keith has a friend named Kim.; 8. Keith gets all A's.; 9. Keith plans to go to college.

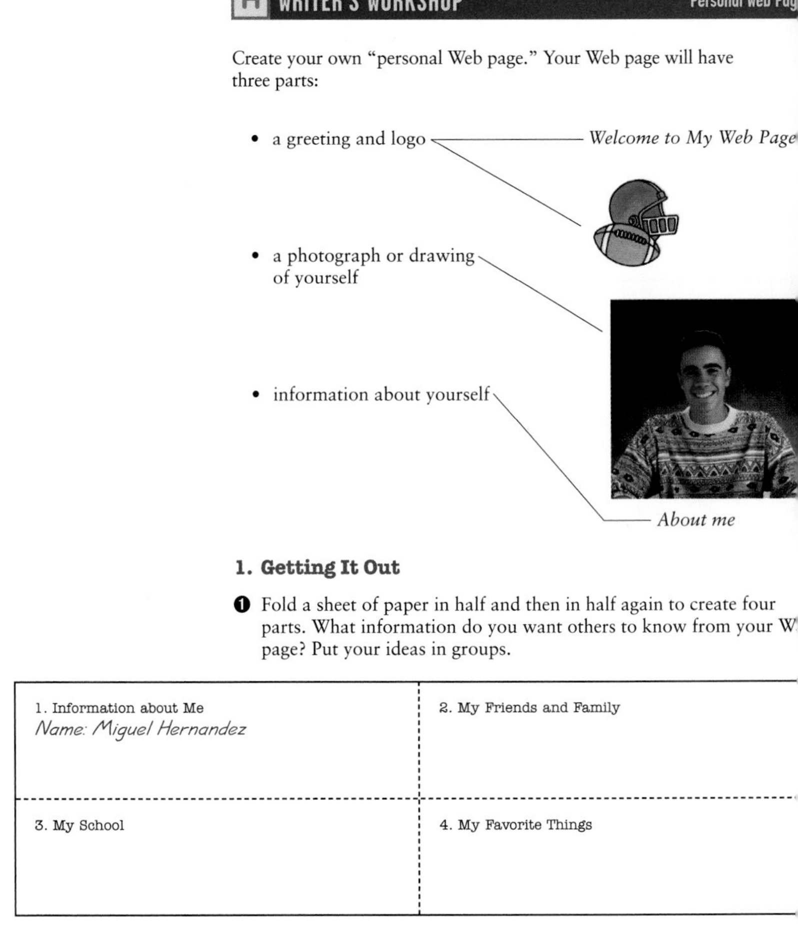
WRITING

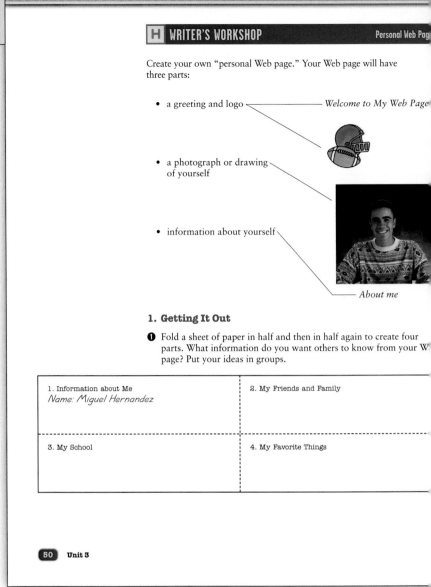

H WRITER'S WORKSHOP — Personal Web Pag

Create your own "personal Web page." Your Web page will have three parts:

- a greeting and logo — *Welcome to My Web Page*
- a photograph or drawing of yourself
- information about yourself — *About me*

1. Getting It Out

1. Fold a sheet of paper in half and then in half again to create four parts. What information do you want others to know from your W page? Put your ideas in groups.

1. Information about Me *Name: Miguel Hernandez*	2. My Friends and Family
3. My School	4. My Favorite Things

50 Unit 3

H WRITER'S WORKSHOP

Standard

- Use the writing process: prewriting

1. Getting It Out

WARM UP

- Tell students that they are going to have the chance to create their own personal Web pages. Explain that they will display their web pages on the wall or bulletin board rather than on the Internet.
- Have students look at Miguel's Web page, identifying the greeting, the logo, the picture, and the information. Ask students to suggest alternative ideas that they might use on their own Web pages in place of the ones on Miguel's page. For example the greeting might be *Let's play!* and the logo might be a soccer ball.

TEACHING TIP If the technology is available at your school and the administration is comfortable with the idea, you might help supervise interested students in placing their Web pages on the school's Web site.

WARM UP

- Ask students what they think will get other people interested in their Web pages. Is it the greeting, the size and color of the print, the artwork, the actual information?

TEACHING THE LESSON

- Ask students to divide a piece of paper into four sections by folding it in quarters (Part 1). Then have them copy one of the numbered headings in the chart into each section of their papers.

Or have students use the form on Practice Book page 29. Have students fill in their information.

Decide what information about you is interesting. Share it with a partner.

My favorite sports are baseball and soccer.
I have two sisters and one brother.
My name is Miguel.
I'm a ninth grader at Kennedy Middle School.

Each "welcome" uses letters with different shapes, sizes, and colors.

Think about your welcome. Which style do you like best? Why?

b.

Meet Miguel

d.

Welcome to Miguel's Web Page!

Look for a photo of yourself. Or draw your own portrait.

- Have students share their charts with a partner, asking for feedback on what is interesting and what is not so interesting (Part 2).
- Have students think about their welcomes. Discuss different types of greetings they might use. Encourage students to suggest other greeting ideas not shown on the page (Part 3).
- Have students bring in photos of themselves or draw their own portraits (Part 4).

WRAP UP

- Ask volunteers to share what they think is the most interesting or exciting information in their charts.

PB PRACTICE BOOK ACTIVITY

See Activity H, Writer's Workshop, on Practice Book page 29.

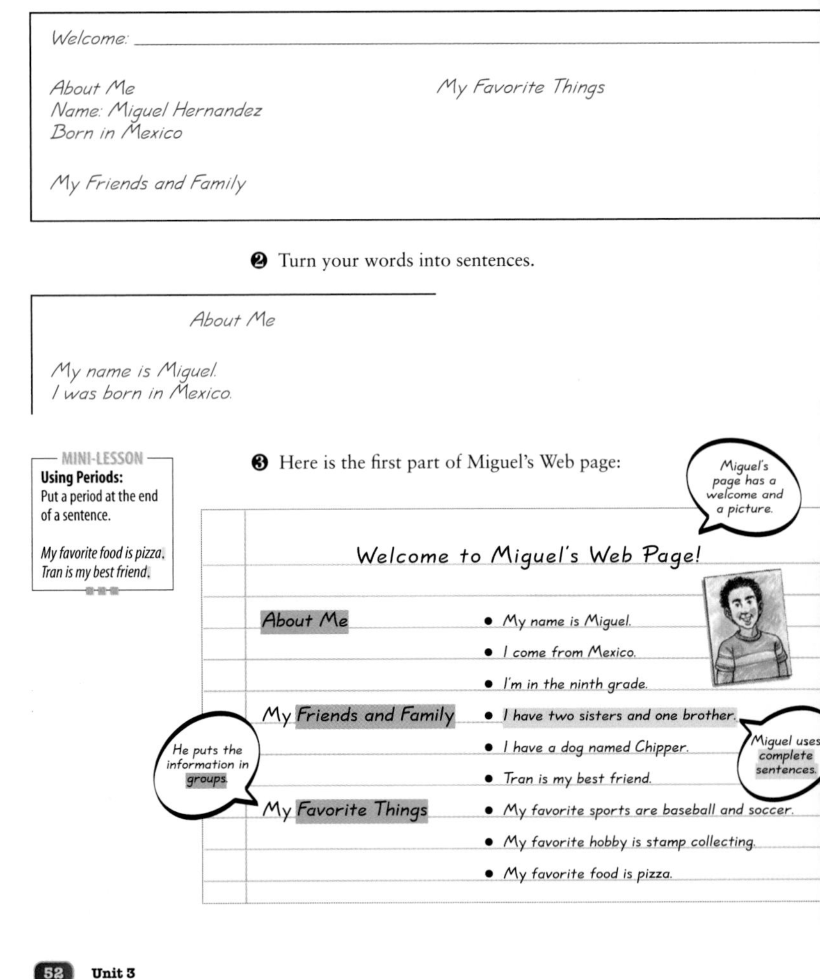

WRITING

2. Getting It Down

❶ Make an outline like this. Use words and phrases that give information about you.

Welcome: ______

About Me
Name: Miguel Hernandez
Born in Mexico

My Favorite Things

My Friends and Family

❷ Turn your words into sentences.

About Me

My name is Miguel.
I was born in Mexico.

MINI-LESSON
Using Periods:
Put a period at the end of a sentence.

My favorite food is pizza.
Tran is my best friend.

❸ Here is the first part of Miguel's Web page:

Miguel's page has a welcome and a picture.
Welcome to Miguel's Web Page!
About Me
• My name is Miguel.
• I come from Mexico.
• I'm in the ninth grade.
My Friends and Family
• I have two sisters and one brother.
• I have a dog named Chipper.
• Tran is my best friend.
My Favorite Things
• My favorite sports are baseball and soccer.
• My favorite hobby is stamp collecting.
• My favorite food is pizza.
He puts the information in groups.
Miguel uses complete sentences.

52 Unit 3

H WRITER'S WORKSHOP

Standards

- Use the writing process: drafting, revising, editing
- Use a simple outline to organize information
- Write complete sentences
- Give a short oral presentation

2. Getting It Down

WARM UP

- Ask: *How is a web page like a story? How is it different?* Elicit students' ideas.

TEACHING THE LESSON

- As students copy the outline onto a separate sheet of paper, copy it on the board (Part 1). Then have students look at the first part of Miguel's outline, *About Me.* Ask a volunteer to read the information aloud. Then have students find similar kinds of information in their own Getting It Out charts. Have a volunteer share as you enter his or her information in the outline on the board.
- Now have students complete their own outlines (Part 2). Remind students to use single words and phrases in their outlines.
- It's time for students to turn their outlines into their own Web pages (Part 3). Point out how Miguel turned his notes into complete sentences. Ask volunteers to read different notes from the chart on the board and turn them into complete sentences.
- Point out how Miguel used a picture and bullets to make his Web page attractive and easy to read. Supply colored markers and invite students to use the same techniques.
- Help students identify the strengths in Miguel's Web page. Use the comments in the speech bubbles to guide the discussion.
- Give students time in class to complete their Web pages.

Mini-Lesson on Conventions Point out the Mini-Lesson box. Ask students to point out where Miguel used periods and didn't use periods on his Web page.

WRAP UP

- Tell students that they will have a chance to revise their work during the next session. Have them locate the ChecBric for this unit in the Student Book or Practice Book. Have them prepare for Getting It Right by reviewing the ChecBric on their own, underlining indicators they're not sure about.

Getting It Right Take a careful look at your Web page. Use this ide to revise your writing.

Question to Ask	How to Check	How to Revise
1. Will other students want to read my Web page?	Show your greeting to a partner. Ask if it is interesting.	Add a picture or change the size, shape, or color of the letters and words.
2. Is the information in groups?	Look at each group and make sure the information goes together.	Move some information to a different group.
3. Do I tell a lot about myself?	Make sure each group has two or three sentences.	Add more information about yourself to each group.
4. Do I use complete sentences?	Underline the subject and circle the complement in each sentence.	Add missing words to make complete sentences.

Presenting It Share your Web page design with the class. Take a allery walk" around the classroom and read your classmates' Web pages.

Make a note-taking chart like this one. List the name of each classmate on the chart.

My Classmates	One Interesting Fact
Carlos	
Tran	
Lori	

Help your teacher post the Web page designs along a bulletin board or wall.

Read each Web page design. Take notes on your chart. Write one interesting fact about each person.

Share one interesting fact you learned about a classmate with the class.

3. Getting It Right

WARM UP

- Guide students through the ChecBric for this unit in the Student Book or Practice Book. Explain that they will use the ChecBric to prepare a final draft of their writing.
- Have volunteers explain, in their own words, what each indicator in the ChecBric means.

TEACHING THE LESSON

- Have students use the chart and the ChecBric to revise their work.
- Now have students share their Web pages with a partner. Have students tell one thing they like about their partner's Web page.

Group Share Model how students will share their Web pages. Have several volunteers practice giving feedback on a classmate's Web page.

WRAP UP

- Tell students that they will present their Web pages by displaying them in a classroom "gallery" where all students can walk around and look at them.

Help students complete the ChecBric on Practice Book page 105. Ask them to attach it to the back of their Web pages before putting them in their portfolios.

4. Presenting It

WARM UP

- Help students create their own gallery by displaying their Web pages on bulletin boards and other wall surfaces in the classroom (Part 2).

TEACHING THE LESSON

- Have students make a note-taking sheet (Part 1).
- Have students take a gallery walk, looking at each Web page and taking notes (Part 3).
- Have students share interesting things they learned about other students from their Web pages (Part 4).

> TEACHING TIP Save student Web pages for display on Back-to-School Night.

✓ WRAP UP

Outcome Sentence Have students complete this sentence stem, then share:

I liked ____________'s Web page because ________________.

I BEYOND THE UNIT

Standards

- Make a bar graph to express information visually
- Read and respond to poetry
- Write a simple poem based on a model

1. On Assignment

WARM UP

- Do a quick survey of how many right-handed and left-handed students there are in the class and write the results on the board. Then create a simple column graph comparing the two types of students. Ask a volunteer to explain briefly how a column graph works.

TEACHING THE LESSON

- Use 3×5 index cards or similar sized pieces of paper as answer cards. Give six to each student (Part 1).
- Have students complete an answer card for each of the six questions (Part 2). Collect all the answer cards, sorting them by question.
- Ask students to form six groups (Part 3). Supply each group with large chart paper and colored markers. Give each group all the answer cards for a particular question (sport, hobby, TV show, etc.).

Team Talk Have each group write down the various answers to their question and make tally marks showing how many people chose each answer (Part 4).

- Have each group of students make a column graph using the results of the tallying activity (Part 5). Supply a ruler so that they can mark off the bars in equal increments. Have them shade in each bar using a different color marker.

I BEYOND THE UNIT

1. On Assignment Make a column graph that shows your favorite things.

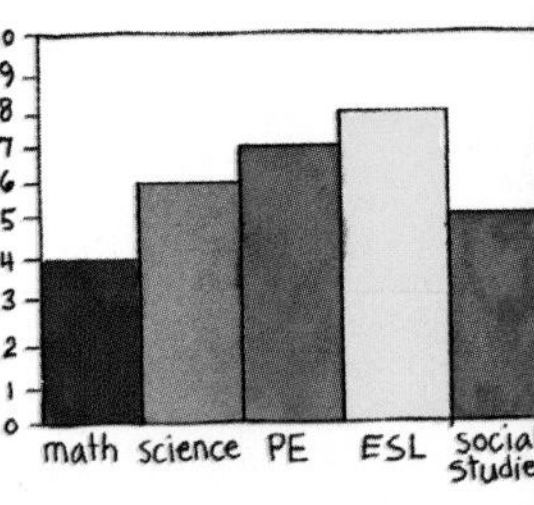

❶ Your teacher will give you six "answer cards." Label each card with one of these subjects:

Sport
Hobby
TV show
Food
School subject
Singer

❷ Fill out an answer card for each of the following questions:

What is your favorite sport?
What is your favorite hobby?
What is your favorite TV show?
What is your favorite food?
What is your favorite subject in school?
Who is your favorite singer?

❸ Divide up into six groups. Each group will get all the completed answer cards for *one* of the questions.

❹ Count up, or tally, how your class answered the question assigned to your group.

EXAMPLE:

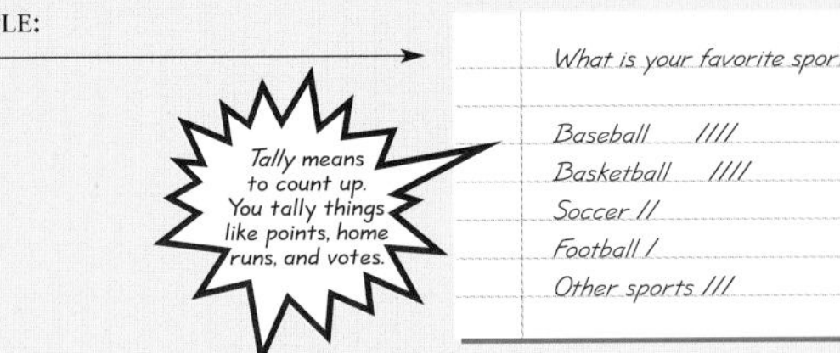

Tally means to count up. You tally things like points, home runs, and votes.
What is your favorite sport?
Baseball ////
Basketball ////
Soccer //
Football /
Other sports ///

❺ Make a column graph with the information from Step 4. Use a big piece of paper and colored markers. Share your graph with classmates.

54 Unit 3

- Have students share their graphs with their classmates.

WRAP UP

- Choose one or two graphs. Help students make pie charts that convey the same information.

Link to Literature

SHARED READING Read the autobiography poem written by Mikey L, who attends school in Edina, Minnesota.

LET'S TALK Answer the following questions.

1. What is one thing about Mikey that is just like you?
2. What is one thing about Mikey that is different from you?
3. What do you like about the poem? Why?

JUST FOR FUN Write your own autobiography poem. Use this planner to help you with organization.

1st line: Your first name only
2nd line: Three or four words that tell something about you
3rd line: Brother/Sister/Son/Daughter of ___________
4th line: Who loves ___________, ___________, and ___________
5th line: Who feels ___________, ___________, and ___________
6th line: Who fears ___________, ___________, and ___________
7th line: Who would like to see ___________, ___________, and ___________
8th line: Your last name (or initial) only.

Mikey

Funny, nice, fun, and fast
Son of Nancy
Who loves popcorn, family, and the end of the school year
Who feels that school is too long, base-ball is fun,and summer is too short
Who fears heights, breaking a bone, and lots of homework
Who would like to see the Vikings win the Super Bowl, school end, and New York
L

Source: edina.k12.mn.us

heights—high places
Vikings—Minnesota's football team
Super Bowl—the championship football game played every year in January

2. Link to Literature

WARM UP

- Write the words *autobiography* and *biography* on the board. Tell students that a biography tells someone's life story. Help students figure out what an *autobiography* is.

TEACHING THE LESSON

- **Shared Reading** Read the autobiography poem "Mikey" aloud as students follow along. Model oral expression and use pauses to help clearly communicate the meaning of each line.
- Now play the tape or CD, or read the poem all the way through. Then go through it again, one line at a time. After each line, pause and ask a volunteer to explain what the line means in his or her own words.
- Have volunteers read the poem aloud. Encourage students to read with expression. Answer any questions students may have about new vocabulary words.
- **Let's Talk** Use the questions to lead a discussion of the poem.

JUST FOR FUN

Have students use the planner in the Practice Book to write their own autobiography poems.

✓ WRAP UP

Have students read their poems to the class.

PB PRACTICE BOOK ACTIVITY

See Activity I, Responding to Literature, on Practice Book page 30.

✓ UNIT WRAP UP

Outcome Sentence Write these sentence stems on the chalkboard:

I think that Mikey ______.

I wonder if Mikey ______.

Have students look back at the poem, complete the sentences, and then share out.

Where Are We?

Unit Overview

Section	At a Glance	Standards
Before You Begin	Students examine a picture of two people and imagine the conversation they may be having.	■ Derive meaning from visual information
A. Connecting to Your Life	Students sort address descriptions from the most specific to the least specific.	■ Listen for details ■ Organize information in a logical sequence
B. Getting Ready to Read	Students talk about places in the community and learn content area vocabulary.	■ Use context to figure out the meaning of new words ■ Use content-area vocabulary (maps)
C. Reading to Learn	Students look at several maps and learn how to read a legend. PRACTICE BOOK: Students complete sentences about map-making and map symbols.	■ Read and understand simple sentences ■ Use content-area vocabulary (maps)
D. Word Work	Students explore common antonym pairs. PRACTICE BOOK: Students complete sentences with antonyms.	■ Use knowledge of antonyms to derive meaning from text ■ Identify sound/spelling relationships
E. Grammar	Students learn how to form plural nouns. PRACTICE BOOK: Students complete sentences with plural nouns.	■ Form plurals
F. Bridge to Writing	Students learn more about maps and places in the community. PRACTICE BOOK: Students practice taking Reading Vocabulary and Reading Comprehension tests. PRACTICE BOOK: Students practice new vocabulary.	■ Read and understand connected sentences

Section	At a Glance	Standards
G. Writing Clinic	Students learn mapping conventions (use of color, shapes, and abbreviations). PRACTICE BOOK: Students read directions and trace a route on a map. They also label symbols on the map. PRACTICE BOOK: Students write abbreviations for a variety of addresses and state names.	■ Read and understand maps ■ Use mapping conventions (font, color, abbreviations)
H1. Writer's Workshop: Getting It Out	Students choose a location to map, gather materials, and make a rough draft map of the area.	■ Use the writing process: prewriting
H2. Writer's Workshop: Getting It Down	Students create maps, labeling important places and adding a legend, a scale bar, and a title. PRACTICE BOOK: Students sketch their maps.	■ Use the writing process: drafting ■ Understand and use content-area vocabulary (maps)
H3. Writer's Workshop: Getting It Right	Students revise and edit their maps.	■ Use the writing process: revising and editing
H4. Writer's Workshop: Presenting It	Students present their maps to their classmates and give each other feedback.	■ Give a short oral presentation
I. Beyond the Unit	Students learn about various types of maps. Students read and respond to a poem. PRACTICE BOOK: Students add words in their first language to a poem written in English.	■ Read and understand maps ■ Read and respond to poetry ■ Recognize cognates

BEFORE YOU BEGIN

Standard

- Derive meaning from visual information

- Have students look at the picture on page 57. Note that we see Juan and his brother. Ask: *What are they doing? What is Juan looking at?*
- Read the caption under the picture. Ask volunteers to explain what it means.

Shared Writing Ask students to imagine what Juan and his brother are saying. Help students create a short dialog on the board. Have volunteers act out the dialog.

TEACHING TIP In this unit, it will be helpful if you can have various types of maps to show students.

Unit 4 Where Are We

Read...

- Selections from *Looking at Maps and Globes* by Carmen Bredeson. Learn about maps and globes—and how to use them.

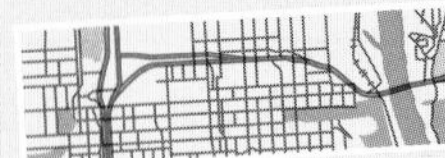

Link to Literature

- "Door Number Four," a poem by Charlotte Pomerantz.

Objectives:

Reading:
- Understanding maps and symbols
- Understanding captions that describe or explain
- Strategy: Connecting visuals with text
- Literature: Reading poetry

Writing:
- Making maps
- Labeling
- Choosing colors, fonts, and abbreviations
- Writing titles

Vocabulary:
- Learning names for places at school and in the community
- Recognizing antonyms
- Understanding basic map terminology

Listening/Speaking:
- Understanding a conversation
- Following directions for getting somewhere

Grammar:
- Making plural nouns

Spelling and Phonics:
- Spelling the /s/ sound as in *kiss* and *city*.

We're Lost!

EFORE YOU BEGIN

lk with your classmates.

1. Look at the picture. What are Juan and his brother doing? What is Juan looking at?
2. Read the caption. What is happening?
3. What are Juan and his brother saying to each other? Help your teacher write on the board the words they might be saying.

A CONNECTING TO YOUR LIFE

Standards
- Listen for details
- Organize information in a logical sequence

WARM UP

- Invite students to tell about times when they got lost. Ask: *What did you do?*

TEACHING THE LESSON

1. Tuning In

- Tell students that they will now hear Juan talking with his brother. Ask students to listen for what the problem is. Play the tape or CD, or read the script as students listen.

  Now have students listen one more time. Ask them to tell you what the problem is.

2. Talking It Over

- Ask students what street they live on. Then have them tell what neighborhood they live in (if your city's neighborhoods have names). Elicit a variety of responses. Note that neighborhoods have many streets and that your city has many neighborhoods.

Heads Together Have students look at the pictures with captions. Explain that they are out of order. Read each caption aloud as students follow along. Have partners number the captions in the correct order, from smallest to largest. Then have volunteers read the captions aloud, in the correct order.

Heads Together Have students work in pairs as they rewrite the eight sentences to describe their own lives. Elicit one or two examples from students and write them on the board. For example: *I live on Center Street.*

READING

A CONNECTING TO YOUR LIFE

1. Tuning In Listen to the conversation between Juan and his brothe[r]. What is the problem?

- ☐ Juan is too young to drive.
- ☐ Juan forgot the address.
- ☐ Juan lost the map.

2. Talking It Over Work with a partner. Put the pictures and captio[ns] in the correct order. Then rewrite the sentences to tell where you live.

__1__ Jay lives in a house. His house is on Washington Street.

_____ Jay lives in the United States. The United States is on a continent: North America.

_____ Jay lives on Washington Street. Washington Street is in a neighborhoood.

_____ Jay lives in Columbus. Columbus is in the state of Nebraska.

_____ Jay lives in Nebraska. Nebraska is in a country: the United States.

_____ Jay lives in a neighborhood. His neighborhood is in the city of Columbus.

Read the title of this unit. What do you think the unit is probably about? Check (✓) the correct answer.

_____ 1. It's about people getting lost.

_____ 2. It's about knowing how to read maps and globes.

_____ 3. It's about following directions.

58 Unit 4

Center Street is in the Fairmont neighborhood. The Fairmont neighborhood is in Tulsa. Invite volunteers to share with the class.

- Read the unit title aloud. Have students use finger signals to tell what they think the unit might be about.

WRAP UP

- Have several volunteers who are recent arrivals from other cities or countries tell you the street, neighborhood, state/province, country, and continent where they used to live.

ANSWER KEY

Tuning In: Juan forgot the address.

Talking It Over: Row 1: 1, 6, 2; Row 2: 4, 5, 3.

Talking It Over: 2.

B GETTING READY TO READ

. Learning New Words Read the sentences below. Try to figure ut the meanings of the underlined words.

1. Tran doesn't know if Lori's house is north or south of his house. He doesn't know which direction her house is in.
2. A baseball, basketball, and volleyball are not square, they're round.
3. Zaida's house is like a box. It has a flat roof.
4. When you throw a football, it curves in the air.
5. Venus and Mars are planets. The Earth is a planet, too.
6. Jorge takes the bus to school. He can't walk there because he lives two miles away.
7. Miguel's dog Chipper has short legs. He is only one foot tall.
8. Chipper has a very short tail. It is only an inch long.

Aatch each word on the left with the correct definition on the right.

1. direction	a. without any high or low areas
2. round	b. a U.S./English unit used to measure long distances (= 5,280 feet or 1.6 kilometers)
3. flat	c. the way someone or something is facing, moving, or located in relation to you
4. curve	d. a unit for measuring length (= 12 inches or 30.5 centimeters)
5. Earth	e. a unit for measuring short lengths (= 1/12 of a foot or 2.54 centimeters)
6. mile	f. the planet we live on
7. foot	g. shaped like a ball or the letter "o"
8. inch	h. to move like part of a circle

. Talking It Over Work with a partner. On a separate piece of aper, make a list of places in the community you see every day or almost very day.

B GETTING READY TO READ

Standards

- Use context to figure out the meaning of new words
- Use content-area vocabulary (maps)

WARM UP

- Ask a few volunteers to name one building or other place in the community they passed on the way to school today. List them on the board.

TEACHING THE LESSON

1. Learning New Words

Team Talk Write the new words on the board. Have students work in groups of three, defining at least three words they know (or think they know).

- Have volunteers read aloud the sentences with underlined words. Ask other students to talk about or show what each underlined word means. Encourage students to make up their own sentences using the vocabulary word.
- Now have students complete the activity in their books by matching each word to its definition. Review the correct answers with the class.

2. Talking It Over

Heads Together Have students work in pairs as they list as many places as they can that they pass on their way to school every day. Encourage students to list places in order.

- Ask students to save their lists of places for the next lesson.

✓ WRAP UP

Outcome Sentence Write these sentence stems on the board:

On my way home, I walk past ______.
I see ________________.

Have students share, using complete sentences.

Access for All Students with strong spatial intelligence are able to represent the real world using images in their minds. Ask which students in the class can always tell where north is and very rarely get lost. Have them explain how they know where they are.

ANSWER KEY

Learning New Words: 1. c; 2. g; 3. a; 4. h; 5. f; 6. b; 7. d; 8. e.

C READING TO LEARN

READING STRATEGY
Using Pictures:
When you see pictures and words together, the pictures can help you understand the meaning of the words.

1. Before You Read Working in pairs, explain to a partner how to get from school to your house or apartment.

2. Let's Read Read the following information about maps. Look at and think about each picture as you read the caption.

Maps are flat drawings of areas of land that show us where to find different places.

1.

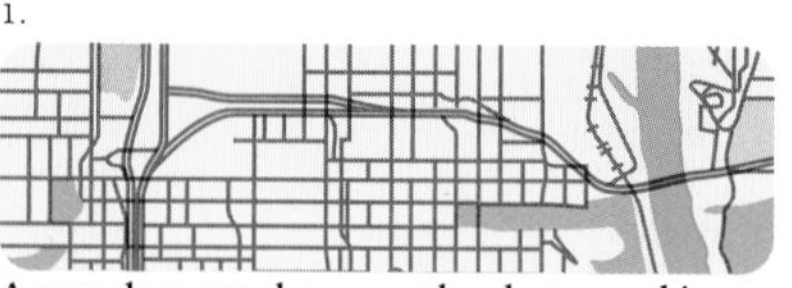

A map does not show exactly what something looks like.

2.

It is not like a photograph.

3.

Maps use symbols. Symbols are small pictures that mean different things. On this map, ▲ is the symbol for mountains; the tree-and-table symbol is the symbol for parks.

4.

Map Legend

The map legend shows what each symbol means.

5.

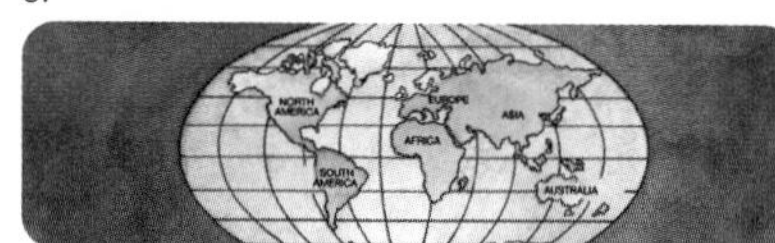

There are many kinds of maps. A world map shows the whole Earth.

6.

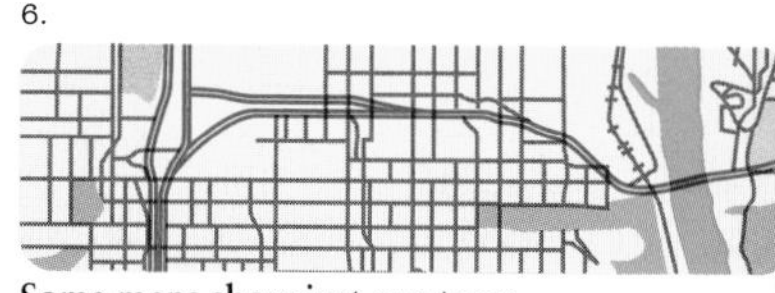

Some maps show just one town.

7.

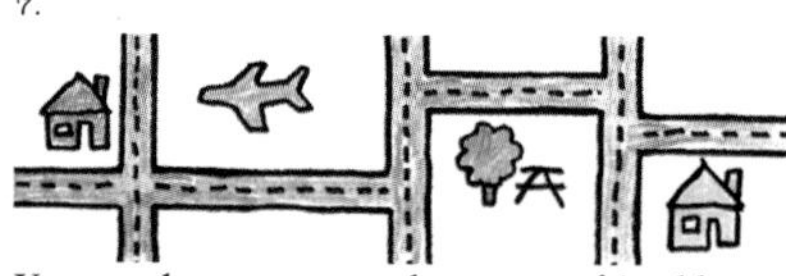

You can draw a map to show a new friend how to get to your house.

8.

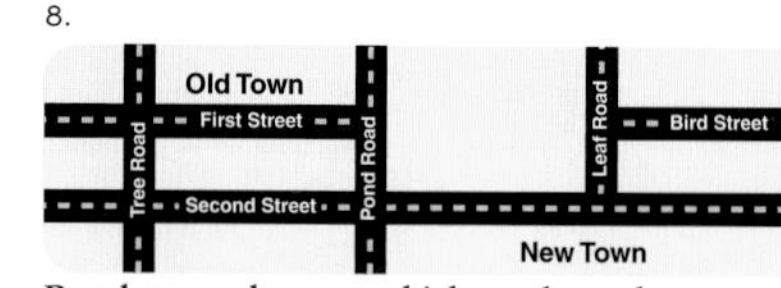

Road maps show us which road to take to get to another town.

C READING TO LEARN

Standards

- Read and understand simple sentences
- Use content-area vocabulary (maps)

WARM UP

- Brainstorm a list of different kinds of maps. Note all student responses on chart paper and save it for later use. Help students think of a wide variety of maps such as road, street, subway, bus, weather, shopping mall, etc.

TEACHING THE LESSON

1. Before You Read

Heads Together Ask students to take out the list of places between home and school that they made during the previous lesson. Have them work in pairs, describing the route they take from home to school. Suggest that they use their lists as a guide.

Interactive Writing Write these terms on the board: *turn right, turn left, walk straight, pass by.* Ask two or three volunteers to dictate the routes they take, as you draw maps that follow their directions. Help students use these terms, and other direction words and phrases, as they talk.

2. Let's Read

Explain that pictures and images can help you figure out what something is about (Reading Strategy box). For example, the mountain symbol helps explain the word *mountain.*

My Turn: Read Aloud/Think Aloud Read the captions aloud to the class. As you read, stop to comment on language and ideas.

Outcome Sentence Now play the tape or CD, or read the captions. Write these sentence stems on the board:

Symbols are _______ *A legend is* _______

Have students listen for information about each, then complete each sentence stem. (Symbols are tiny pictures that represent large objects. A legend tells you what each symbol means.)

Our Turn: Interactive Reading Now have students help read each caption. As students read, ask questions, and make comments.

- **Build Fluency** Have pairs of students take turns reading the captions to each other.

Your Turn: Independent Reading Have students read the captions to themselves. The ask them to complete this sentence stem:

✓ *Something I learned about maps is* ______________________.

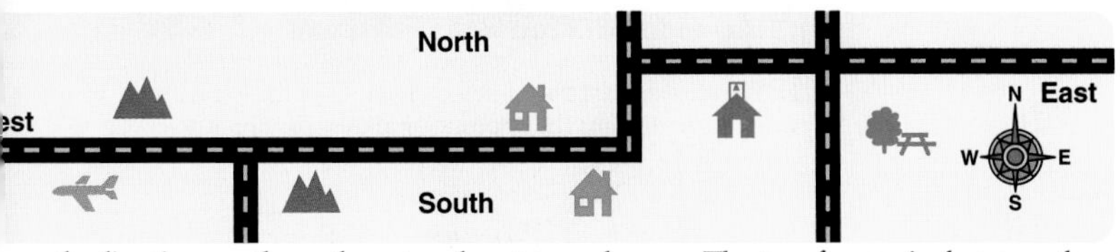

use the directions north, south, east, and west to read a map. The top of a map is always north. bottom of a map is south. East is to the right. West is to the left.

Source: *Looking at Maps and Globes* by Carmen Bredeson

Unlocking Meaning

Identifying the Purpose Which phrase explains the main purpose of this unit? Check (✓) the correct answer.

_____ 1. to teach us how to go from one place to another

_____ 2. to teach us how to read maps

_____ 3. to teach us how to draw symbols

Finding Details Complete the legend below. Match each symbol with a word.

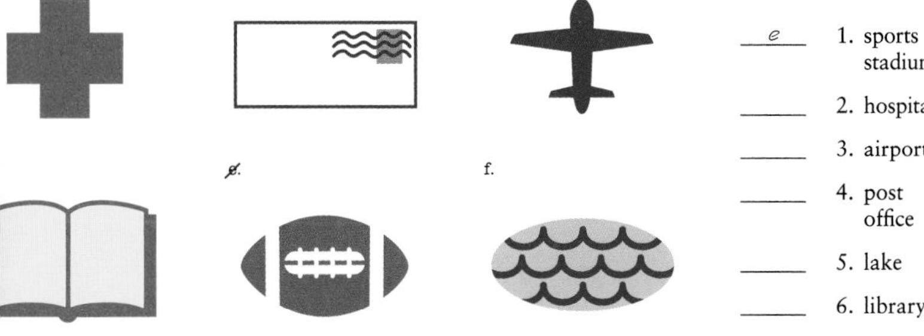

__e__ 1. sports stadium

_____ 2. hospital

_____ 3. airport

_____ 4. post office

_____ 5. lake

_____ 6. library

Think about It Work in four groups. Make a map for *one* quadrant, or ¼-part, of your classroom. Then put the four parts together.

Before You Move On Draw a map that shows how to get from school to your home.

3. Unlocking Meaning

✓ IDENTIFYING THE PURPOSE

Have students use finger signals to tell you which sentence tells the main purpose of this unit.

FINDING DETAILS

- Have students complete the activity by matching the letter of each picture to the number of the correct meaning.

THINK ABOUT IT

- Divide the class into four groups. If you have a large class, you may wish to divide students into two or three sets of four groups each. Divide the classroom into four quadrants using masking tape on the floor, or simply show students where the dividing lines are. Then assign one quadrant to each group and have them work together to draw their maps. Remind students to make up their own symbols for things such as desks, wall maps, computers, etc. When they finish, have each set of four groups place their maps together and comment on each other's work.

> TEACHING TIP Consider, as an alternative, having students map each quadrant of your school campus.

BEFORE YOU MOVE ON

- Have students use the lists of places they made in the previous lesson to create maps that show how they get from school to their homes.

WRAP UP

Heads Together Invite volunteers to share their maps.

PB PRACTICE BOOK ACTIVITY

See Activity A, Revisit and Retell, on Practice Book page 31.

ANSWER KEY

Identifying the Purpose: 2.

Finding Details: 1. e; 2. a; 3. c; 4. b; 5. f; 6. d.

D WORD WORK

Standards
- Use knowledge of antonyms to derive meaning from text
- Identify sound/spelling relationships

WARM UP

- Write the following pairs of antonyms on the board and ask students what each pair of words has in common.

  beautiful—ugly
  boring—interesting

TEACHING THE LESSON

1. Word Detective

- Have students work with partners to complete the activity by matching each word in the first column with its opposite in the second column.

2. Word Study

- Explain that many words have an opposite, or *antonym,* for example, *big* and *little.* Then have students use dictionaries to check their matches in the previous activity. Review the answers from Activity 1.

3. Word Play

Heads Together Have students work in pairs as they write an antonym for each word on the list. Then have them write sentences using the words and their antonyms.

JUST FOR FUN

Have a student make up a sentence using a word from the pairs they have studied. This student then calls on a classmate to make up a true sentence using an antonym. For example:

S1: *The pizza at Benny's is hot.*
S2: *The pizza at Joe's is cold.*

READING

D WORD WORK

1. Word Detective Match each word on the left with the word on the right that means the opposite or almost the opposite.

1. round	a. west
2. top	b. little
3. east	c. flat
4. long	d. short
5. big	e. bottom

2. Word Study An antonym is a word with the opposite, or almost opposite, meaning of another word. Look at the examples below.

A map is flat.	A globe is round.
Canada is north of the U.S.	Mexico is south of the U.S.

3. Word Play Work with a partner. Write an antonym for each of th words below. Then write pairs of sentences using all the words. You ca use your dictionary.

1. long *short*	2. new	3. fast	4. narrow
5. dark	6. hot	7. high	8. easy

1. *I have long hair. My brother has short hair.*
2.
3.
4.
5.
6.
7.
8.

SPELLING AND PHONICS: To do this activity, go to page 183.

62 Unit 4

Spelling and Phonics

- Read each word aloud. Have students tell you what they notice about the letters in red. (They all sound the same, like /s/.) Have students complete each word on a separate piece of paper. Encourage them to use their dictionaries to check their work.

✓ WRAP UP

- Write the following words on the board and ask students to find at least two antonyms for each: *old, short, large.*

PB PRACTICE BOOK ACTIVITY

See Activity B, Word Work, on Practice Book page 32.

ANSWER KEY

Word Detective: 1. c, 2. e, 3. a, 4. d, 5. b.

Spelling and Phonics: a. mouse; b. miss; c. Francisco; d. classes; e. whistle; f. Christmas; g. cents; h. address; i. face.

GRAMMAR — Plural Nouns

Listen Up Listen to each sentence. Point your thumb up if it ...nds correct. Point your thumb down if it sounds wrong.

1. I'll have two cheeseburger.
2. The library is two blocks away.
3. I am taking five class at school.
4. I can't see! I lost my glasses.
5. This is a map.
6. One bird is sitting on the fence and two birds are sitting in the tree.

Learn the Rule Adding one or two letters to nouns makes them ...ral. Read the rules for making singular nouns plural. Then repeat ...ivity 1.

PLURAL NOUNS

. A final *–s* or *–es* is added to a noun to make it plural.

Singular		Plural	
This is a map.	This is a dish.	These are map*s*.	These are dish*es*.

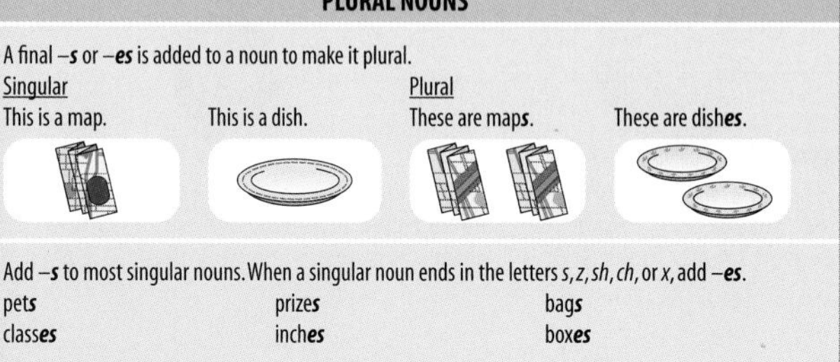

. Add *–s* to most singular nouns. When a singular noun ends in the letters *s, z, sh, ch,* or *x*, add *–es*.

pet*s*	prize*s*	bag*s*
class*es*	inch*es*	box*es*

Practice the Rule Work with a partner. Complete each sentence ...h the plural form of the underlined noun.

1. Lori won a prize. Mario won two ______.
2. My favorite class is math. Juan's favorite ______ are PE and science.
3. One car is parked in the garage and two ______ are parked in the driveway.
4. Stefan has a dog. His friend William has a cat and two ______.
5. There's a fox in the yard. There are two more ______ in the woods.
6. I have four good ______. My best friend is Tran.

E GRAMMAR

Standard

- Form plurals

WARM UP

- Hold up one classroom object (e.g., pencil, piece of chalk). Ask: *What is this?* Next hold up two of the same objects. Ask: *What are these?*

TEACHING THE LESSON

1. Listen Up

- Ask students to listen carefully. Then play the tape or CD, or read the sentences aloud. Have students point their thumbs up if the sentence sounds correct, and point them down if it sounds wrong.

2. Learn the Rule

- Use the chart to teach the three rules about how plurals are formed in English. Explain: *Sometimes the* –s *ending sounds like /s/ and sometimes it sounds like /z/. However, the* –es *ending always sounds like /z/.*

Heads Together Have students write original examples of the two types of plurals on a piece of paper. Then have them share with a partner and check each other's work. Make a two-column chart on the board with the headings *–s* and *–es* and have students take turns writing their examples in the correct column.

- Repeat the Listen Up activity, reteaching as necessary.

3. Practice the Rule

- Read the instructions and have students complete the activity with a partner.

TEACHING TIP Here is a list of common words whose plurals are formed using *–es: dress, bus, kiss, wish, rash, bush, match, peach, watch, sandwich, badge, judge, fax, six.*

WRAP UP

- Have students look around the classroom and write down three things they see that are plural. Have them share their lists.

PB PRACTICE BOOK ACTIVITY

See Activity C, Grammar, on Practice Book page 33.

ANSWER KEY

Listen Up: Correct sentences: 2, 4, 5, 6.

Practice the Rule: 1. prizes; 2. classes; 3. cars; 4. dogs; 5. foxes; 6. friends.

F BRIDGE TO WRITING

Standard
- Read and understand connected sentences

WARM UP

- Draw a large circle on the board. Explain that this is the earth. Then draw a horizontal line through the circle: the equator. Have students copy your drawing.
- Ask students to write the name of a continent they think is north of the equator, then one that is south of the equator.
- Ask them to write the name of a country they think is north of the equator, then one that is south of the equator.
- Have students share, as you record on your globe. Then, have volunteers look at your world map or globe, circling responses that are correct.

TEACHING THE LESSON

1. Before You Read

- Point to both a world map and a globe in your classroom. Have students compare them. Record students' ideas—perhaps using a Venn diagram—on the board.

2. Let's Read

My Turn: Read Aloud/Think Aloud Begin by reading the captions aloud. Model correct phrasing and expression and fluent reading. As you read, stop to comment on individual words and ideas. For example: *"Take up" means "cover."*

- Now play the tape or CD, or read the captions. Ask: *Which shows the earth better, a map or a globe?* Have students explain why.

WRITING

READING STRATEGY
Using Pictures:
When you see pictures and words together, the pictures can help you understand the meaning of the words.

F BRIDGE TO WRITING

Map

1. Before You Read Look around your classroom. What kinds of maps do you see?

2. Let's Read Read more about maps. Use these pictures to help you understand each caption.

1.

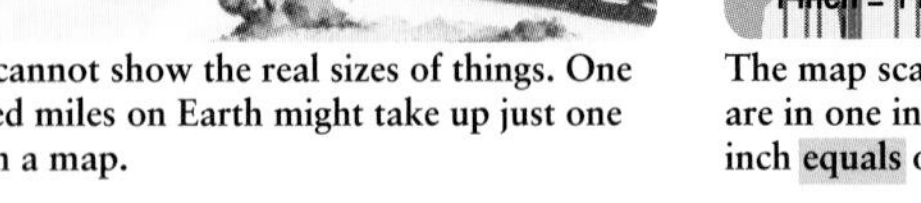

Maps cannot show the real sizes of things. One hundred miles on Earth might take up just one inch on a map.

2.

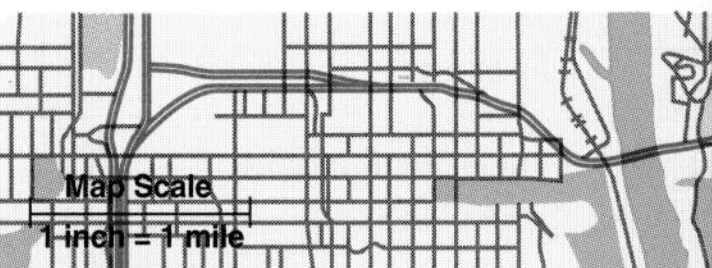

The map scale shows us how many real miles are in one inch on the map. On this scale, one inch **equals** one mile.

3.

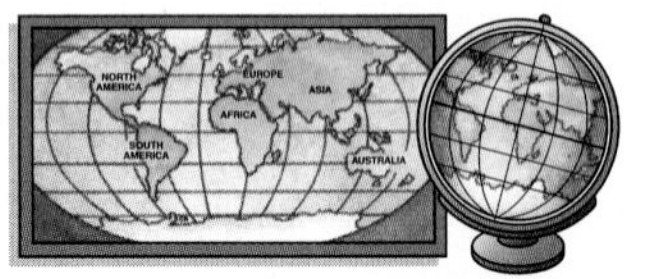

It is hard to show the round Earth on a flat map. A flat piece of paper does not curve. A round globe shows us how the world really looks. It curves like the Earth.

4.

The top of the globe shows us the part of the Earth called the North Pole. The bottom of the globe shows us the South Pole.

5.

The **imaginary** line that **wraps around** the middle of the globe is called the equator. Find the United States on the globe. Is it above or below the equator?

6.

It is fun to find places on the globe. You can **travel** around the world with just your finger!

Source: *Looking at Maps and Globes* by Carmen Brede

equal—to be the same as
imaginary—not real
wrap around—to go all the way around
travel—to go places

64 Unit 4

Our Turn: Interactive Reading Now have students help you read the captions. As they read, focus on the glossed words, ask questions, and make comments. For example: *Show me with your hands what a "curve" looks like.*

- **Build Fluency** Have students take turns reading the captions under the pictures aloud to each other.

Your Turn: Independent Reading Have students read the captions on their own. As they read, ask them to think of one question to ask a partner. Then have pairs take turns asking each other a question about each caption.

TEACHING TIP Have students bring in postcards from different places in the world, then arrange them around a world map. Connect each postcard with its location on the map, using yarn or string.

Making Content Connections Draw a simple map that shows
to get from your house to a classmate's house. Your classmate
ıld make the same map. Compare your maps. How are they the
e? How are they different?

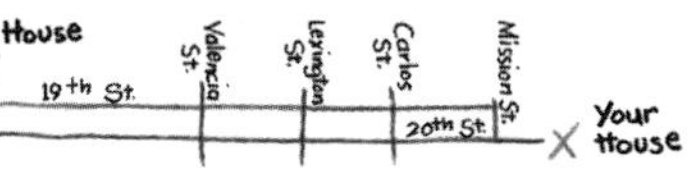

From my house to your house.

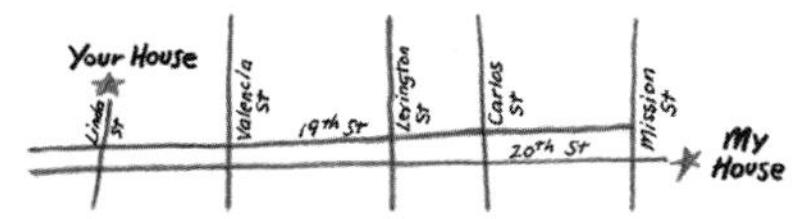

From your house to my house.

Expanding Your Vocabulary A map sometimes shows
dings and other landmarks. Match each item in the map below with
ame.

c	1. library	______	7. bakery
______	2. hotel	______	8. movie theater
______	3. health club	______	9. playground
______	4. car dealership	______	10. supermarket
______	5. post office	______	11. newsstand
______	6. museum	______	12. fast food restaurant

Access for All Have students with strong logical-mathematical skills redraw a simple map, doubling or tripling the scale.

✓ WRAP UP

Sentence Synthesis Write these words on the board: *map, globe, earth.* As a class, have students make a sentence that uses all three words.

PB PRACTICE BOOK ACTIVITY

See Activity D, Test-Taking Practice, on Practice Book pages 34 and 35.

See Activity E, Using New Vocabulary, on Practice Book page 36.

ANSWER KEY

Expanding Your Vocabulary: 1. c; 2. b; 3. j; 4. e; 5. h; 6. a; 7. f; 8. d; 9. g; 10. i; 11. l; 12. k.

3. Making Content Connections

- Tell students that it's time to return to their own neighborhoods.

Heads Together Have pairs of students draw maps showing how to get from one of their houses to the other. Then ask them to look at the maps together and discuss what things are the same on the two maps and what things are different.

- Have them save their maps for later.

4. Expanding Your Vocabulary

- Read the directions and point out where the library is on the map. Look for the hotel (b) together as a class. Ask how we know it's a hotel (fancy entrance, tall building).

Heads Together Ask students to complete the matching activity in pairs.

G WRITING CLINIC

Standards
- Read and understand maps
- Use mapping conventions (font, color, abbreviations)

WARM UP

- Have students look once again at the maps they drew for getting from one house to another. Have them tell you what their maps show (streets, various landmarks, etc.).
- Say: *You want to go somewhere. You have the address. What kind of map would you look at?* (a route map, a road map, a street map)

TEACHING THE LESSON

1. Think about It

- Point out that there are other kinds of maps beside road maps. Ask: *Where do you find maps?* Elicit or explain that *atlases* have maps that show continents, countries, and major bodies of water. *Newspapers* have weather maps and maps showing where important stories are talking place. A *history textbook* often has maps that show battles.
- Consider showing students the types of maps that an atlas contains.

2. Focus on Organization

- Have students look at the route map. Have them identify important elements.

Modeled Writing Have students look back at the maps once again. Ask a volunteer if you can borrow his/her map. Copy it on the board. Model how you might add new elements to the map, including:

a title
a compass rose
symbols and legend, as needed
a scale

- Give students time to modify their own maps.

PB PRACTICE BOOK ACTIVITY

See Activity F, Focus on Organization, on Practice Book page 37.

3. Focus on Style

Heads Together Read the question and the three choices and ask students to give the thumbs up signal for the correct answer (Part 1). Ask students to explain why the route is highlighted in purple.

WRITING

G WRITING CLINIC

1. Think about It Where are three places you often find maps?

☐ in an atlas ☐ in a novel ☐ in your history textbook
☐ in a teen magazine ☐ in the newspaper ☐ on a CD cover

2. Focus on Organization

A route map shows how to get from one place to another. Look at this route map. The sentences below the map explain what the purpose of each part is.

① Route Map for Getting from Scho
to Maria's House

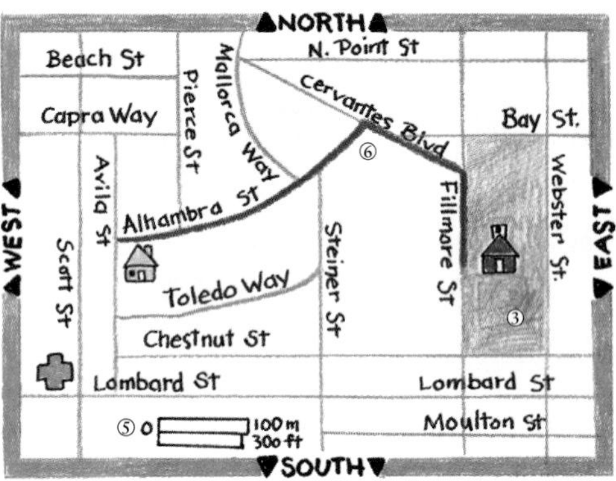

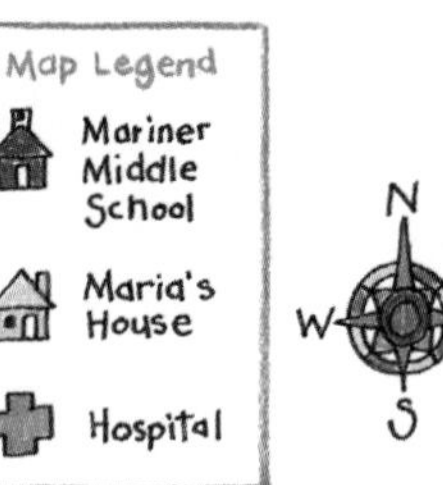

① The map has a title.
② A compass shows direction.
③ The map uses symbols.
④ A legend shows what the symbols mean.
⑤ The map shows the scale.
⑥ The route is easy to follow.

3. Focus on Style

❶ Many maps use colors, shapes, and lines to improve understanding. Colors can help show different places and routes. Look again at the map. What do you think the green area probably shows?

☐ a parking lot ☐ a swimming pool ☐ a park or sports f

Why is the route highlighted in purple? Talk with a partner.

Vhich colors would you use on a map? Match each color on the left vith a place on the right.

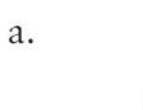

. blue	a. a freeway, road, or street
. green	b. a place with lots of snow
. gray	c. a warm place with lots of sun (like a beach)
. white	d. a park or recreational area
. red	e. water (an ocean, lake, or river)
. yellow	f. a place that gets little rain (like the desert)
. brown	g. a fire station

Iaps often use symbols to show where buildings and landmarks are ocated. Match each building or landmark on the left with the correct ymbol on the right.

. airport — a.

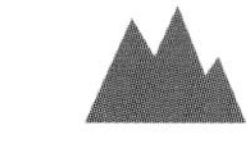

. school — b.

. mountain — c.

Iaps tell the names of streets and roads. They use a font, or print yle, that is easy to read. Which of these do you think is the best font or a street map?

. *Main Street*	3. *Main Street*
. Main Street	4. MAIN STREET

Iaps also use abbreviations, or short forms of words, to name ifferent types of streets. Match each abbreviation on the left with a ıll word on the right.

. Blvd.	a. Street
. Ave.	b. Road
. Hwy.	c. Boulevard
. Rd.	d. Avenue
. St.	e. Highway

PB PRACTICE BOOK ACTIVITY

See Activity G, Focus on Style, on Practice Book page 38.

ANSWER KEY

Think about It: in an atlas, in the newspaper, in your history textbook.

Focus on Style 1: a park or sports field; Purple is different from any other color on the map so the route stands out clearly.

Focus on Style 2: 1. e; 2. d; 3. a; 4. b; 5. g; 6. c; 7. f.

Focus on Style 3: 1. b; 2. c; 3. a.

Focus on Style 4: 2.

Focus on Style 5: 1. c; 2. d; 3. e; 4. b; 5. a.

- Have students match each numbered color with the type of place it would probably stand for on the map (Part 2).
- Next have students match the name of each building or landmark with its symbol (Part 3).
- Have students circle the font they think is the best for a street map (Part 4). Ask volunteers to say which one they chose and why. Guide them to understand that simplicity and clarity are more important than prettiness when labeling things on a map.
- Complete the activity orally (Part 5). Have students spell out each abbreviation (capital B, l, v, d, period) and then say the full form it stands for (Boulevard).

WRAP UP

- Once again, have students revisit their route maps. Have them share things they might do differently with their next maps based on what they learned in this lesson.

H WRITER'S WORKSHOP

Imagine that you are a *cartographer*, or mapmaker. Create a class map book. Work with a partner.

1. Getting It Out

❶ Decide what kind of map you will make. Choose a small area to m[ap] out, one you can easily walk to.

❷ Gather the materials you will need.

1. sketchpad
2. sheet of chart paper or white construction paper
3. pencil
4. ruler
5. colored marking pens
6. calculator (optional)

❸ Walk around the area. Make a rough drawing as you walk.

Each block is
about 250 steps.
That's about
our map will be
10 inches by 12 inches.
Each inch will equal
500 feet.

Estimate, or guess, sizes and distances by walking. Each step equals about two feet.

Write down the names of each street and label buildings and important places.

❹ Decide on the scale of your map.

H WRITER'S WORKSHOP

Standards

- Use the writing process: prewriting, drafting
- Understand and use content-area vocabulary (maps)

1. Getting It Out

WARM UP

- Write these map-making steps on the board and ask students to suggest the correct sequence:

gather map-making materials	(2)
choose a scale for your map	(4)
choose an area to map	(1)
make a rough drawing	(3)

- Explain that in this lesson, pairs of students will create their own maps which will then be gathered into a class map book.

TEACHING TIP You may wish to limit the map making to your school campus. In this case, you can have pairs measure different areas and buildings on campus. Then the pairs can compare their maps.

TEACHING THE LESSON

Heads Together Ask pairs of students to brainstorm different areas they might like to map out and choose one (Part 1).

- Supply the necessary materials as listed in the Student Book (Part 2). Students can make their preliminary sketches using the form on Practice Book page 39.
- Explain that a "rough drawing" is a quick sketch which includes the main routes and key places that will appear on the map (Part 3). Demonstrate the process of recording distances between key places by pacing off the width of the classroom and then converting your "steps" into feet. Remind students to record all distances and draw symbols to represent all key places on their sketches.
- Show students how to convert the actual distances they measured into the correct distances on their maps (Part 4). Say: *Let's say you measure our school and it is 300 feet long and you decided on a scale of 1 inch = 100 feet. You divide the length of the school (300 feet) by the number of feet that equal 1 inch (100 feet). The answer is three. So on your map, the 300-foot-school is three inches long. That will fit on your map.*

WRAP UP

- Invite volunteers to describe parts of the map-making process that they particularly enjoyed or that were particularly challenging for them.

PB PRACTICE BOOK ACTIVITY

See Activity H, Writer's Workshop, on Practice Book page 39.

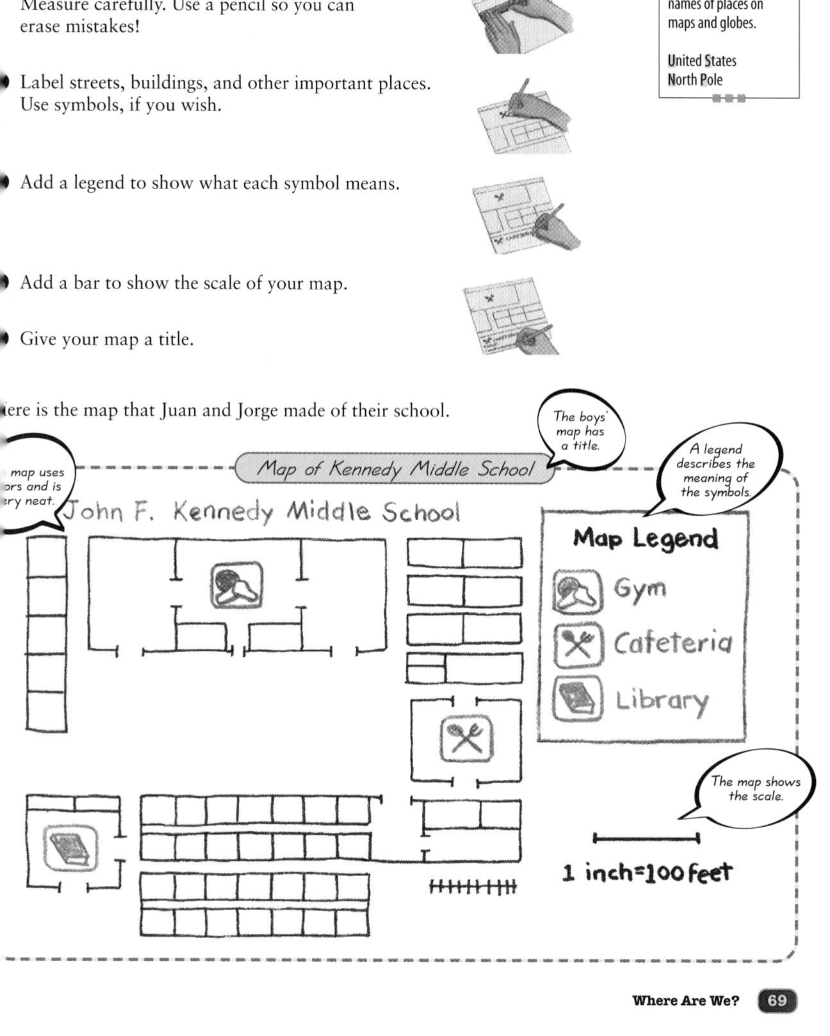
WRITING

. Getting It Down

- Use your rough drawing to lay out your map. Measure carefully. Use a pencil so you can erase mistakes!
- Label streets, buildings, and other important places. Use symbols, if you wish.
- Add a legend to show what each symbol means.
- Add a bar to show the scale of your map.
- Give your map a title.

MINI-LESSON
Capitalizing Place Names: Capitalize the names of places on maps and globes.

United States
North Pole

ere is the map that Juan and Jorge made of their school.

The boys' map has a title.
Map of Kennedy Middle School
map uses ors and is ery neat.
John F. Kennedy Middle School
A legend describes the meaning of the symbols.
Map Legend
Gym
Cafeteria
Library
The map shows the scale.
1 inch=100 feet

Where Are We? 69

2. Getting It Down

WARM UP

- It's time for students to turn their sketches into maps! Have several volunteers share their sketches with classmates. Then explain that the next step will be to add some details that will make their maps easier to understand and more interesting to look at.

TEACHING THE LESSON

- Copy a volunteer's map onto an overhead transparency or draw it on the board or on large chart paper. Use this map to model the steps in this section.
- Remind students to use a pencil so they can fix any errors they make as they lay out their maps (Part 1). Remind them to leave space for the legend.
- Encourage students to make up their own symbols for buildings and other landmarks (Part 2).
- Remind students to include in the legend a guide to all the symbols they have used on the map (Part 3).
- Suggest that they place the scale bar at the bottom of the map near the legend (Part 4).
- Ask students why they might need a calculator when they're making their maps. (A lot of math is involved in converting their real measurements into distances on the map.)
- Finally, have them add a title (Part 5).
- Have students take a careful look at Juan and Jorge's map, noting the title, the symbols, and labels they used, and explaining what each item in the legend means. Help them use the scale to convert the distances on the map into real-world distances.

Mini-Lesson on Conventions
Point out the Mini-Lesson box. Explain that names of cities, countries, and other places usually start with a capital letter. Invite students to take turns writing other place names on the board.

WRAP UP

- Tell students that they will have a chance to revise their work during the next session. Have them locate the ChecBric for this unit in the Student Book or Practice Book. Have them prepare for Getting it Right by reviewing the ChecBric on their own, underlining indicators they're not sure about.

H WRITER'S WORKSHOP

Standards
- Use the writing process: revising and editing
- Give a short oral presentation

3. Getting It Right

WARM UP

- Guide students through the ChecBric for this unit in the Student Book or Practice Book. Explain that they will use the ChecBric to prepare a final draft of their writing.
- Have volunteers explain, in their own words, what each indicator in the ChecBric means.

TEACHING THE LESSON

- Have students use the questions and suggestions in the chart and the ChecBric to revise their work (Part 1).
- Now have students share their maps with a partner. Have students tell one thing they like about their partner's map.

Group Share Model how students will share their maps. Have several volunteers practice giving feedback on a classmate's Web page.

- Using a volunteer's map as a model, demonstrate the steps for revising it (Part 2). If you wish, have the entire class complete each step before you move on to the next one.

WRAP UP

- Tell students they are now ready to present their maps to the class. Suggest that they practice pointing at various parts of the map as they rehearse their presentations so that they will feel more comfortable when they present to the class.

Help students complete the ChecBric on Practice Book page 107. Ask them to attach it to the back of their maps before putting them in their portfolios.

WRITING

3. Getting It Right

❶ Take a careful look at your map. Use this guide to help you revise your work.

Question to Ask	How to Check	How to Revise
1. Does our map have a title?	Ask your partner to read the title aloud.	Add a title that begins, "Map of ____________."
2. Is our map to scale?	Ask an adult, such as your teacher, if your map appears to be to scale.	Change the sizes of buildings or the lengths of streets. Add a scale bar to show what one inch equals.
3. Do we use symbols? If so, does our map have a legend?	Lightly circle each symbol in pencil.	Add symbols for common places. Include a legend.
4. Is our map accurate and easy to follow?	Ask other students if they understand your map.	Make changes, based on the feedback you get.

❷ Develop your final draft.

- Trace over pencil lines with marking pen
- Add color
- Make sure that your map is neatly drawn

70 Unit 4

Presenting It

Share your map with your classmates.

- Ask for feedback.

- Compare your map with similar maps that your classmates made.

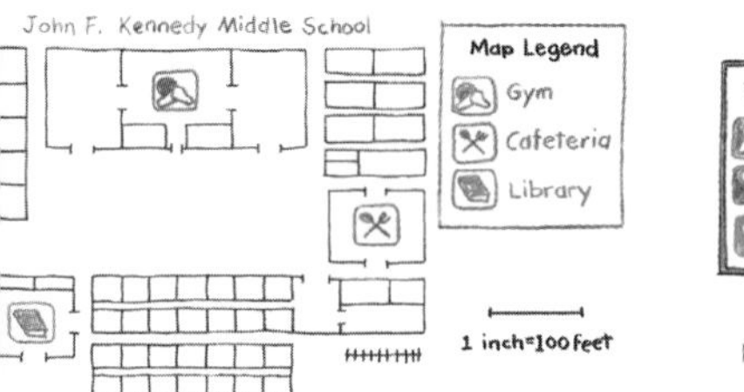

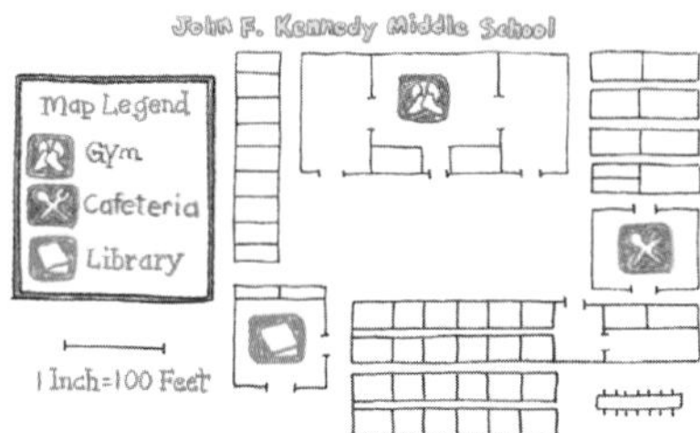

4. Presenting It

WARM UP

- Suggest that students take note of the strong points in their classmates' presentations as they go along and think about how they can incorporate some of these elements into their own presentations.
- As a class, develop a simple presentation checklist. Focus on content, organization, speaking skills (poise, expression, volume, posture, eye contact), enthusiasm, use of visuals, creativity, involvement of the audience, and length of presentation.

TEACHING THE LESSON

- Tell students that you want them to pay attention to these things as they present their work:

  1. Use a loud and clear voice.
  2. Read slowly.
  3. Show your audience your work as you present.
  4. Ask for feedback.

- Have students take turns presenting their maps to their classmates. Remind them to point out all key parts of the map itself, including streets or highways, buildings, landmarks, symbols, etc. Suggest that they also explain briefly the scale they used and tell what the other items in the legend mean.
- Review the sample language for giving positive feedback. Invite students to suggest other phrases they might use. Have students ask their classmates to give them feedback on their maps at the end of their presentation.
- Help students display their maps on the walls of the classroom. Have them do a galley walk, noting the similarities and differences between their maps and other students' maps. Invite volunteers to share their findings with the class.

WRAP UP

- Congratulate students on a job well done.
- Ask students to bring newspapers with maps in them to the next class meeting. Bring in extra newspapers in case some students forget.

I BEYOND THE UNIT

1. On Assignment Learn more about different types of maps. Look in the newspaper to find examples.

❶ Almost every issue of the newspaper has maps. How many different types of maps can you find? Find examples to share with classmates.

1.

Political maps show countries, states, and cities.

2.

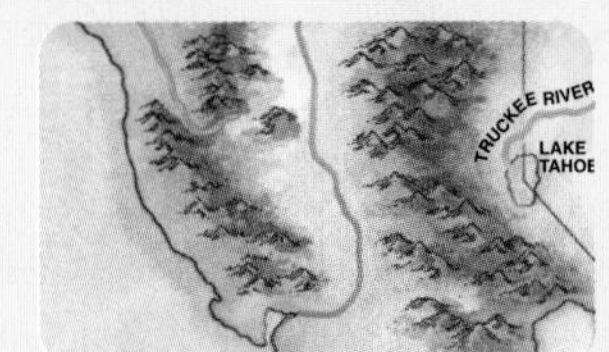

Physical maps show natural features, like mountains, oceans, lakes, and rivers.

3.

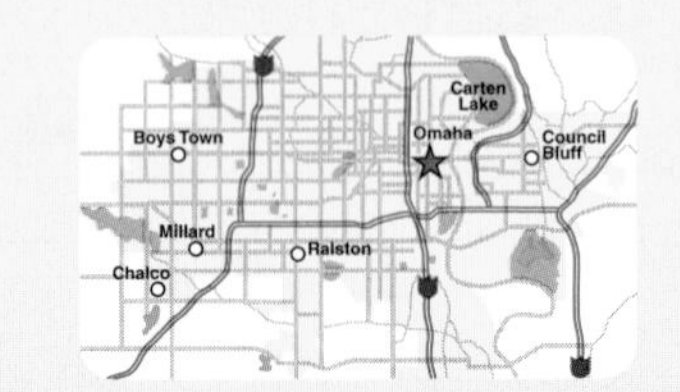

Road maps show types of roads and where places are located.

4.

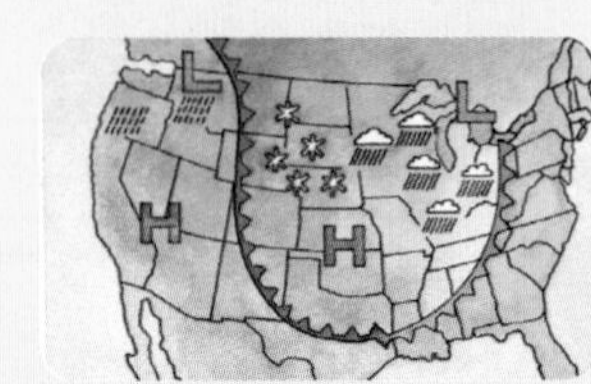

Weather maps show rain, sleet, and snow.

❷ Choose a map from a recent edition of your local newspaper. Show the map to your classmates and explain it to them.

This is a weather map.

What kind of map is it?

Why was this map in the newspaper?

Is it a good map? Could it be better? How?

72 **Unit 4**

I BEYOND THE UNIT

Standards
- Read and understand maps
- Read and respond to poetry
- Recognize cognates

1. On Assignment

WARM UP

- Show students several types of maps found in the newspapers students brought to class, or in an atlas. Name each type of map (weather, political, physical, etc.). Tell students that they are going to learn more about different types of maps.

TEACHING THE LESSON

- Help students understand the symbols and other features used on the maps pictured in the Student Book. Ask students to take turns reading a caption aloud. Then ask questions and make comments.

  Are all the names of countries, states, and cities the same size and color?

  What color are oceans, rivers and lakes?

  How does the cartographer show mountains on the map?

  How can you tell a main road or highway from a side road?

  What does the symbol for snow look like? For clouds? For rain?

- Give students time to look through their newspapers for maps. Distribute the newspapers you brought in to students who didn't bring one to class. Explain that they are to find an example of a map then discuss what type of map it is and what the map tells us. Ask them to talk about whether the map is easy to read and explain why or why not.
- Have students share the maps, as well as their ideas, with classmates.

Technology Tip Students with Internet access can find a wide range of interesting map resources besides the local newspaper. Weather maps are available at www.weather.com. A wide variety of political maps is available through the United Nations Web site. Go to www.un.org and click on Documentation and Maps. Road maps can be found on such Web sites as www.mapquest.com.

WRAP UP

- Tell students to pretend that they have been offered a high-paying job as a mapmaker. Have them tell which type of maps—political, physical, road, or weather—they would like to work on and why.

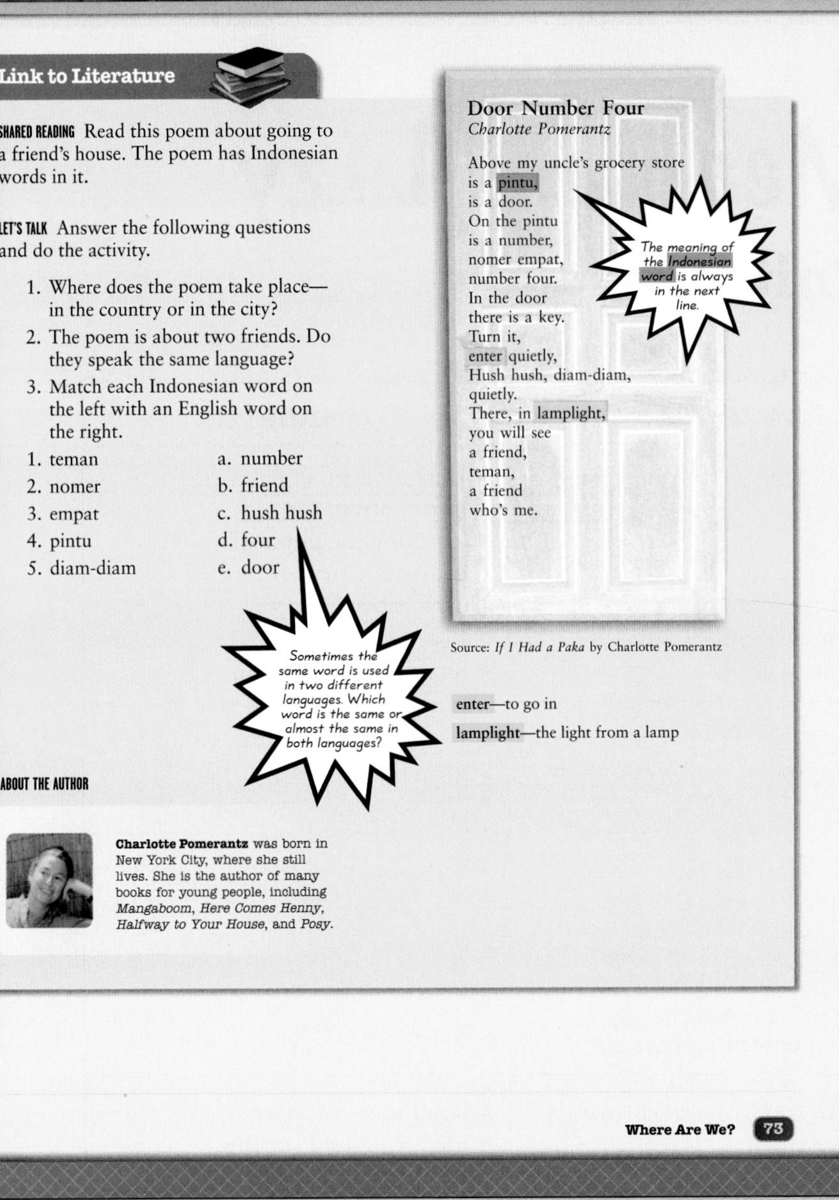

Link to Literature

SHARED READING Read this poem about going to a friend's house. The poem has Indonesian words in it.

LET'S TALK Answer the following questions and do the activity.

1. Where does the poem take place—in the country or in the city?
2. The poem is about two friends. Do they speak the same language?
3. Match each Indonesian word on the left with an English word on the right.

1. teman	a. number
2. nomer	b. friend
3. empat	c. hush hush
4. pintu	d. four
5. diam-diam	e. door

Door Number Four
Charlotte Pomerantz

Above my uncle's grocery store
is a pintu,
is a door.
On the pintu
is a number,
nomer empat,
number four.
In the door
there is a key.
Turn it,
enter quietly,
Hush hush, diam-diam,
quietly.
There, in lamplight,
you will see
a friend,
teman,
a friend
who's me.

The meaning of the Indonesian word is always in the next line.
Sometimes the same word is used in two different languages. Which word is the same or almost the same in both languages?

Source: *If I Had a Paka* by Charlotte Pomerantz

enter—to go in
lamplight—the light from a lamp

ABOUT THE AUTHOR

Charlotte Pomerantz was born in New York City, where she still lives. She is the author of many books for young people, including *Mangaboom, Here Comes Henny, Halfway to Your House,* and *Posy.*

Where Are We? 73

2. Link to Literature

WARM UP

- Ask students to give examples of words from their native language that they hear native speakers of English using from time to time.

TEACHING THE LESSON

Shared Reading Read the poem "Door Number Four" aloud as students follow along. Model oral fluency and expression. Ask students to identify the Indonesian words and guess what they mean.

- **Build Fluency** Practice reading for fluency. Have students read each line aloud after you have read the line.
- Have volunteers read the poem aloud. Encourage students to read with expression.

Let's Talk Use the discussion questions to lead a discussion of the poem.

- Ask students to locate each Indonesian word from item 3 in the poem. Then have them look at the English words that come right after it. Help them match each Indonesian word in the first column of item 3 with the correct English word in the second column.

WRAP UP

- Ask students to make up original sentences using the Indonesian words. Have them say the English sentence first and then repeat it using Indonesian words. For example: *Close the door quietly. Close the pintu diam-diam.*

PB PRACTICE BOOK ACTIVITY

See Activity I, Responding to Literature, on Practice Book page 40.

✓ UNIT WRAP UP

Outcome Sentence Have students complete this sentence stem in their **notebooks:**

I learned to make maps. What I enjoyed most was _______________.

ANSWER KEY

Let's Talk: 1. b; 2. a; 3. d; 4. e; 5. c.

Mean and Lazy

Unit Overview

Section	At a Glance	Standards
Before You Begin	Students describe a Bengal tiger.	■ Derive meaning from visual information ■ Describe the physical characteristics of something
A. Connecting to Your Life	Students match animal names to their pictures.	■ Listen for details ■ Share information and ideas
B. Getting Ready to Read	Students discuss the characteristics of various animals and learn useful vocabulary.	■ Use context to figure out the meaning of new words ■ Share information and ideas
C. Reading to Learn	Students read about three "mean" animals: the Komodo dragon, the anaconda, and the praying mantis. PRACTICE BOOK: Students answer interview questions about the animals in the reading passage.	■ Read and understand simple sentences
D. Word Work	Students learn measurement words for size, length, and weight. PRACTICE BOOK: Students complete sentences using the correct measurement words.	■ Read information in charts ■ Identify sound/spelling relationships
E. Grammar	Students learn subject–verb agreement rules. PRACTICE BOOK: Students practice using correct present tense verb forms.	■ Recognize and use third person singular *–s*
F. Bridge to Writing	Students read about three "lazy" animals: the cow, the hippopotamus, and the cat. PRACTICE BOOK: Students practice taking Reading Vocabulary and Reading Comprehension tests. PRACTICE BOOK: Students match animals with facts about them.	■ Read and understand simple sentences

Section	At a Glance	Standards
G. Writing Clinic	Students examine the organization and contents of a field guide, then use adjectives to make sentences more interesting. PRACTICE BOOK: Students read passages about animals and then organize the information in outline form. PRACTICE BOOK: Students use adjectives to make writing more interesting	■ Identify the structural features of a field guide ■ Use adjectives to make writing lively
H1. Writer's Workshop: Getting It Out	Students choose an animal to write about, answer questions about it, draw a picture of it, and make a map showing where it comes from. PRACTICE BOOK: Students use a form to plan their field guide pages.	■ Use the writing process: prewriting
H2. Writer's Workshop: Getting It Down	Students make a page plan to use when writing their reports.	■ Use the writing process: drafting
H3. Writer's Workshop: Getting It Right	Students revise and edit their reports.	■ Use the writing process: revising and editing
H4. Writer's Workshop: Presenting It	Students present their reports to their classmates and give each other feedback.	■ Give a short oral presentation
I. Beyond the Unit	Students contribute to a class picture dictionary of animals and read and respond to an alphabet poem. PRACTICE BOOK: Students respond to and rewrite an alphabet poem.	■ Identify the letters of the alphabet ■ Read and respond to poetry

BEFORE YOU BEGIN

Standards

- Derive meaning from visual information
- Describe the physical characteristics of something

- Ask students to look at the picture on page 75 and tell what they see. Then ask what they would do if they came face to face with this kind of animal.
- Have them read the caption and name the animal.

 **Interactive Writing** Ask students to describe the Bengal tiger. As they speak, write their words on the board.

- Tell students that tigers can be *mean*, or cruel and nasty. Help them list other animals that are mean.

Unit 5 Mean and Laz

Read...

- Selections from *The Meanest: Amazing Facts about Aggressive Animals* and *The Laziest: Amazing Facts about Lazy Animals* by Mymi Doinet.

Learn about animals who would rather bite than make friends and creatures that are the couch potatoes of the animal kingdom.

Link to Literature

- "Wild Animals," an alphabet poem written by students.

Objectives:

Reading:
- Understanding information about animals in texts and charts
- Strategy: Finding details
- Literature: Responding to poetry

Writing:
- Writing complete sentences
- Contributing a page to a class field guide
- Using adjectives to enliven writing
- Helping to write a class picture dictionary about animals
- Helping to create a class alphabet poem about animals

Vocabulary:
- Learning word groups: Size, height, and weight
- Learning names of wild animals

Listening/Speaking:
- Understanding an oral narrative
- Answering questions about information in a chart
- Telling about and describing animals
- Giving others feedback

Grammar:
- Understanding subject-verb agreement

Spelling and Phonics:
- Pronouncing words with the letter *a*

A Bengal tiger

[B]EFORE YOU BEGIN

[Tal]k with your classmates.

1. Look at the picture. What do you see? What would you do if you met one of these animals?
2. Read the caption. What type of tiger is this?
3. What does the Bengal tiger look like? Help your teacher write a description.

A CONNECTING TO YOUR LIFE

Standards
- Listen for details
- Share information and ideas

WARM UP

- Ask students to name some scary animals.

TEACHING THE LESSON

1. Tuning In

- Tell students that they are going to hear a frightening story.
- Ask students to listen for what happened to Eduardo and Brian. Play the tape or CD, or read the script as students listen. Now read the three statements and have students hold up one finger if they think the first statement is correct, two fingers for the second, and three fingers for the third.
- Play the audio or read the script again. This time, ask students to listen for which man was almost killed and which man saved the other's life. After students listen, elicit answers.
- Ask several volunteers to retell the entire story.

2. Talking It Over

- Have students match the pictures to the animals' names. Review the correct answers with the class.

Heads Together Have a volunteer define, in his/her own words, the words *mean* and *lazy*. Then have students work in pairs, deciding whether each pictured animal is mean or lazy.

- Have students share out, explaining their answers. For example, some may feel cats are mean because they kill mice, while others may feel that killing mice is not mean, it's just natural for cats.

READING

A CONNECTING TO YOUR LIFE

1. Tuning In Listen to the conversation. Eduardo and Brian are talking about a time when something exciting happened. What happene

□ They killed a huge snake. □ A snake almost killed them. □ They took a pictur of a snake.

2. Talking It Over How many of these animals do you recognize? Match the pictures with the names.

_____ 1. Komodo dragon _____ 4. hippopotamus
_____ 2. anaconda _____ 5. praying mantis
_____ 3. cow _____ 6. cat

a.

b.

c.

d.

e.

f.

Talk with a partner. Decide which of these animals are *mean* and which animals are *lazy*.

Read the title of this unit. What do you think the unit is probably abou Check (✓) the correct answer.

_____ 1. It's about kids you know who you don't like.
_____ 2. It's about people who are mean to others.
_____ 3. It's about animals that are scary and animals that sleep a lot.

76 Unit 5

- Read the title of the unit again. Have students use finger signals to tell what they think the unit might be about. (It's about animals that are scary and animals that sleep a lot.)

✓ WRAP UP

- Ask students to tell which animal in these pictures they think is the meanest and which is the laziest. Ask them to tell why.

TEACHING TIP Stock your classroom libraries with copies of nature magazines like *National Geographic, National Geographic Kids*, or *Ranger Rick*.

ANSWER KEY

Tuning In: A snake almost killed them.
Talking It Over: 1. f; 2. b; 3. c; 4. e; 5. a; 6. d.
Talking It Over: 3.

B GETTING READY TO READ

Learning New Words Read the sentences below. Try to figure
t the meanings of the underlined words.

1. Fred lives on Mansfield Street. His address is 4876 Mansfield Street.
2. Erik has very big feet. He wears a size 13 shoe.
3. An elephant is very heavy. It has the same weight as a truck.
4. My German shepherd is a big dog. He weighs almost 100 pounds.
5. Many people have golden retrievers. They're a popular breed.
6. Cats are pets that live indoors with people. They are domestic animals.

atch each word on the left with its correct definition on the right.

1. address	a. how heavy or how light something is
2. size	b. a unit used to measure weight (= 16 ounces or 454 grams)
3. weight	c. the street name and number where someone lives or works
4. pound	d. used to describe an animal that lives with people or works on a farm
5. breed	e. how big or how small something is
6. domestic	f. a type of animal

Talking It Over Talk with a partner. Which of the animals below
good pets? Which are bad pets? Why?

Goldfish

2.

A rabbit

3.

Baby alligators

A chimpanzee

5.

A parakeet

6.

A cat

B GETTING READY TO READ

Standards

- Use context to figure out the meaning of new words
- Share information and ideas

WARM UP

- Write these words on the board as headings for a simple column chart: *pet, pest.* Explain that a pet is an animal you keep at home—one that you like or even love. A pest is a small animal that people don't like.
- Help students think of examples of pets...and pests, as you record their ideas on the board.

TEACHING THE LESSON

1. Learning New Words

- Help volunteers read aloud items 1–6. After each student reads, paraphrase the sentences. Then focus on each underlined word and ask students to try to define it.
- Now ask a volunteer to read aloud the lettered list of definitions. Then have students complete the activity.
- Review the correct answers.

2. Talking It Over

- Have students share what kinds of pets they have at home. Ask students who do not have pets: *If you could get a family pet, what would you choose?* Encourage students to share.
- Help students discover things that might make an animal a good pet or a bad pet. Ask questions such as: *Which ones are easy to take care of? Which ones would fit comfortably in your house?*

 **Heads Together** Have students work in pairs to discuss which animals make good or bad pets.

CULTURE NOTE

Explain that different cultures have different ideas about pets. In China, cats bring good luck. In Arab countries, people believe that dogs are unclean. The Inuit Eskimos of Northern Canada keep bear cubs, foxes, and baby seals. Animals are rarely kept as pets in many parts of Africa.

✓ WRAP UP

- Have students write a short description of a favorite pet and then share this information about it: pet, size, weight.

ANSWER KEY

Learning New Words: 1. c; 2. e; 3. a; 4. b; 5. f; 6. d.

C READING TO LEARN

Standard

- Read and understand simple sentences

WARM UP

- Ask students to share which animal scares them more than any other. Ask any students who have been close to the animal that scares them to describe when and where it happened.

TEACHING THE LESSON

1. Before You Read

- Have students look at the pictures of the Komodo dragon, the anaconda, and the praying mantis. Then ask whether animals like these usually live in the city, in the jungle, or underneath houses. Have them hold up one, two, or three fingers to show whether they think the first, second, or third answer is correct.

2. Let's Read

- Tell students they are going to learn about some more mean animals. Ask them to keep this question in mind as they read: *Which animal do you think is the meanest and why?*
- Begin by playing the tape or CD, or read the field guides. Ask students to listen for information that tells which animal is biggest and which is smallest. (The anaconda is the biggest and the praying mantis is the smallest.)

My Turn: Read Aloud/Think Aloud Read the field guides aloud. As you read, comment on words and ideas. For example, stand 9.5 feet from the wall and say: *This is how long 9.5 feet is.*

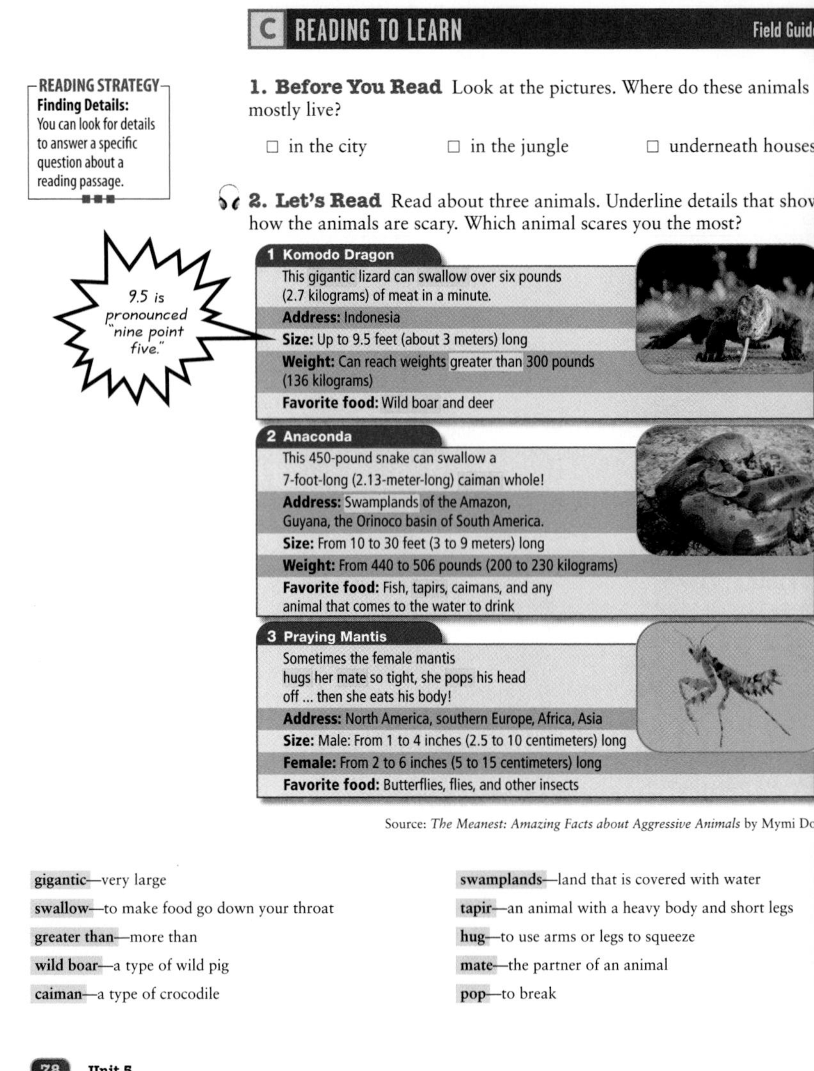

READING

C READING TO LEARN Field Guide

READING STRATEGY
Finding Details:
You can look for details to answer a specific question about a reading passage.

1. Before You Read Look at the pictures. Where do these animals mostly live?

☐ in the city ☐ in the jungle ☐ underneath houses

2. Let's Read Read about three animals. Underline details that show how the animals are scary. Which animal scares you the most?

9.5 is pronounced "nine point five."

1 Komodo Dragon
This gigantic lizard can swallow over six pounds (2.7 kilograms) of meat in a minute.
Address: Indonesia
Size: Up to 9.5 feet (about 3 meters) long
Weight: Can reach weights greater than 300 pounds (136 kilograms)
Favorite food: Wild boar and deer

2 Anaconda
This 450-pound snake can swallow a 7-foot-long (2.13-meter-long) caiman whole!
Address: Swamplands of the Amazon, Guyana, the Orinoco basin of South America.
Size: From 10 to 30 feet (3 to 9 meters) long
Weight: From 440 to 506 pounds (200 to 230 kilograms)
Favorite food: Fish, tapirs, caimans, and any animal that comes to the water to drink

3 Praying Mantis
Sometimes the female mantis hugs her mate so tight, she pops his head off ... then she eats his body!
Address: North America, southern Europe, Africa, Asia
Size: Male: From 1 to 4 inches (2.5 to 10 centimeters) long
Female: From 2 to 6 inches (5 to 15 centimeters) long
Favorite food: Butterflies, flies, and other insects

Source: *The Meanest: Amazing Facts about Aggressive Animals* by Mymi Do

gigantic—very large
swallow—to make food go down your throat
greater than—more than
wild boar—a type of wild pig
caiman—a type of crocodile
swamplands—land that is covered with water
tapir—an animal with a heavy body and short legs
hug—to use arms or legs to squeeze
mate—the partner of an animal
pop—to break

78 Unit 5

- Point out the starburst. Write some other numbers with decimals on the board and ask students to read them aloud.

Our Turn: Interactive Reading Have students help read the descriptions of the Komodo dragon, the anaconda, and the praying mantis. As they read, focus on the glossed words, ask questions, and make comments:

What do lizards look like? What special body parts do they have?

What can you tell about the anaconda just by looking at the picture?

Why do you think the praying mantis eats her mate's body?

- **Build Fluency** Have students read each caption after you. Encourage them to read fluently and with expression.

✓ **Your Turn: Independent Reading** Ask students to read all three descriptions on their own. Then have students complete this sentence stem:

I would be most afraid of the ________ *because* ________.

Unlocking Meaning

Identifying the Main Idea What are the reading selections about? Check (✓) the correct answer.

_____ 1. animals that eat people

_____ 2. animals that attack, or hurt and kill, other animals

_____ 3. animals that are all very large

Finding Details Read the sentences below. Write *T* for True or *F* for False.

_____ 1. The Komodo dragon is an insect.

_____ 2. The Komodo dragon is very large.

_____ 3. The Komodo dragon weighs more than most people.

_____ 4. The anaconda is a large snake.

_____ 5. The anaconda eats butterflies and other insects.

_____ 6. The anaconda lives near water.

_____ 7. The praying mantis is an insect.

_____ 8. The praying mantis lives mostly in South America.

_____ 9. The male praying mantis kills and eats the female.

Think about It Talk with a partner. Which of the animals you read about is most likely to harm or kill people? Why?

Before You Move On Can you guess why the type of mantis in the picture is called the *praying* mantis?

3. Unlocking Meaning

IDENTIFYING THE MAIN IDEA

- Have students use finger signals to choose the sentence that tells what the three selections are about. Have a volunteer explain the correct answer.

✓ FINDING DETAILS

- Have each student complete the activity, deciding whether each statement is true or false. Have students share and discuss.

THINK ABOUT IT

Heads Together Have students talk with a partner. Have them discuss and then decide which animal is most likely to harm or kill a person. Have students share out.

- Ask: *What do you think is the most dangerous animal on earth?* List students' ideas. Tell students that many people believe that the tiny mosquito is the most dangerous. Explain that mosquitoes carry diseases like malaria. Over 300 million people get malaria each year. Over 1 million die of malaria each year.

Access for All Have a volunteer who is good at searching the Internet find out how many people each year are killed by anacondas, then report back to the class. Which animal kills more people—anacondas or mosquitoes?

BEFORE YOU MOVE ON

- Ask students to show with their hands what people do when they pray. Then have them look at the picture and tell what it is about the insect that makes people call it the "praying mantis."

✓ WRAP UP

Outcome Sentence Have students complete this sentence stem.

The _______ *is "mean" because* _______.

PB PRACTICE BOOK ACTIVITY

See Activity A, Revisit and Retell, on Practice Book page 41.

ANSWER KEY

Before You Read: in the jungle

Identifying the Main Idea: 2.

Finding Details: 1. F; 2. T; 3. T; 4. T; 5. F; 6. T; 7. T; 8. F; 9. F.

D WORD WORK

Standards

- Read information in charts
- Identify sound/spelling relationships

WARM UP

- Ask students to think of words that describe size, length, or weight, such as *big* and *long*. Record their suggestions in three columns (with the headings *Size, Length,* and *Weight*) on the board.

TEACHING THE LESSON

1. Word Detective

- Have students study the information in the chart on their own. Tell students that they are going to hear descriptions of some of the animals in the chart. Play the tape or CD, or read the script twice. Have students point their thumbs up if the sentence is true or point them down if it is false.
- Play the tape or CD, or read the script again, and discuss the correct responses.

2. Word Study

- Have students write sentences using words from the chart. Ask volunteers to read their sentences to the class.

3. Word Play

Heads Together Have students use the measurement words on the chart to write true sentences about their own lives. They ask them to share their sentences with a partner.

Spelling and Phonics

- Have students listen to the words and tell you what they notice about them. (The letter *a* is pronounced differently in each word.) Say the words and ask students to repeat.
- Have students complete the chart. Review the correct answers with the class.

D WORD WORK

1. Word Detective Look at the measurement chart below. Listen to the sentences. Point your thumb up if the sentence is right. Point your thumb down if it is wrong.

SPELLING AND PHONICS: To do this activity, go to page 184.

2. Word Study It is sometimes helpful to learn words in groups. Look at the chart below for groups of words that describe size, length, and weight. Write three sentences using the information in the chart below.

EXAMPLE: *The thread snake is tiny.*

Measurement Word Groups

	Size	Length	Weight
Thread snake	tiny	very short (3 inches or 7.6 centimeters)	very light (several ounces or between 100 and 200 grams)
Brown snake	small	short (9 to 12 inches or 22.9 to 30.5 centimeters)	light (less than a pound or half a kilogram)
Kingsnake	medium size	medium length (36 to 72 inches or 91.4 to 182.9 centimeters)	medium weight (2 to 3 pounds or 0.9 to 1.4 kilograms)
Boa constrictor	big/large	long (over 8 feet or 2.4 meters)	heavy (30 pounds or 13.6 kilograms)
Anaconda	huge/gigantic	very long (up to 30 feet or 9.1 meters)	very heavy (up to 500 pounds or 227 kilograms)

3. Word Play Work with a partner. Write three sentences about your own life using the words in the word families.

✓ WRAP UP

- Have students look again at the pictures of the Komodo dragon, the anaconda, and the praying mantis. Have them write a sentence about each animal, using a measurement word.

PB PRACTICE BOOK ACTIVITY

See Activity B, Word Work, on Practice Book page 42.

ANSWER KEY

Word Detective: Correct sentences: 1, 2, 4, 6, 7.

Spelling and Phonics: cat: have, mantis, (alligator), gigantic, Africa, anaconda; **snake:** praying, (alligator), Asia, male; **yawn:** swallow, talk, small.

GRAMMAR Subject-Verb Agreement

Listen Up Listen to each sentence. Point your thumb up if it ...nds correct. Point your thumb down if it sounds wrong.

1. Dogs chases cats.
2. My cat loves to eat mice.
3. Anacondas can kills alligators.
4. Anacondas live in South America.
5. A Komodo dragon weigh over 300 pounds.
6. The praying mantis like to eat butterflies.

Learn the Rule In a good sentence, the subject and the verb must ...ee. Read the following rules to learn how to make present tense verbs ...ee with the subjects. Then do Activity 1 again.

SUBJECT-VERB AGREEMENT WITH PRESENT TENSE VERBS
. When the subject of a sentence is a singular noun (praying mantis, alligator), the verb ends in *-s* or *-es*. *A female praying mantis* ***eats*** *its mate.* *The anaconda* ***squeezes*** *its victim to death.*
. When the subject is a plural noun (anacondas), the verb does not end in *-s* or *-es*. *Anacondas* ***live*** *in South America.*
. When *can* comes before the verb, the verb does not end in *-s* or *-es*. *An anaconda can* ***swallow*** *a human in one bite!*

Practice the Rule Look at the sentences below. Circle the correct ...m of each verb.

1. The Komodo dragon (live/lives) in Indonesia.
2. Komodo dragons (kill/kills) other animals.
3. The anaconda (reach/reaches) 30 feet in length.
4. It (weigh/weighs) up to 500 pounds.
5. Baby anacondas can (eat/eats) baby birds.
6. The female praying mantis (hug/hugs) her mate to death.
7. The praying mantis can (change/changes) color from green to brown.

I'm home, honey.
Let me give you a hug!

E GRAMMAR

Standard

- Recognize and use third person singular *–s*

WARM UP

- Write the verbs *eat* and *live* on the board. Ask students to make up sentences about animals using these words. Record exactly what students say, without correcting. Save for later.

TEACHING THE LESSON

1. Listen Up

- Ask students to listen carefully. Then play the tape or CD, or read the sentences twice. Have students point their thumbs up if the sentence sounds correct, and down if it sounds wrong.

2. Learn the Rule

- Use the chart to present and teach subject–verb agreement with present tense verbs. Write examples on the board such as *My cat likes me* and *My dog chases my cat.* Circle the *–s* and *–es* endings. Write examples such as *My cats like me* and *My dogs chase my cat.* Point out that there are no *–s* or *–es* verb endings.
- Explain that there is no *–s* or *–es* ending on a present tense verb when it follows *can.* Say: *"My dog can swim" is correct. "My dog can swims" is not correct.*
- Revisit the sentences that students generated. Do they follow the subject-verb agreement rules? Have students help you correct any that do not.
- Repeat the Listen Up activity. Reteach as necessary.

3. Practice the Rule

- Have students complete the activity and read their sentences aloud. Offer corrections, as needed.

✓ WRAP UP

- Write these word pairs on the board: *anaconda/anacondas, tiger/tigers, dog/dogs.* Ask volunteers to make a pair of present tense statements about each animal. Have other students listen for the correct use of present tense verb endings. Guide students to use verbs other than *be.*

PB PRACTICE BOOK ACTIVITY

See Activity C, Grammar, on Practice Book page 43.

ANSWER KEY

Listen Up: Correct sentences: 2, 4.

Practice the Rule: 1. lives; 2. kill; 3. reaches; 4. weighs; 5. eat; 6. hugs; 7. change.

F BRIDGE TO WRITING

Standard

- Read and understand simple sentences

WARM UP

- Have students look back at the pictures of the Komodo dragon, the anaconda, and the praying mantis on page 78 and then look at the pictures of the cow, the hippo, and the cat. How are the two groups of animals *different*?

TEACHING THE LESSON

1. Before You Read

- Ask: *What are all of the pictured animals doing?* Have a volunteer explain.

2. Let's Read

Tell students that if you have a specific question about a subject, you can look for details in a reading to answer it (Reading Strategy box).

My Turn: Read Aloud/Think Aloud Read the information about the animals aloud. As you read, comment on words and ideas:

Point to your shoulders and say, *These are my shoulders.*

Cows eat different food in summer and in winter. Why?

The hippo stays underwater all day. Why?

Domestic is the opposite of wild. Domestic cats are sometimes called "house cats."

- Now play the tape or CD, or read the field guides twice. As students listen, ask them to note which animal is heaviest (male hippo) and which is lightest (domestic cat).

WRITING

F BRIDGE TO WRITING — Field Guid

READING STRATEGY
Finding Details: You can look for details to answer a specific question about a reading passage.

1. Before You Read Look at the pictures below. What do you noti about these animals?

2. Let's Read Read about three "lazy" animals. Underline details th show how the animals are lazy.

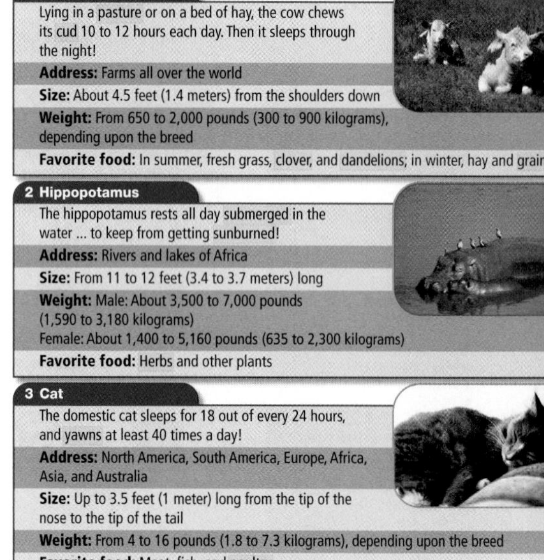

1 Cow
Lying in a pasture or on a bed of hay, the cow chews its cud 10 to 12 hours each day. Then it sleeps through the night!
Address: Farms all over the world
Size: About 4.5 feet (1.4 meters) from the shoulders down
Weight: From 650 to 2,000 pounds (300 to 900 kilograms), depending upon the breed
Favorite food: In summer, fresh grass, clover, and dandelions; in winter, hay and grain

2 Hippopotamus
The hippopotamus rests all day submerged in the water ... to keep from getting sunburned!
Address: Rivers and lakes of Africa
Size: From 11 to 12 feet (3.4 to 3.7 meters) long
Weight: Male: About 3,500 to 7,000 pounds (1,590 to 3,180 kilograms)
Female: About 1,400 to 5,160 pounds (635 to 2,300 kilograms)
Favorite food: Herbs and other plants

3 Cat
The domestic cat sleeps for 18 out of every 24 hours, and yawns at least 40 times a day!
Address: North America, South America, Europe, Africa, Asia, and Australia
Size: Up to 3.5 feet (1 meter) long from the tip of the nose to the tip of the tail
Weight: From 4 to 16 pounds (1.8 to 7.3 kilograms), depending upon the breed
Favorite food: Meat, fish, and poultry

Source: *The Laziest: Amazing Facts about Lazy Animals* by Mymi Dc

pasture—grassland where cattle feed
cud—food already eaten once, then brought back into the mouth
clover—a grasslike plant with three round leaves
dandelion—a plant with tiny yellow flowers
grain—crops like corn, wheat, or rice
submerged—under water
sunburned—used to describe skin that is burned by the sun
herb—a plant used for flavor in cooking
yawn—to open your mouth wide when you are sleepy
poultry—birds like chickens and turkeys

82 Unit 5

Our Turn: Interactive Reading Take turns having individual students read the information. As they read, focus on the glossed words, ask questions, and make comments:

What is a pasture?

How does skin look when it is sunburned?

Why do we yawn? Is it polite or impolite to yawn in front of people?

Do domestic cats ever kill their own meat? Give an example.

- **Echo Reading** Have a different student read each word or phrase after you. Encourage them to copy your pronunciation and intonation.

Your Turn: Independent Reading Have students read about the animals on their own. Ask them to underline details that show that the animals are lazy and decide which of the three animals is the laziest. When they finish, invite volunteers to share with the class.

. **Making Content Connections** Work with a partner. Choose e mean animal and one lazy animal. Compare the two. How are they fferent? Complete the chart below.

	Mean Animal: ________	Lazy Animal: ________
What is one interesting fact about it?		
Where does it live?		
How big does it get?		
What does it eat?		

. **Expanding Your Vocabulary** Match each animal name on the t with a picture on the right. Write the letters on the lines.

h 1. giraffe
____ 2. tiger
____ 3. leopard
____ 4. lion
____ 5. gorilla
____ 6. dingo
____ 7. orangutan
____ 8. rhinoceros

a. b. c. d. e. f. g. h.

JUST FOR FUN

Practice animal vocabulary. Play Lingo Bingo. Divide students in groups of four. Have each group fold a piece of paper in four parts one way and then four parts the other way, making 16 squares. As you write the name of an animal on the board, each group copies the name in any square. Provide 16 animal names. In random order, describe each animal without naming it. As each group guesses the animal, they put an X in that animal's square. The first group with a complete row of four Xs, whispers, "Lingo Bingo!"

✓ WRAP UP

Outcome Sentence Have students complete this sentence stem, then share:

To me, the most interesting animal is the __________ because __________.

PB PRACTICE BOOK ACTIVITY

See Activity D, Test-Taking Practice, on Practice Book pages 44 and 45.

See Activity E, Using New Vocabulary, on Practice Book page 46.

ANSWER KEY

Before You Read: Answers will vary.

Making Content Connections: Answers will vary.

Expanding Your Vocabulary: 1. h; 2. d; 3. g; 4. a; 5. e; 6. b; 7. f; 8. c.

3. Making Content Connections

Heads Together Ask students to work in pairs. Have them choose two animals, then complete the chart.

Interactive Writing Copy the chart on the board. Invite volunteers to take turns filling in their responses in the second and third columns.

4. Expanding Your Vocabulary

- Have students complete the activity individually by matching the animal names and pictures.

G WRITING CLINIC

Standards
- Identify the structural features of a field guide
- Use adjectives to make writing lively

WARM UP

- Have students look at the field guide and explain that this kind of book gives us basic information about a lot of different animals and usually contains a picture of each animal.

TEACHING THE LESSON

1. Think about It

Heads Together Ask students which of the six people would be most interested in reading about wild animals. Although the best answer is "someone interested in nature," invite students to give reasons why a student or a scientist might want to read a field guide.

2. Focus on Organization

- Ask students to study the picture, the text, and the numbered notes below the picture (Part 1).
- Have students match the numbered statements under the field guide page with the related information on the page.
- Now have students, on their own, identify the parts of the selection on anacondas (Part 2). Have them share out.

PB PRACTICE BOOK ACTIVITY

See Activity F, Focus on Organization, on Practice Book page 47.

G WRITING CLINIC — Field Guides

1. Think about It Who would probably like to read a field guide?

- ☐ a scientist
- ☐ an airline pilot
- ☐ a police officer
- ☐ a lawyer
- ☐ a student
- ☐ someone interested in natur

2. Focus on Organization

❶ A field guide often gives us information about an animal.

① **1 The Komodo Dragon** ②
③ This gigantic lizard can swallow over six pounds (2.7 kilograms) of meat in a minute.
④ **Address:** Indonesia
Size: Up to 9.5 feet (about 3 meters) long
⑤ **Weight:** Can reach weights greater than 300 pounds (136 kilograms)
Favorite food: Wild boar and deer

① Here is the name of the animal.
② Here is a picture of the animal
③ Here is an amazing fact about the animal.
④ This tells where the animal lives.
⑤ Here is basic information about the animal.

❷ Answer these questions by writing the numbers from the Anaconda field guide below on the lines.

_4_ 1. What part tells where the animal lives?
____ 2. What part shows what the animal looks like?
____ 3. What part tells us the name of the animal?
____ 4. What part gives the reader basic information about the animal?
____ 5. What part tells us an amazing fact about the animal?

① **The Anaconda** ②
③ This 450-pound snake can swallow a 7-foot-long (2.13-meter-long) caiman whole!
④ **Address:** Swamplands of the Amazon, Guyana, the Orinoco basin of South America.
Size: From 10 to 30 feet (3 to 9 meters) long
⑤ **Weight:** From 440 to 506 pounds (200 to 230 kilograms)
Favorite food: Fish, tapirs, caimans, and any animal that comes to the water to drink

Focus on Style

Adjectives help make your writing interesting. Circle the adjective in each of these sentences.

1. The Komodo dragon is a gigantic lizard.
2. The anaconda wraps its large body around its victim.

ferocious

2.

hungry

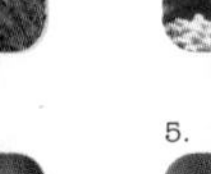

3.

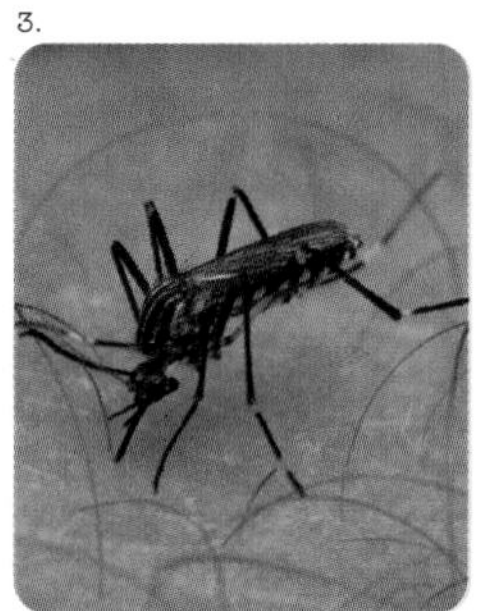

~~tiny~~

colorful

5.

ugly

6.

huge

Complete the following sentences with words from the pictures above.

1. The ___*tiny*___ mosquito bites people.
2. The ________________ lion is king of the jungle.
3. The ________________ elephant weighs several tons.
4. A ________________ shark sometimes kills people.
5. The vampire bat has a very ________________ face.
6. The mandrill is a ________________ animal.

✓ WRAP UP

Outcome Sentence Write the following sentence starter on the board and say: *Choose a wild animal. Write an amazing fact about the animal. Use an adjective in your sentence.*

Amazing fact about __________:

________________________________.

PB PRACTICE BOOK ACTIVITY

See Activity G, Focus on Style, on Practice Book page 48.

ANSWER KEY

Think about It: a scientist; a student; someone interested in nature.

Focus on Organization 2: 1. 4; 2. 2; 3. 1; 4. 5; 5. 3.

Focus on Style, 1: gigantic; large.

Focus on Style, 2: 1. tiny; 2. ferocious; 3. huge; 4. hungry; 5. ugly; 6. colorful.

3. Focus on Style

- Ask students to locate the adjective in each sentence. Then ask: *What does an adjective add to a sentence? How does it make a sentence better?* (It adds detail. It helps to create a clear picture in a person's mind.)
- Use the adjective label under each picture to make a statement about the animal. For example: *This lion looks angry and ferocious!* Then paraphrase the description or add similar information, or invite students to do so. For example: *He really looks violent. This is not a gentle animal.* Repeat for the other adjectives.
- Write the six adjectives on the board. Ask students to count off from 1 to 6. The 1s write a sentence with *ferocious*, the 2s use the word *hungry* in a sentence, etc. Have students write their sentences on the board. Then ask students to work individually as they complete the activity. Have students share their answers.

H WRITER'S WORKSHOP — Field Guides

Imagine that your class is writing a field guide about the *meanest* animal on Earth. Make a page for the book.

1. Getting It Out

❶ Choose an animal to write about. Look at the pictures below for idea or choose another creature.

1 Great White Shark

- **Facts:** Loves to eat meat
- Sometimes eats other sharks
- Lives in the Pacific Ocean and Atlantic Ocean
- Is 12 to 21 feet (3.7 to 6.4 meters) long
- Weighs about 5,000 pounds (2,300 kilograms)
- Eats seals, sea turtles, and dolphins

2 Vampire Bat

- **Facts:** Drinks blood at night from sleeping animals (must have blood every 48 hours)
- Lives in Mexico and South America
- Is 2.5 to 4 inches (6.4 to 10 centimeters) long
- Very light: weighs 0.5 to 1.75 ounces (14 to 50 grams)
- Loves the blood of cattle (cows and bulls)

3 Crocodile

- **Facts:** One of the world's most dangerous reptiles
- Lives in rivers, lakes, and bays
- Can be as long as 25 feet (7.6 meters)
- Loves to eat humans
- Has very powerful jaws
- Usually drowns its victims

4 Bengal Tiger

- **Facts:** Teeth are like knives and over 3 inches (7.6 centimeters) long
- Hunts at night
- Lives in India, Nepal, and Myanmar
- Almost 10 feet (3 meters) long
- Male weighs 375 to 550 pounds (170 to 250 kilograms)
- Female weighs 220 to 330 pounds (100 to 150 kilograms)
- Eats deer, buffalo, pigs, and baby elephants

Source: *The Meanest: Amazing Facts about Aggressive Animals* by Mymi Doi

H WRITER'S WORKSHOP

Standard

- Use the writing process: prewriting

1. Getting It Out

WARM UP

- Brainstorm a list of the meanest animals on Earth. Encourage students to go beyond those mentioned in the book.

TEACHING THE LESSON

- Focus on the Great White Shark (Part 1). Read the information aloud or ask a student to do so. Then ask volunteers what is interesting or surprising about this shark. Ask them to read about the other animals and share which one they think is the most interesting and why.
- Then have students choose different animals to write about. Have them think about one question they have about the animal that is not answered in the fact file. Encourage them to use the Internet or library to find the answer to their question.

Access for All Encourage more proficient students to choose an animal that is not pictured. Have them use the Internet, or other information resources, to do their research on the animal.

Technology Tip Students with Internet access can use it to research an animal that interests them. Have them gather the same types of information they used earlier in the lesson: address, size, weight, and favorite food, as well as other interesting information. The San Diego Zoo Web site (www.sandiegozoo.org) has information on an interesting assortment of wild animals such as koalas, sea lions, bats, and even wild cattle. Students can also try www.kidsplanet.org.

- Take out a sheet of paper. Print the name of the animal you chose at the top. Fold the paper in half and then in half again to create four sections. Number each section and copy the questions from the chart below.

Here is what Graciela wrote. What do you think?

Mosquito

1. What is one amazing fact about the animal? *The female flaps her wings 800 times a second when looking for skin to bite.*	*2. Where does it live?* *It lives in every part of the world, especially in places with warm weather.*
3. How big/heavy is it? *It's 0.16 to 0.4 inches long.*	*4. What is its favorite food?* *Fresh blood!*

- Draw a picture of the animal or cut out a photograph from a magazine.

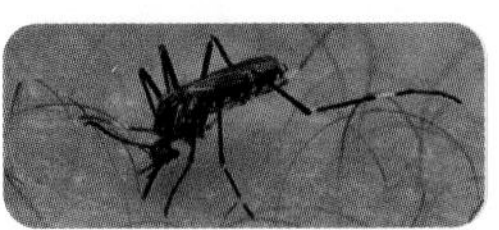

- Look at the map below. Shade in the places where your animal lives. Print the name of each shaded-in place on your map.

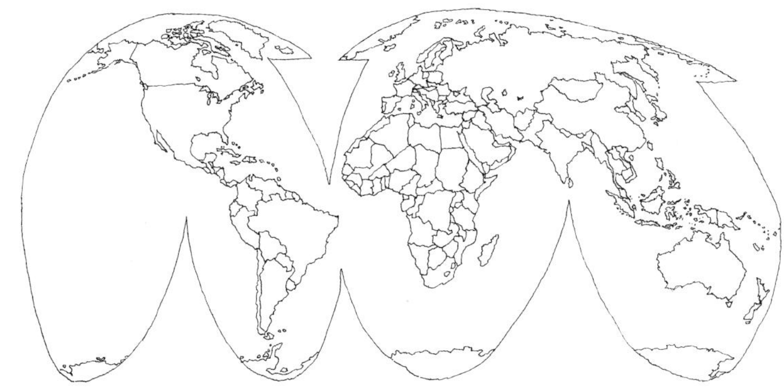

- For Part 2 have students fold a sheet of paper in four parts. Then ask them to write the name of the animal they have chosen at the top, number each of the four sections, and add each question to the appropriate section. They can copy the section questions from the sample chart in the book or they can use the form on page 49 of the Practice Book.
- Focus students on Graciela's work as a sample. Ask volunteers to read the questions and information aloud. Have them say what they think about Graciela's notes. Are they thorough? Do they have any questions?

TEACHING TIP If possible, have several books and magazines that tell about animals available in the classroom for students to use as references. Be sure the materials are written at a level that is appropriate for your students.

- Have students cut out or copy a picture of their animal to use in their reports.
- Have students label a map to show where their animal is found.

WRAP UP

- Have students share their work with a partner.

PB PRACTICE BOOK ACTIVITY

See Activity H, Writer's Workshop, on Practice Book page 49.

H WRITER'S WORKSHOP

Standards

- Use the writing process: drafting, revising, and editing
- Give a short oral presentation

2. Getting It Down

WARM UP

- Tell students that it's time to turn their notes into a "page plan."

TEACHING THE LESSON

- Make a copy of the plan on the board (Part 1). Ask students to volunteer information for the chart based on Graciela's notes. Write the information on the chart.
- Remind students that they should use single words and phrases on their page plans to save time, and so they can focus on their ideas and not worry about getting the spelling and grammar perfect at this point. Then have students complete their own plans.
- Help students examine Graciela's page, referring to the comments in speech bubbles (Part 2). Then have students turn their plans into actual pages.

Mini-Lesson on Conventions
Point out the Mini-Lesson box. Explain that you use a colon before a list of things of the same type. Ask students to point out where colons are used in Graciela's sample. Invite a volunteer to write on the board another example of a category, followed by a colon, followed by items that fit that category. (For example: *footwear: shoes, socks, boots*)

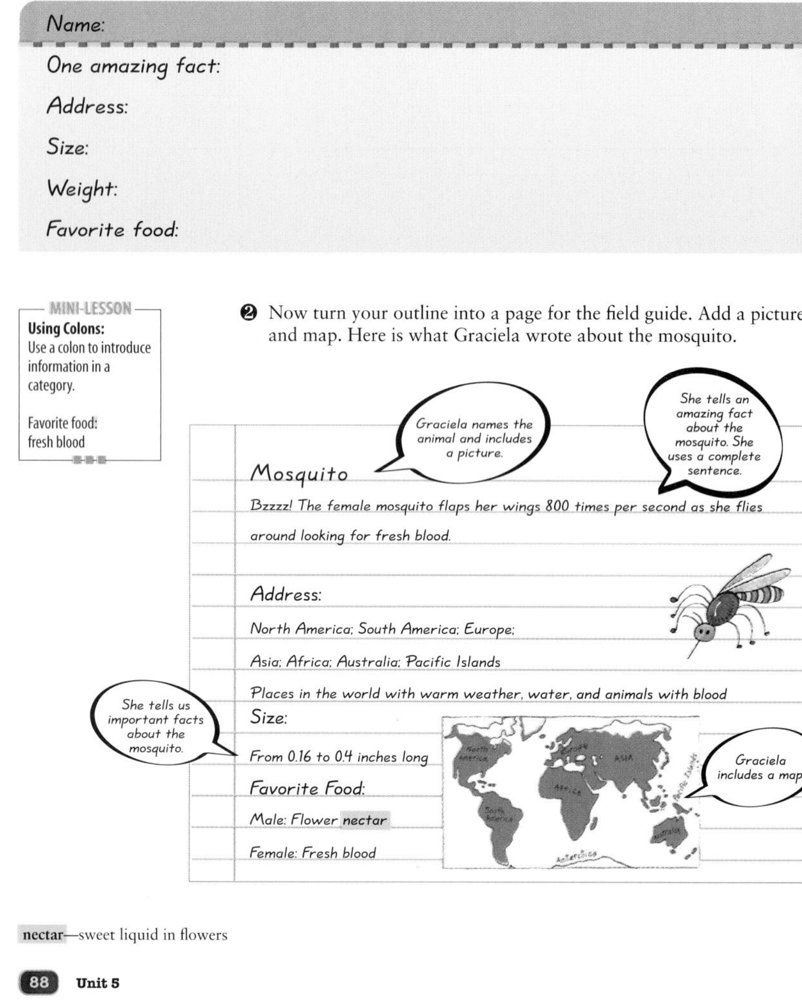

WRITING

2. Getting It Down

❶ Copy the plan below and create an outline about your animal.

Name:
One amazing fact:
Address:
Size:
Weight:
Favorite food:

MINI-LESSON
Using Colons:
Use a colon to introduce information in a category.

Favorite food:
fresh blood

❷ Now turn your outline into a page for the field guide. Add a picture and map. Here is what Graciela wrote about the mosquito.

nectar—sweet liquid in flowers

88 Unit 5

WRAP UP

- Tell students that they will have a chance to revise their work during the next session. Have them locate the ChecBric for this unit in the Student Book or Practice Book. Have them prepare for Getting it Right by reviewing the ChecBric on their own, underlining indicators they're not sure about.

. Getting It Right Now take a careful look at what you have ritten. Use this guide to revise your page.

Question to Ask	How to Check	How to Revise
1. Does my page name the animal?	Underline the name of the animal.	Add a title with the animal's name to your page.
2. Do I use a complete sentence to tell an amazing fact?	Put a check mark (✓) in front of the sentence that tells an amazing fact.	Add a verb or direct object to your sentence to make it complete.
3. Does the verb agree with the subject?	Reread the rule for subject-verb agreement on page 81.	Add *-s* or *-es* to the verb, if you need to.
4. Does my page have a picture and map?	Put a star (★) next to the picture and a check mark (✓) next to the map.	Add a picture and/or map if you don't have them.

. Presenting It Share your page for the field guide with our classmates.

- Begin by showing your page and saying which animal you chose to write about.
- Read your page aloud. Read slowly and speak clearly.
- Ask if anyone has any questions.

- Tell your classmates what you like about their reports.

3. Getting It Right

WARM UP

- Guide students through the ChecBric for this unit. Explain that they will use the ChecBric to prepare a final draft of their writing.
- Have volunteers explain, in their own words, what each indicator in the ChecBric means.

TEACHING THE LESSON

- Have students use the chart and the ChecBric to revise their work.
- Now have students share their field guides with a partner. Have students tell each other one thing they like about their partner's field guide.

Group Share Model how students will share their field guides.

WRAP UP

- Tell students they are now ready to present their field guides to the class. Suggest that they imagine the kinds of questions their classmates may ask them and think about possible answers ahead of time.

Help students complete the ChecBric on Practice Book page 109. Ask them to attach it to the back of their field guides before putting them in their portfolios.

4. Presenting It

WARM UP

- Survey the class to find out which animals students are going to talk about. Consider having students share in groups, balanced to avoid repetition.
- As a class, develop a simple presentation checklist.

TEACHING THE LESSON

- Tell students that you want them to pay attention to these things as they present their work:
  1. Use a loud and clear voice.
  2. Read slowly.
  3. Show your audience your work as you present.
  4. Ask for feedback.
- Have students ask for questions and feedback after their presentations.

WRAP UP

- Post student pages on the bulletin board or wall. Have students choose the pages with "best art," "best information," and "best layout."

I BEYOND THE UNIT

Standards
- Identify the letters of the alphabet
- Read and respond to poetry

1. On Assignment

WARM UP

- Write these words on the board: *aardvark, quetzal, xenops,* and *yak.* Ask: *What do these words all have in common?* (They are all names of animals.) Explain that many speakers of English have never seen some of these words. In order to understand what each is, they would need to look at a picture dictionary.

TEACHING THE LESSON

- Write the letters of the alphabet in vertical columns on the chalkboard and have students brainstorm an animal name of each letter of the alphabet (Part 1). Here is a list of possible responses: *anaconda, bear, cat, deer, eel, frog, goose, hippo, iguana, jackal, Komodo dragon, leopard, mosquito, newt, octopus, pelican, quetzal, rhino, stork, turtle, unicorn, vicuna, wildebeest, xenops, yak, zebra.*
- Ask students to choose a letter and find as many different animal names as possible for that letter (Part 2). They can use the list on the board as a starting point. Encourage them to use dictionaries.
- Have students alphabetize the animal names for a given letter and check their work with a partner (Part 3).
- Point out that we sometimes have to look at the second or even the third letter of a word when arranging words that start with the same letter in alphabetical order. Write the three examples from the Student Book on the board and first cover everything but

I BEYOND THE UNIT

1. On Assignment Make a class picture dictionary of animals.

❶ Help your teacher make a list of animals from A to Z. The followin chart will help you with some of the more difficult animals to name

A: anaconda
B: ______
C: cat, cow
D: ______
E: eel
F: ______
G: ______
H: hippopotamus
I: ______
J: ______
K: Komodo dragon
L: ______
M: mosquito
N: ______
O: ______
P: ______
Q: quetzal
R: ______
S: ______
T: ______
U: unicorn
V: vulture
W: ______
X: xenops
Y: yak
Z: ______

A quetz

A xenops

A ya

❷ Choose a letter from the alphabet. Find as many names as you can for animals that begin with this letter.

antelope
aardvark
anaconda

90 Unit 5

the first letter *a*. Then uncover the first and second letters and show that both *anaconda* and *antelope* have the same first and second letters. Then uncover the third letters.

- Ask students to make picture dictionary pages for all the animals they found for a given letter, writing the animal's name under each picture (Part 4).
- Have students put the pages together into a book (Part 5).

WRAP UP

- Display the animal page of a picture dictionary (such as the *Oxford Picture Dictionary*) and invite students to comment on it.

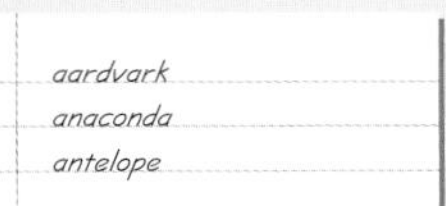

❸ Make a page for the animal dictionary. Put your animals in alphabetical order.

Make a page for each animal. Find a picture of each animal or draw your own picture. Label the pictures with the animal names.

Put the pages in alphabetical order and attach them to each other to make a book.

Link to Literature

SHARED READING Read this alphabet poem written by students.

LET'S TALK Answer the following questions and do the activity.

1. Why is this poem called an alphabet poem?
2. What does each line in the poem begin with?
3. Find three adjectives in the poem.

JUST FOR FUN Write a class alphabet poem about animals.

1. Look again at the page you made for your class picture dictionary.
2. Choose one animal. Write a sentence about the animal.
3. Place your line in the right place in the alphabet to make your class poem.

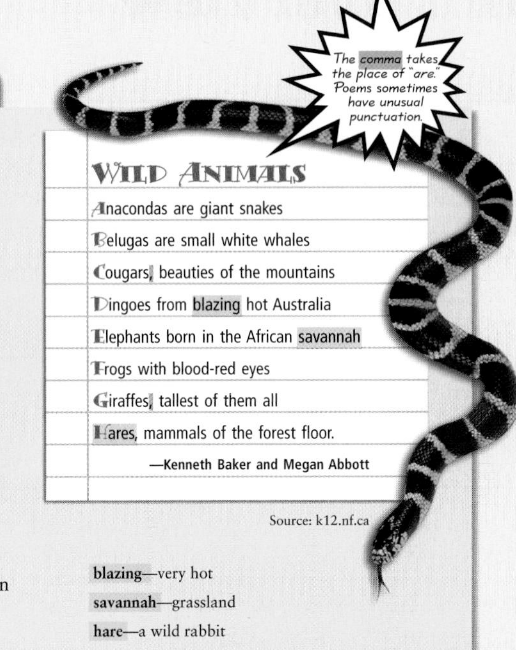

The comma takes the place of "are." Poems sometimes have unusual punctuation.

WILD ANIMALS

Anacondas are giant snakes
Belugas are small white whales
Cougars, beauties of the mountains
Dingoes from blazing hot Australia
Elephants born in the African savannah
Frogs with blood-red eyes
Giraffes, tallest of them all
Hares, mammals of the forest floor.

—Kenneth Baker and Megan Abbott

Source: k12.nf.ca

blazing—very hot
savannah—grassland
hare—a wild rabbit

2. Link to Literature

WARM UP

- Have students close their books. See if the class, working together, can remember an animal name for every letter of the alphabet.

TEACHING THE LESSON

Shared Reading Read the poem "Wild Animals" aloud, or play the tape or CD, as students follow along. Model oral expression and use pauses and nonverbal cues to help clearly communicate the meaning of each line.

- **Build Fluency** Have students take turns reading each line aloud with fluency and expression.
- Read the comment in the starburst. Explain that poems don't always follow the usual rules of punctuation. Ask students what else, besides the commas, is unusual about the punctuation of this poem. (There is no punctuation at the end of any line except the last one.)

Let's Talk Use the questions to lead a discussion of the poem. Ask what makes it an alphabet poem. Have students look at the first letter of each line. Ask students to point out three adjectives in the poem.

JUST FOR FUN

Write the letters of the alphabet down one side of a long strip of butcher paper that you have attached to the wall. Invite students to suggest lines for an animal alphabet poem which you then record on the paper. When the poem is finished, invite students to use colored markers to illustrate their line of the poem.

WRAP UP

- Invite students to take turns reading aloud their line of the poem as they point to it.

PB PRACTICE BOOK ACTIVITY

See Activity I, Responding to Literature, on Practice Book page 50.

UNIT WRAP UP

- Have students reflect upon what they learned in this unit in their **notebooks.** Consider collecting and responding to notebook entries.

You Can Cook!

Unit Overview

Section	At a Glance	Standards
Before You Begin	Students talk about a picture of boy attempting to cook.	■ Derive meaning from visual information
A. Connecting to Your Life	Students talk about the ingredients in a "super burrito."	■ Share information and ideas
B. Getting Ready to Read	Students learn the names of various cooking utensils.	■ Use context to figure out the meaning of new words ■ Share information and ideas
C. Reading to Learn	Students learn how to make quesadillas, using a recipe. PRACTICE BOOK: Students rewrite the steps in a recipe in the correct order.	■ Read and understand simple directions
D. Word Work	Students use compound words that describe cooking utensils. PRACTICE BOOK: Students use compound words to complete a conversation.	■ Use knowledge of compound words to determine word meaning ■ Identify sound/spelling relationships
E. Grammar	Students learn to use prepositions that tell where. PRACTICE BOOK: Students look at pictures and complete sentences with the correct prepositions of place.	■ Use locative prepositions
F. Bridge to Writing	Students read how to make "Nostalgic Meatloaf." They also learn food idioms. PRACTICE BOOK: Students practice taking Reading Vocabulary and Reading Comprehension tests. PRACTICE BOOK: Students practice new vocabulary.	■ Read and understand instructions ■ Recognize idioms

Section	At a Glance	Standards
G. Writing Clinic	Students put the steps in a recipe in the correct order, then choose interesting names for recipes. PRACTICE BOOK: Students identify different parts of a recipe and then number the steps in the correct order. PRACTICE BOOK: Students add descriptive words to food names.	■ Identify the structural features of how-to instructions ■ Organize information in time order
H1. Writer's Workshop: Getting It Out	Students begin planning a recipe they are going to write. PRACTICE BOOK: Students use a form to take notes as a friend or family member describes a recipe.	■ Use the writing process: prewriting
H2. Writer's Workshop: Getting It Down	Students turn their notes into an outline and then turn the outline into a recipe.	■ Use the writing process: drafting ■ Use an outline to draft writing
H3. Writer's Workshop: Getting It Right	Students revise and edit their recipes.	■ Use the writing process: revising and editing
H4. Writer's Workshop: Presenting It	Students present their recipes to their classmates.	■ Give a short oral presentation
I. Beyond the Unit	Students learn how to safely prepare a dish and set a place setting. They also read a recipe poem. PRACTICE BOOK: Students write an original recipe poem.	■ Read and understand safety rules ■ Read and respond to poetry

BEFORE YOU BEGIN

Standard

- Derive meaning from visual information

- Point to the boy in the picture on page 93 and ask students what he is doing.
- Read the words under the picture and ask students what the cook's name is.
- Have students describe what they see in the illustration. Encourage them to share what the boy must be thinking. Record what students say on the board.

Unit 6 You Can Cook!

Read...

- Recipes for every meal from *The Everything® Kids' Cookbook.* From quesadillas to s'mores—learn about all you need to have fun in the kitchen.

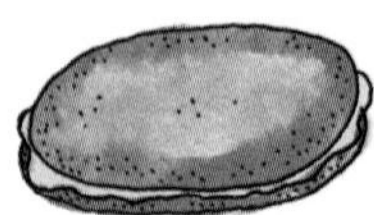

Link to Literature

- "A Recipe for Weather" by an unknown poet.

Objectives:

Reading:
- How-to instructions: Understanding recipes
- Strategy: Visualizing as you read
- Literature: Reading a recipe poem

Writing:
- Writing a recipe for a class cookbook
- Listing steps of a process in time order
- Writing interesting names for recipes

Vocabulary:
- Learning names of cooking utensils and ingredients
- Noticing words borrowed from other languages
- Recognizing compound words
- Idioms with food words

Listening/Speaking:
- Understanding the purpose of a conversation
- Explaining steps in a process
- Demonstrating a recipe

Grammar:
- Understanding prepositions that indicate location

Spelling and Phonics:
- Spelling the /k/ sound as in *king* and *cat*

92 Unit 6

Chef Miguel

EFORE YOU BEGIN

k with your classmates.

1. Look at the picture. What is the boy doing?
2. Read the caption. Who is the cook?
3. What is happening? Help your teacher write sentences about the picture.

A CONNECTING TO YOUR LIFE

Standard

- Share information and ideas

WARM UP

- Ask students to name foods they know how to make.

TEACHING THE LESSON

1. Tuning In

- Tell students they will hear a woman teaching her son to do something. Play the tape or CD, or read the script. Have students listen for what the woman is teaching the boy to do. Then have them share their conclusions.
- Have students listen a second time. This time, ask them to listen for the two different types of cooking methods that are used.

2. Talking It Over

- Tell students that they will be deciding what they think should go into a perfect burrito and making a list of these items. Point out the ingredients in the sample recipe and explain the meaning of any unfamiliar words.
- Referring to the starburst, help students understand the term "ingredient."

Heads Together Have students work in pairs. Give them time to make their lists of ingredients. Then ask volunteers to share their lists with the whole class.

TEACHING TIP If possible, take students to a cooking classroom and have them make burritos together. This would raise the interest level tremendously and start the unit off with a bang.

READING

A CONNECTING TO YOUR LIFE

1. Tuning In Listen to the conversation between a woman and her son. What is the woman teaching her son to do?

☐ make a burrito ☐ use the microwave oven ☐ eat a burrito

2. Talking It Over

Work with a partner. Make a "Super Burrito"—the best burrito in the world!

List the ingredients you will put into your burrito. Share the list with your classmates.

Read the title of this unit. What do you think the unit is probably about? Check (✓) the correct answer.

_____ 1. It's about how people grow our foods.

_____ 2. It's about reading and writing *recipes*, or directions, for making different dishes.

_____ 3. It's about foods that are good for you and bad for you.

94 Unit 6

- Have a volunteer read the title of the unit aloud. Have students use finger signals to show what they think the unit is about.
- Explain that we use the word *food* to describe anything we eat, prepared or unprepared. For example: *Apples are a healthy food. My favorite food is macaroni and cheese.*

WRAP UP

- Ask students to name foods they would like to learn how to make.

ANSWER KEY

Tuning In: make a burrito.

Talking It Over: 2.

GETTING READY TO READ

Learning New Words Match each cooking utensil in the picture with a description below.

b 1. a machine used to heat food very quickly
____ 2. a metal pan used to cook or bake food in the oven
____ 3. a machine used to bake or broil food
____ 4. tools used to measure small amounts
____ 5. a sharp tool used to cut food into small pieces
____ 6. a tool used to lift, turn, or flip pieces of food
____ 7. a flat dish used to serve food on
____ 8. a tool made of wood and used to stir or mix food together
____ 9. a small, deep metal pan used to cook food on the stove
____ 10. a cup used to measure large amounts of ingredients

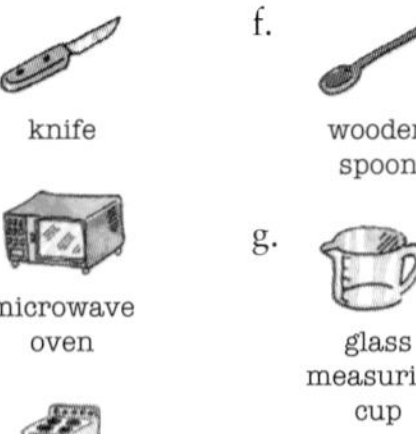

a. knife
b. microwave oven
c. oven
d. plate
e. measuring spoons

f. wooden spoon
g. glass measuring cup
h. baking pan
i. saucepan

j. spatula

Talking It Over Match the items in the box with the recipes below. Write the names of the recipes on the lines.

Egg salad sandwich Smoothie Cookies Tossed green salad

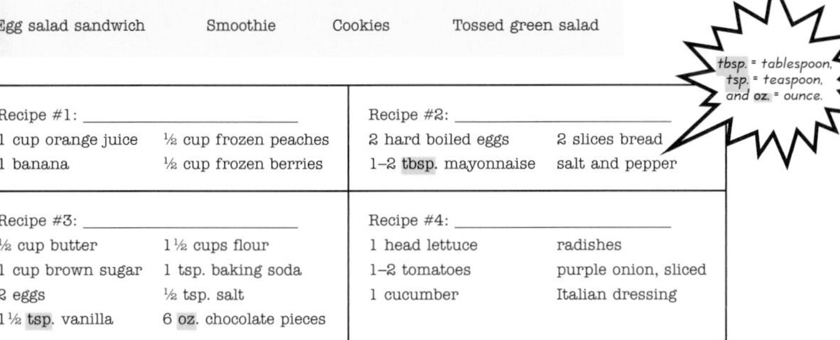

tbsp. = tablespoon, tsp. = teaspoon, and oz. = ounce.

Recipe #1: ____		Recipe #2: ____	
1 cup orange juice	½ cup frozen peaches	2 hard boiled eggs	2 slices bread
1 banana	½ cup frozen berries	1–2 tbsp. mayonnaise	salt and pepper
Recipe #3: ____		**Recipe #4: ____**	
½ cup butter	1½ cups flour	1 head lettuce	radishes
1 cup brown sugar	1 tsp. baking soda	1–2 tomatoes	purple onion, sliced
2 eggs	½ tsp. salt	1 cucumber	Italian dressing
1½ tsp. vanilla	6 oz. chocolate pieces		

B GETTING READY TO READ

Standards

- Use context to figure out the meaning of new words
- Share information and ideas

WARM UP

- Ask students to think of things they find in the kitchen—things they use to prepare food. Have them list as many as they can think of, then share out.

TEACHING THE LESSON

1. Learning New Words

- Have students complete the activity by matching each word to its correct definition. Have students share out.

JUST FOR FUN

Have students play Lingo Bingo. For directions, see page 83. Use the 12 cooking utensils in the book and add these four, explaining what they are if necessary: *can opener, frying pan, blender, bowl.*

2. Talking It Over

- Tell students that the first thing they need to do when they make a new dish is gather the necessary ingredients. Point out the four lists of ingredients in this activity. As you read each word aloud, have students use the thumbs up or thumbs down signal to show whether or not they know the word. Explain any unfamiliar words.
- Point to the starburst and explain the meaning of the three abbreviations: *tbsp*, *tsp*, and *oz*.
- Explain that a recipe is a set of steps that tell you how to prepare a certain kind of food. Point out the names of the four recipes. Ask volunteers to describe what each one is and tell whether or not they like it.

Team Talk Have students work in groups to complete the activity. Ask volunteers to share and explain answers.

✓ WRAP UP

Outcome Sentence Have students complete this sentence stem, then share:

A recipe is a set of instructions for ______________.

ANSWER KEY

Learning New Words: 1. b; 2. h; 3. c; 4. e; 5. a; 6. j; 7. d; 8. f; 9. i; 10. g.

Talking It Over: #1: Smoothie; #2: Egg salad sandwich; #3: Cookies; #4: Tossed green salad.

C READING TO LEARN

Standard

- Read and understand simple directions

WARM UP

- Brainstorm with students a list of places where they can find recipes. Help them think of non-book sources such as magazines, the Internet, and the outsides of food boxes.

TEACHING THE LESSON

1. Before You Read

Heads Together Have students work with a partner and list three things they both like to eat for lunch, then share out.

2. Let's Read

- Ask how many students have eaten quesadillas and invite volunteers to describe what they like about them. Tell students to visualize, or picture, each step of the recipe to help them understand it (Reading Strategy box).

My Turn: Read Aloud/Think Aloud Read the recipe aloud. As you read, comment on words and ideas:

Refried beans are beans that have been cooked twice—first they're boiled and mashed; then they're fried.

Some tortillas are made with wheat flour and some are made with corn flour.

The word "top" is used as a verb here. It means put something on top of something else.

- Now play the tape or CD, or read the recipe twice. Have students take simple notes as they listen, then share.

Our Turn: Interactive Reading Have students read the recipe aloud. Focus on glossed words, ask questions, and make comments.

READING

C READING TO LEARN — Recipe

READING STRATEGY
Visualizing:
Forming pictures in your mind can help you understand what you are reading.

1. Before You Read It's time for lunch! Talk with a partner. Make a list of three things you both like to eat for lunch.

2. Let's Read Read the recipe for quesadillas. Some words, like *quesadillas*, are not English. As you read, find the words that are borrowed or that come from, another language; in this case, the words are borrowed from Spanish. Write them down. Then share them with the class.

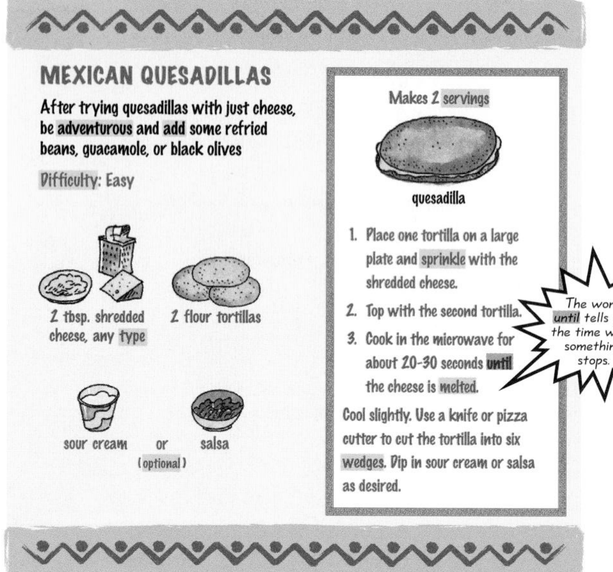

Source: *The Everything® Kids' Cookbook* by Sandra K. Nessenb

adventurous—willing to try new and different things
add—to put something else in with other things
difficulty—how easy or hard it is to do something
type—a kind
optional—possible, but not necessary
serving—the amount of a food that one person eats
sprinkle—to scatter tiny pieces of something on something else
melted—very hot, soft, and gooey
wedge—a piece of something, shaped like a triangle

96 Unit 6

What does "adventurous" mean? Can you find a smaller word inside that gives you a clue?

Show me what you do when you "sprinkle" something.

- **Build Fluency** Have students repeat after you. Encourage them to read with fluency and expression.

Your Turn: Independent Reading Have students write down all the borrowed (Spanish) words in the recipe. Have them share what they find. Ask students to think about how they would change the recipe if they were making it just for themselves. Then have students complete these sentence stems:

I would put ______________________ *in my quesadillas.*

I wouldn't put ______________________ *in my quesadillas.*

Unlocking Meaning

Identifying the Purpose Choose the sentence that explains the main purpose of the recipe. Check (✓) the correct answer.

_____ 1. to make you want to eat quesadillas

_____ 2. to teach you how to make quesadillas

_____ 3. to teach you words that come from Spanish

Finding Details Match each step in the recipe below with the following pictures.

b.

~~c.~~

e.

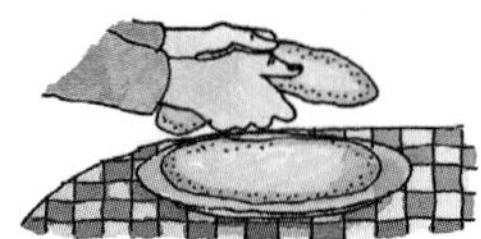

f.

cipe:

__c__ 1. Place one tortilla on a large plate.

_____ 2. Sprinkle with shredded cheese.

_____ 3. Put the second tortilla on top of the first.

_____ 4. Cook in the microwave until the cheese is melted.

_____ 5. Cool and cut into wedges.

_____ 6. Dip in sour cream and salsa.

Think about It Work with a partner. List foods from other countries that people in the U.S. often eat. Tell where each food comes from.

EXAMPLE: *Pizza—Italy*
Burritos—Mexico

Before You Move On Work with a partner. Think of a better name for the recipe than "Mexican Quesadillas." Share your ideas with your classmates.

3. Unlocking Meaning

IDENTIFYING THE PURPOSE

- Have students use finger signals to choose the sentence that explains the main purpose of the recipe. Have a volunteer explain the correct answer.

✓ FINDING DETAILS

- Have students complete the activity by matching the numbered pictures to the corresponding steps in the recipe. Have students share and discuss.

THINK ABOUT IT

- Write these words on the board: *pretzel, quiche, pizza, hot chocolate, sushi, latte, curry.* Help students identify what each one is made of and what country it originated in (Germany, France, Italy, Mexico, Japan, Italy, India).

Heads Together Have students generate a list of additional foods and where they come from, then share out.

BEFORE YOU MOVE ON

Heads Together Have students work in pairs. Ask them to come up with other names for the quesadilla recipe and share them with classmates.

✓ WRAP UP

Outcome Sentence Have students complete these sentence stems.

My favorite food from another country is ______________________.
It comes from ______________________.

PB PRACTICE BOOK ACTIVITY

See Activity A, Revisit and Retell, on Practice Book page 51.

ANSWER KEY

Before You Read: Answers will vary.

Let's Read: Spanish words: quesadillas, guacamole, tortillas, salsa.

Identifying the Purpose: 2.

Finding Details: 1. c; 2. b; 3. e; 4. d; 5. f; 6. a.

Think about It: Possible answers: Croissants (France), Sausage (Germany); Pizza (Italy), Hot dogs (Germany), Sushi (Japan); Roast beef (England), Lasagna (Italy), Roast lamb (Greece).

D WORD WORK

Standards

- Use knowledge of compound words to determine word meaning
- Identify sound/spelling relationships

WARM UP

- Write these sentences on the board: *I dropped one running shoe on the way to the track meet. I found it later at the edge of the playing field.* Circle the words *running shoe, track meet,* and *playing field.* Ask students what these three items have in common. (Each is made up of two separate words.) Tell students that words like these are called compound words.

TEACHING THE LESSON

1. Word Detective

- Have students complete the activity.

2. Word Study

- Write these words on the board: *soup spoon, measuring spoon.* Say: *The first word in a compound can be a noun or a verb.* Point to the words on the board and ask which one starts with a noun (soup spoon) and which starts with a verb (measuring spoon).
- Go over the chart. Point out that the first word makes the meaning of the second word more exact.

3. Word Play

Heads Together Read the directions. Have students work in pairs to complete the activity.

Spelling and Phonics

- Have students listen to the words and tell you what they have in common (they all contain the /k/ sound). Have them complete the activity and share their answers.

READING

D WORD WORK

1. Word Detective You can often understand the meaning of a compound word by thinking about the meaning of each smaller word:

pan for baking things → baking pan

Match each compound word on the left with its correct meaning on the right.

1. measuring cup
2. can opener
3. mixing bowl
4. oven mitt
5. pizza cutter
6. bread knife

a. a tool you use to slice bread
b. a bowl you use to mix ingredients
c. something you wear on your hand when you take a hot pan out of the oven
d. a tool you use to cut pizzas
e. a tool you use to open cans
f. a cup you use to measure ingredients

2. Word Study The first word in a compound sometimes makes the second word more exact. The first word can come from a *verb* or it can come from a *noun*.

FIRST WORD: VERB	FIRST WORD: NOUN
bowl you use to mix things → mixing bowl	sheet (pan) for making cookie(s) → cookie shee
cup you use to measure things → measuring cup	tool for peeling vegetable(s) → vegetable peele

SPELLING AND PHONICS: To do this activity, go to page 184.

3. Word Play Work with a partner. Read each of the following definitions. Then write the compound word that goes with each definition. Begin by guessing the compound word, then check your dictionary to check your answers.

1. pan you use to cook sauces (and other liquids) *saucepan*
2. tool you use to mash potatoes ______
3. spoons you use to measure things ______
4. board you cut things on ______
5. plate you bake pies in ______
6. tool you use to open bottles ______

98 **Unit 6**

WRAP UP

- Have students list three new food compound words, then share. For example: *peanut butter, cottage cheese, orange juice.*

PB PRACTICE BOOK ACTIVITY

See Activity B, Word Work, on Practice Book page 52.

ANSWER KEY

Word Detective: 1. f; 2. e; 3. b; 4. c; 5. d; 6. a

Word Play: 1. saucepan; 2. potato masher; 3. measuring spoons; 4. cutting board; 5. pie plate; 6. bottle opener.

Spelling and Phonics: a. cook; b. stomach; c. quarter; d. keep; e. sick; f. question; g. lucky; h. Could; i. schedule.

E GRAMMAR Prepositions That Tell Where

. **Listen Up** Listen to each sentence. Point your thumb up 👍 if it
ounds correct. Point your thumb down 👎 if it sounds wrong.

👍👎 1. Juan put the ice cream onto the freezer.

👍👎 2. I took the pot off of the stove.

👍👎 3. A sandwich has filling between two slices of bread.

👍👎 4. The pot is on the stove.

👍👎 5. The milk is into the refrigerator.

👍👎 6. Take the milk out of the refrigerator.

. **Learn the Rule** Prepositions often tell us where something is.
earn how "place" prepositions are used by reading the following rules.
hen do Activity 1 again.

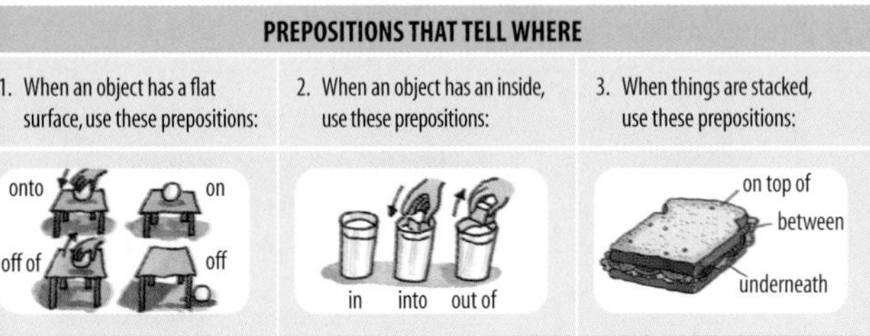

PREPOSITIONS THAT TELL WHERE		
1. When an object has a flat surface, use these prepositions:	2. When an object has an inside, use these prepositions:	3. When things are stacked, use these prepositions:
onto, on, off of, off	in, into, out of	on top of, between, underneath

. **Practice the Rule** Work with a partner. Write a sentence for each
reposition about things in your classroom.

1. (on) ______
2. (onto) ______
3. (on top of) ______
4. (off) ______
5. (off of) ______
6. (out of) ______
7. (in) ______
8. (into) ______
9. (underneath) ______
10. (between) ______

E GRAMMAR

Standard

- Use locative prepositions

WARM UP

- Ask students to follow your directions as you give the following commands: *Put your book between your feet. Put your right hand on your head. Put your left hand on top of your right hand. Take your left hand off of your right hand. Pick the book up off of the floor and put it on your desk.*

TEACHING THE LESSON

1. Listen Up

- Ask students to listen carefully. Then play the tape or CD twice, or read the sentences aloud. Have students point their thumbs up if the sentence sounds correct, and down if it sounds wrong.

2. Learn the Rule

- Read aloud the rule above the first picture. Then ask volunteers to make up sentences using the prepositions to describe the objects in the picture. For example: *The ball is going onto the table. The ball is on the table.* Repeat this activity for the other two types of prepositions.
- Have students take turns placing objects in various positions around the room. As they do this, elicit descriptive sentences using prepositions from other students. For example: *The book is on the top shelf. She's taking the book off of the shelf.*
- Repeat the Listen Up activity, reteaching as needed.

3. Practice the Rule

Heads Together Have students work in pairs, writing sentences that illustrate how to use each of the prepositions in the box.

WRAP UP

JUST FOR FUN

Play "I'm thinking of..." for six to eight objects. Provide clues such as: "I'm thinking of something that is on my desk..." Have students write the name of each object, then share.

PB PRACTICE BOOK ACTIVITY

See Activity C, Grammar, on Practice Book page 53.

ANSWER KEY

Listen Up: Correct sentences: 2, 3, 4, 6.

Practice the Rule: Answers will vary.

WRITING

F BRIDGE TO WRITING — Recipes

READING STRATEGY
Visualizing:
Forming pictures in your mind can help you understand what you are reading.

1. Before You Read Look at the recipe below. What is for dinner?

2. Let's Read Read the following recipe for meatloaf. **Visualize,** or form pictures in your mind, of the steps in the recipe as you read.

NOSTALGIC MEATLOAF
Almost like Grandma's, but a lot easier to make.
Difficulty: Medium
whisk
measuring spoons
oven mitts
wooden spoon
mixing bowl
measuring cup
baking pan
cooking spray
Makes 6 servings
1 lb ground beef
1 egg, beaten
3/4 cup of spaghetti sauce
1 cup seasoned bread crumbs
1/2 tsp. salt
1/4 tsp. pepper
Leave out the word "of" in the list of ingredients.
Preheat oven to 350 degrees.
Spray the baking pan with cooking spray.
spray
In a large bowl, combine all ingredients.
Shape meat mixture into a meat loaf and place it into the pan.
Bake for 50-60 minutes, or until meatloaf is fully cooked.
Let the meatloaf sit for about 5-10 minutes before you slice and serve it, so it has time to set.

Source: *The Everything® Kid's Cookbook* by Sandra K Nessnberg

nostalgic—making you remember happy past times
medium—in between; moderate
seasoned—having flavor from herbs, spices, or salt
crumb—a very small piece of bread or cake
preheat—to heat an oven to a certain temperature before putting food in it
spray—to put a liquid onto something using a pressurized can
shape—to form something with your hands
set—to become solid

100 **Unit 6**

F BRIDGE TO WRITING

Standards
- Read and understand instructions
- Recognize idioms

WARM UP

- Ask students if they have favorite foods that a family member or friend makes or used to make for them.

TEACHING THE LESSON

1. Before You Read

- Ask students to look at the recipe and tell what it is for.

2. Let's Read

Explain that visualizing is allowing words to create pictures in your mind. Tell students that visualizing can help them understand what they are reading (Reading Strategy box). Suggest that students try visualizing each instruction as they read it.

My Turn: Read Aloud/Think Aloud Read the recipe aloud. As you read, comment on words and ideas:

Ground beef is the same thing you use to make hamburgers.

Point out the starburst comment. Have students listen carefully and notice you do not use the word *of* as you read aloud the list of ingredients.

You usually put spaghetti sauce on pasta, but it's good in meatloaf too.

Cooking spray keeps the meatloaf from sticking to the pan.

- Now play the tape or CD, or read the recipe twice. Ask students to be ready to tell you what the first step is.

Our Turn: Interactive Reading Have students read the recipe aloud. As students read, focus on glossed words, ask questions, and make comments:

How difficult is this recipe?

Why do you have to preheat the oven?

Where is the word "spray" used as a noun? Where is it used as a verb?

What does "nostalgic" mean?

- **Build Fluency** If appropriate for your class, have different students repeat sentences from the recipe after you.

Your Turn: Independent Reading Have students read the recipe on their own. Ask them to write down how long they think each step would take, and how long the whole process would take from preheating the oven to serving the meatloaf.

Access for All Have students with artistic ability illustrate the recipe.

3. Making Content Connections Talk with a partner. Do you know how to cook? Think of one dish for each meal or snack that you can make *without* using a recipe. Then complete the chart below.

Meal	You	Your Partner
breakfast		
lunch		
snack		
dinner		

4. Expanding Your Vocabulary When people talk, they often use expressions, or groups of words, with a special meaning. Work with a partner. First, match each of the following highlighted food words or phrases with its definition below. Then write a sentence using each expression.

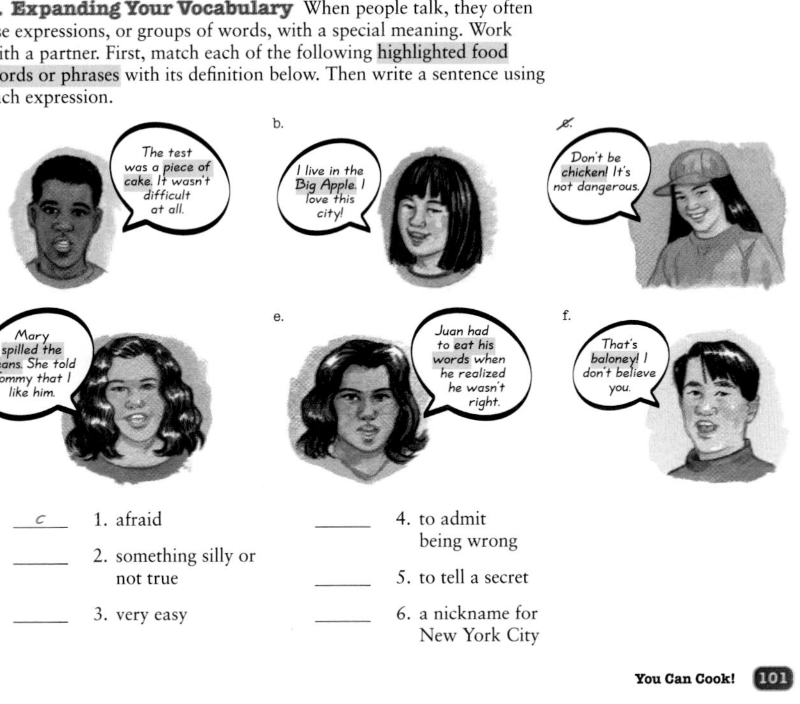

a.
The test was a piece of cake. It wasn't difficult at all.
b.
I live in the Big Apple. I love this city!
c.
Don't be chicken! It's not dangerous.
d.
Mary spilled the beans. She told Tommy that I like him.
e.
Juan had to eat his words when he realized he wasn't right.
f.
That's baloney! I don't believe you.

_c_ 1. afraid
____ 2. something silly or not true
____ 3. very easy
____ 4. to admit being wrong
____ 5. to tell a secret
____ 6. a nickname for New York City

3. Making Content Connections

Heads Together Read the directions. Ask pairs of students to discuss the kinds of foods they can prepare without recipes. Then have them write the names of these dishes in the appropriate sections of their charts.

Interactive Writing Copy the chart on the board. Invite volunteers to take turns filling in responses for each of the four meals.

4. Expanding Your Vocabulary

- Explain that some words and phrases have a second meaning which is very different from their everyday meaning. For example, *When I say "I could eat a horse," I don't mean that I could actually do that. I mean that I am very hungry.*

Heads Together Point out the six lettered speech bubbles and numbered definitions. Have students complete the matching activity with a partner, then write a sentence for each expression.

- Ask different volunteers to give one correct match and read their original sentence. Then ask the student to explain the idiom in his or her own words.

JUST FOR FUN

Ask students to choose one of the idioms and draw a picture of its literal meaning. For example, a student might show an apple cut in half with a person's house inside. (Linda lives in the Big Apple.) Have students display their drawings while other students guess which idioms they represent.

✓ WRAP UP

Outcome Sentence Have students complete this sentence stem and then share:

I want to learn how to make ________.

PB PRACTICE BOOK ACTIVITY

See Activity D, Test-Taking Practice, on Practice Book pages 54 and 55.

See Activity E, Using New Vocabulary, on Practice Book page 56.

ANSWER KEY

Before You Read: Meatloaf.

Making Content Connections: Answers will vary.

Expanding Your Vocabulary: 1. c; 2. f; 3. a; 4. e; 5. d; 6. b.

G WRITING CLINIC

Standards

- Identify the structural features of how-to instructions
- Organize information in time order

WARM UP

- List these words on the board: *steps, difficulty, name, ingredients.* Ask students to number these elements in the order they appear within a recipe format. Write the number next to each. (steps 4, difficulty 2, name 1, ingredients 3)

TEACHING THE LESSON

1. Think about It

Heads Together Ask students to think of three places where they can find recipes.

2. Focus on Organization

- Read the recipe aloud one section at a time (Part 1). As you finish each section, have a student read aloud the description of that part of the recipe. After each section, ask simple comprehension questions to make sure everyone understands both the recipe and the description. For example: *What is a campfire? What does "a quick version" mean? What is an introduction?*
- For Part 2, read the directions and have students complete the task. Then ask for volunteers to share answers.

Technology Tip Students who are interested in reading other recipes can go to www.foodfit.com and click on the recipes. Another useful Web site is www.anniesrecipes.com. This site contains not only recipes, but also a table of abbreviations and other useful information.

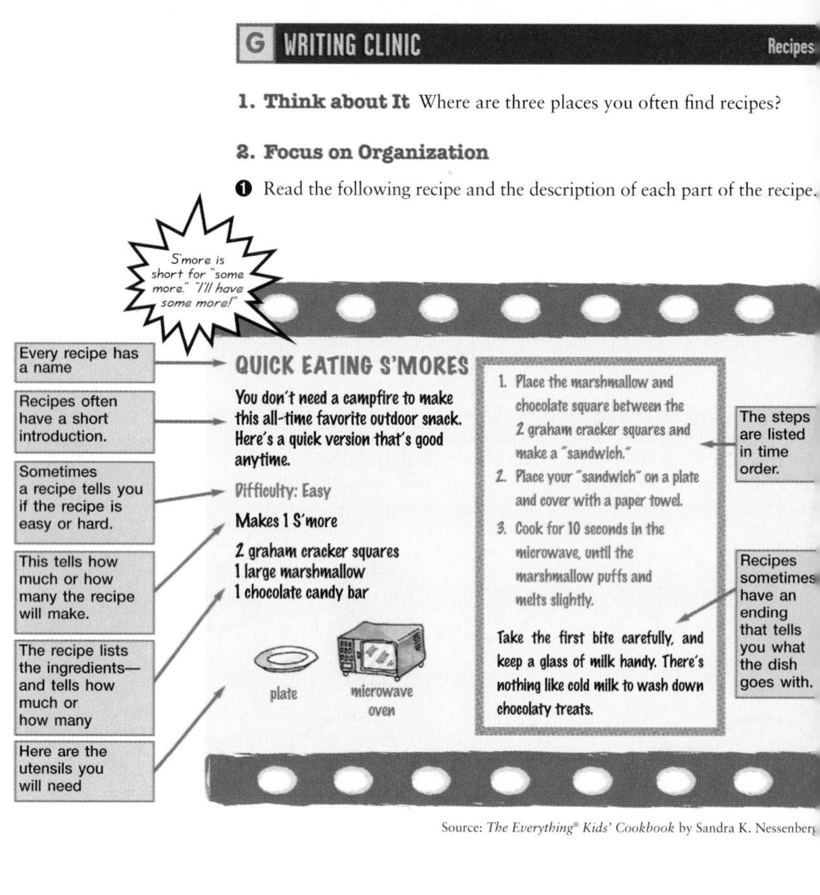
WRITING
G WRITING CLINIC
Recipes
1. Think about It Where are three places you often find recipes?
2. Focus on Organization
1 Read the following recipe and the description of each part of the recipe.
S'more is short for "some more." "I'll have some more!"
Every recipe has a name
Recipes often have a short introduction.
Sometimes a recipe tells you if the recipe is easy or hard.
This tells how much or how many the recipe will make.
The recipe lists the ingredients—and tells how much or how many
Here are the utensils you will need
QUICK EATING S'MORES
You don't need a campfire to make this all-time favorite outdoor snack. Here's a quick version that's good anytime.
Difficulty: Easy
Makes 1 S'more
2 graham cracker squares
1 large marshmallow
1 chocolate candy bar
plate
microwave oven
1. Place the marshmallow and chocolate square between the 2 graham cracker squares and make a "sandwich."
2. Place your "sandwich" on a plate and cover with a paper towel.
3. Cook for 10 seconds in the microwave, until the marshmallow puffs and melts slightly.
Take the first bite carefully, and keep a glass of milk handy. There's nothing like cold milk to wash down chocolaty treats.
The steps are listed in time order.
Recipes sometimes have an ending that tells you what the dish goes with.
Source: The Everything® Kids' Cookbook by Sandra K. Nessenberg
102 Unit 6

PB PRACTICE BOOK ACTIVITY

See Activity F, Focus on Organization, on Practice Book page 57.

Imagine that you are writing a recipe for making hard-boiled eggs. Number the steps below so that they are in the correct time order from step 1 to step 5.

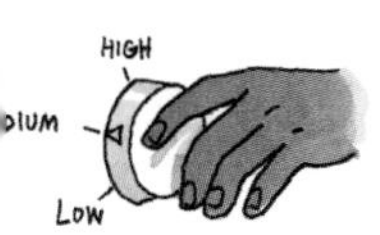

_____ a. When the water boils, turn the heat to medium and let the water simmer (cook slowly) for 12–15 minutes.

_____ b. Gently crack the eggshells and peel them off.

_____ c. Put the saucepan over high heat and bring the water to a boil.

__1__ d. Put the eggs in a small saucepan, and fill the pan with enough water to cover the eggs.

_____ e. Take the saucepan off the heat and pour cold water into the pan to cool the eggs. Cool the eggs for several minutes.

Focus on Style Recipes often have interesting names that make em sound delicious. Match the description of each dish on the left with correct name on the right.

1. Dish with beans and beef you eat in a bowl
2. Sandwich with melted cheese and tuna, served hot
3. Round and golden, you eat them for breakfast with syrup
4. Dish with beans, rice, and meat wrapped in a tortilla
5. Soup you love on a cold day
6. Dish you often serve with chicken or other meat at dinner
7. Fruit-flavored party drink

a. Super Burrito Grande
b. Old Fashioned Mashed Potatoes
c. Texas Chili
d. Tropical Punch
e. Fluffy Buttermilk Pancakes
f. Tasty Tuna Melt
g. Creamy Clam Chowder

3. Focus on Style

- Write on the board the name of a food with an interesting name that students are familiar with, such as "Whopper." Ask a student to describe what a Whopper hamburger is. (It's a very big hamburger with a lot of different toppings.) Then ask another student to explain what the word "whopper" means all by itself. (It's something that is very big.)
- Do the matching activity with the whole class. First read the name of a food on the right and ask a student to explain what the adjectives mean. For example, "Super" means very special and "Grande" means large in Spanish. Then have a student summarize what the name means. (A Super Burrito Grande is a very special, very large burrito.) Ask a third student to find the description at the left that matches that summary (4. Dish with beans, rice, and meat wrapped in a tortilla). Repeat these steps for all six items.
- Ask students to think of other names of popular foods. Have them say the name, explain what the words in the name mean, and then describe the food. For example: *Crispy Chicken Fingers. "Crispy" means hard or crunchy. Here "fingers" means pieces of meat the shape and size of fingers. Crispy Chicken Fingers are finger-shaped pieces of chicken that are fried until they are crunchy.*

WRAP UP

- List these recipe parts on the board leaving space between each: *Name, Difficulty level, Ingredients, Steps.* Ask students to tell where the following parts of a recipe fit in: *Introduction* (after the name), *Utensils* (after the difficulty level), *Servings* (after the utensils), *What the dish goes with* (at the end).

PB PRACTICE BOOK ACTIVITY

See Activity G, Focus on Style, on Practice Book page 58.

ANSWER KEY

Think about It: Possible answers: in the newspaper, in a cookbook, on a package or box, in a magazine, on the Internet.

Focus on Organization 2: a. 3; b. 5; c. 2; d. 1; e. 4.

Focus on Style: 1. c; 2. f; 3. e; 4. a; 5. g; 6. b; 7. d.

H WRITER'S WORKSHOP

Standard

- Use the writing process: prewriting

1. Getting It Out

WARM UP

- Show students a favorite cookbook, talking about how recipes are organized. Tell students that they are going to make their own class cookbook.

TEACHING THE LESSON

- Focus students on the pictures. Have a volunteer or two read the captions. Ask: *How many of you know how to make any of these dishes?*
- Ask students to study the pictures and captions and look up any foods they aren't familiar with in the dictionary. Ask them to think of at least two more foods they like for each category (Part 1). Review the six categories with the whole class and have students share some of their additions to each list with the class.
- Ask students to use the questions to choose which dish they will contribute to the cookbook (Part 2). Tell them to choose something they think others will enjoy making. This means choosing something that most people will want to eat. Guide them to pick something they already know how to make or something a friend or family member can show them how to make. Suggest that they pick a recipe that is easy to describe in words.

H WRITER'S WORKSHOP Recipe

Create a class cookbook. Contribute your favorite recipe. *Important*: Write your own recipe. Do not copy the recipe from another cookbook.

1. Getting It Out

❶ Decide what you will make. Make a list of dishes you like. Here are some possibilities.

1\. *pancakes, muffins, scrambled eggs*

Breakfast

2\. *sandwich, burrito, salad*

Lunch

3\.

tacos fried rice spaghe

Dinner

4\.

nachos, guacamole dip, lumpia

Appetizers

5\.

trail mix, cookies, popcorn

Snacks

6\. *cake, banana split, pie*

Desserts

❷ Choose two or three dishes on your list. Then, to help decide which dish you will teach others to make, ask yourself a few questions:

1. Is this a dish others might like to make?
2. Do I already know how to make this dish? Is there someone in my family that can show me how to make the dish?
3. Is it easy to explain in words how to make this dish?

Here is how Juan answered these questions. Which dish do you think Juan should choose?

Possible Recipes	Is this a dish others would like to make?	Do I know how to make this?	How easy is it to explain how to make this?
Hard-boiled egg	Probably not.	Yes	Very easy
Chocolate peanut butter pudding	YES!!!	Dad knows how to make this. He can help me.	Probably easy.
Fried rice	Not sure.	No. (We always get take out.)	Hard. Lots of ingredients.

Learn how to make the dish you have chosen from your list of recipes. Get help from an adult. Ask questions and take notes. Read Juan's notes below.

Is this easy or hard to make?
What utensils will I need? What ingredients will I need?
What are the steps?

Chocolate Peanut Butter Pudding

–Really easy to make

–Need large bowl, measuring cup, whisk, spatula, saucepan

–Ingredients: 1 package of instant chocolate pudding

MINI-LESSON
Use numbers to show time order:
1. Prepare...

- Have students make a chart to answer the questions. Explain that the chart will help them decide which recipe they will choose (Part 3).
- Help students read Juan's chart. Invite volunteers to tell which dish they think he should make and why. (He should probably make the chocolate pudding because other people would like to learn how to make it, his father can show him how, and it is probably easy to explain.)
- Give students time to make their charts. Have several volunteers share their choices.
- Have students name the best cook in their family. Suggest that they ask this person to help them learn how to make their dish (Part 4). Before they talk to the person, have them review the questions Juan asks his father, along with the notes Juan took.
- Have students make their own notes about questions they may want to ask on separate paper, leaving enough space to take notes.

Students can use the form on page 59 of the Practice Book to take notes.

Mini-Lesson on Conventions
Point out the Mini-Lesson box. Ask students to number the steps in their recipes to show time order.

WRAP UP

- Ask volunteers to name and briefly describe the dish they've decided to make as you record. Save for later.

PB PRACTICE BOOK ACTIVITY

See Activity H, Writer's Workshop, on Practice Book page 59.

H WRITER'S WORKSHOP

Standards

- Use the writing process: drafting, revising, and editing
- Use an outline to draft writing
- Give a short oral presentation

2. Getting It Down

WARM UP

- Revisit the list of the dishes students identified as recipes. Ask them to tell you why they selected each.

TEACHING THE LESSON

Interactive Writing Copy the outline on the board (Part 1). Invite volunteers to help you complete the chart using information from Juan's recipe at the bottom of the page. Then have students complete the chart using information from their notes.

- Have students analyze Juan's recipe, referring to the speech bubble comments (Part 2). Then have them turn their outlines into recipes.

WRAP UP

- Tell students that they will have a chance to revise their work during the next session. Have them locate the ChecBric for this unit in the Student Book or Practice Book. Have them prepare for Getting it Right by reviewing the ChecBric on their own, underlining indicators they're not sure about.

TEACHING TIP If some boys say they never cook, or are reluctant to admit that they cook, remind them that many of the greatest cooks on TV are men. Point out chefs like Wolfgang Puck, Emeril Lagasse, and Bobby Flay.

2. Getting It Down

❶ Turn your notes into an outline. Complete the outline below.

Recipe for: ____________

Difficulty: ____________
Servings: ____________
Utensils needed:
____________ ____________
____________ ____________

Ingredients needed:
____________ ____________
____________ ____________
____________ ____________

Directions:
1. ____________
2. ____________
3. ____________
4. ____________

❷ Now, turn your outline into a recipe. Here is the recipe Juan wrote. What do you think? Do you want to make Chunky Chocolate Peanut Butter Pudding?

Juan's recipe has a cute name. He begins with a sentence that makes you hungry. He tells you the recipe is easy to make.

Chunky Chocolate Peanut Butter Pudding
This is so good you'll eat the whole thing!
Difficulty: Easy
Makes 4 servings
Utensils: bowl, measuring cup, wire whisk, spatula, saucepan

Juan lists the utensils you will need.

1 package instant chocolate pudding *1/2 cup peanut butter*
2 cups cold milk *1/4 cup chopped nuts (optional)*

Juan lists the ingredients. He tells you how many and how much. He tells how many servings the recipe will make.

1. Prepare the pudding. Follow the directions on the package.
2. Use the whisk to stir the peanut butter into the pudding.
3. Pour the pudding into serving dishes.
4. Sprinkle with chopped nuts.

Refrigerate until ready to serve.

The steps are in time order. They are easy to understand.

Getting It Right Take a careful look at what you have written. this guide to help you revise your recipe.

Question to Ask	How to Check	How to Revise
. Does my recipe have a name and short introduction?	Circle the name and underline the introduction.	Add a cute name or write a sentence that makes the cook want to make your recipe.
. Did I list the utensils and ingredients? Did I tell how much or how many?	Put a check mark (✓) next to each utensil, ingredient, and amount.	Add utensils, ingredients, and the amount next to each ingredient.
. Did I remember each step? Are the steps in time order?	Pretend that you are following the recipe. Act out each step in your head.	Add a step or change the order.

Presenting It

Share your recipe with your classmates.

Ask for volunteers to repeat each step in your recipe, using their own words.

As you listen to others, take notes. Use a note-taking guide like this one.

tensils:	Ingredients:
______	______
______	______
______	______

teps:

______

______

______

3. Getting It Right

WARM UP

- Guide students through the ChecBric for this unit.

TEACHING THE LESSON

- Have students use the chart and the ChecBric to revise their work.

Heads Together Have students share their recipes with a partner and give each other positive feedback.

WRAP UP

- Encourage students to bring utensils and key ingredients to use as visual aids as they share their recipes with the class.

Help students use the ChecBric on Practice Book page 111 to revise their recipes. Ask them to attach the ChecBrics to their recipes before putting them in their portfolios.

4. Presenting It

WARM UP

- Call out the six types of recipes (breakfast, lunch, dinner, appetizer, snack, and dessert) and help students form groups based on the type of recipe they wrote. Then form new groups, each of which includes a variety of meal types.
- As a class, develop a simple presentation checklist.

TEACHING THE LESSON

- Tell students that you want them to pay attention to these things as they present their recipes:

  1. Use a loud and clear voice.
  2. Read slowly.
  3. Share any utensils or ingredients you have brought in.

Group Share Model how students will paraphrase the steps in each other's recipes.

- Have students make several copies of the note-taking form or provide them with photocopies.
- When students finish making presentations in groups, work with the whole class. Ask volunteers to use their notes to share some of the recipes others have presented.

✓ WRAP UP

Outcome Sentence Write this sentence stem on the board, then have students share their sentences:

I learned how to make ______________.

I BEYOND THE UNIT

Standards
- Read and understand safety rules
- Read and respond to poetry

1. On Assignment

WARM UP

- Ask a volunteer to describe a cooking show they have seen on television. Who is the chef? Does s/he have a studio audience? Does the chef talk a little or a lot? What is the kitchen like?

TEACHING THE LESSON

- Have students close their books as the class brainstorms safety rules for working in the kitchen (Part 1). Record students' ideas on the board. Then have students open their books and compare their list to the list in the Student Book. Expand on vocabulary items as necessary. For example, have students name several *appliances* and describe the difference between *potholders* and *oven mitts.*
- Choose a chef who is a "showperson." As he or she reads his or her recipe, interrupt the reading and have students say what utensils the chef will be using and what ingredients he or she will need (Part 2).
- Remind students not to talk and to clap softly at appropriate moments (Part 3).
- For Part 4, ask students to look at the picture and say what one important thing is missing (the dinner plate). Then ask students to take turns describing where to place the various items. For example: *The place mat goes under the plate. The fork goes to the left of the plate. The knife goes to the right of the plate.*

I BEYOND THE UNIT

1. On Assignment Does your school have a classroom with kitc appliances? Choose a volunteer "head chef" to show your class how make a dish.

1. Before you begin, listen as your teacher helps the class understand basic safety and kitchen rules.
2. Listen as the chef reads the recipe aloud. Which utensils will he or she need? What are the ingredients?
3. Watch carefully as the chef shows how to prepare the dish. Clap quietly, but do not talk or interrupt.
4. Who will set the table? Look at the picture. What do you think is missing?

Safety and Kitchen Rule
Wash your hands before touching food.
Start with a clean cooking area.
Learn how to use each appliance.
Be careful with knives.
Be careful using electric gas appliances.
Always use potholders c oven mitts.
Keep the cooking area clean as you work.

5. Time to eat! Ask the chef if you may taste the dish.
6. Compliment the chef. Say something nice about the dish.

It's delicious!

Very tasty!

My compliment to the chef!

108 Unit 6

- Have students take turns asking to taste the dish (Part 5). Model phrases such as: *May I have some? Could I try a little. Can I have a taste?*
- Have students practice complimenting the chef (Part 6).

WRAP UP

- Ask students to share what they think would be the best thing and the worst thing about being a chef.

Link to Literature

SHARED READING Read the following recipe poem. The poet is unknown.

LET'S TALK Answer the following questions.

1. Look again at the verbs in the poem. Why is this called a "recipe poem"?
2. What is the "large blue bowl" in the first line?
3. Can you think of one more thing you might "mix" into the weather poem?

JUST FOR FUN Write a recipe poem of your own with four lines.

1. Choose a topic. Use one of these of think of your own.
   ______ school
   ______ friends
   ______ learning English
2. Begin each line with a cooking verb.
   Take ______________________
   Add ______________________
   Stir in ______________________
   Mix ______________________

A Recipe for Weather

Begin with a large blue bowl
Take a sprinkle of yellow sun
Cover it with dark clouds
Add swirling winds
Pour falling rain
Stir in loud crashing thunder
Mix together with a feather
And you've made a day of weather.

Source: humanitiessoftware.com

swirling—going around and around
crashing—making a sudden noise
feather—one of the light, soft things that cover a bird

You Can Cook! 109

2. Link to Literature

WARM UP

- Write these words on the board: *use, pour, sprinkle.* Brainstorm with students a list of other verbs that are commonly used in recipe instructions (add, spray, shape, bake, mix, cook, put, cool, place, etc.).

TEACHING THE LESSON

Shared Reading Read "A Recipe for Weather" aloud as students follow along. After you read it through once, read it again, asking a question about each line. For example: *What is the bowl in the poem?* (The sky.) *Why does the poet say "a sprinkle" of sun.* (Because the sun shines down from up above.) *What do the dark clouds cover?* (The sky. The sun.) *How does the wind move?* (In circles.) *Why does the poet say "Pour falling rain"?* (Because it's like pouring water.) *What does "stir in" mean here?* (Add. Include.) *Why does the poet use a feather to mix things up?* (Because it's part of nature and it rhymes with the word "weather.")

- Have volunteers read the poem aloud. Encourage them to read with expression.

Let's Talk Use the questions to lead a discussion of the poem. Ask: *In what ways is the poem similar to a recipe? What is it about the sky that makes it look like a bowl? What else would you add to a recipe poem about the weather?*

- Copy the poem frame onto the board. Ask students to suggest a topic. Write the topic above the chart. Then elicit lines for the poem from various students. Have a volunteer read the completed poem aloud to the class.

JUST FOR FUN

Have students use the form on Practice Book page 60 to write their own recipe poems. Suggest that they use one of the topics provided or choose a completely different one.

PB PRACTICE BOOK ACTIVITY

See Activity I, Responding to Literature, on Practice Book page 60.

✓ WRAP UP

- Invite volunteers to share their original recipe poems with the class.

✓ UNIT WRAP UP

Quick Write Have students reflect on this question, then share:

Do really good cooks need to follow a recipe? Why or why not?

The Top Five

Unit Overview

Section	At a Glance	Standards
Before You Begin	Students examine a picture of a woman and guess what her job might be.	■ Derive meaning from visual information
A. Connecting to Your Life	Students share their favorite flavors of ice cream.	■ Share preferences
B. Getting Ready to Read	Students learn the language of opinion surveys, then rank their own preferences.	■ Use context to figure out the meaning of new words ■ Share and discuss preferences
C. Reading to Learn	Students read short articles that present survey findings about favorite flavors of ice cream and favorite beverages. PRACTICE BOOK: Students conduct their own surveys.	■ Read and understand a short survey report ■ Identify the main idea and details in text
D. Word Work	Students explore words that can be used as both nouns and verbs. PRACTICE BOOK: Students identify a word in a sentence as a noun or a verb and then write a new sentence using the other part of speech.	■ Identify parts of speech ■ Identify sound/spelling relationships
E. Grammar	Students practice forming *yes/no questions* and questions with *what, who,* and *which.* PRACTICE BOOK: Students complete questions with *what, who,* or *which.*	■ Ask well-formed questions
F. Bridge to Writing	Students read and take notes on surveys showing kids' favorite school subjects and favorite books. PRACTICE BOOK: Students practice taking Reading Vocabulary and Reading Comprehension tests. PRACTICE BOOK: Students practice using fractions, decimals, and percentages.	■ Read and understand a short survey report

Section	At a Glance	Standards
G. Writing Clinic	Students examine the features of a survey report. PRACTICE BOOK: Students use information to complete an article. PRACTICE BOOK: Students add original questions to survey introductions.	■ Identify the structural features of a survey report ■ Use content-area vocabulary (mathematics)
H1. Writer's Workshop: Getting It Out	Students choose a survey idea, choose the people they will interview, take notes as they interview them, and tally the results.	■ Use the writing process: prewriting
H2. Writer's Workshop: Getting It Down	Students outline their survey results and then turn their outlines into reports. PRACTICE BOOK: Students use a form to outline their survey results.	■ Use the writing process: drafting ■ Use an outline to draft writing
H3. Writer's Workshop: Getting It Right	Students revise and edit their reports.	■ Use the writing process: revising and editing
H4. Writer's Workshop: Presenting It	Students present their reports to their classmates and give each other feedback.	■ Give a short oral report
I. Beyond the Unit	Students turn their survey results into pie charts and share them with their classmates. They also read a list poem written by a student. PRACTICE BOOK: Students write their own list poems.	■ Understand and use graphs to express information ■ Read and respond to poetry

BEFORE YOU BEGIN

Standard

- Derive meaning from visual information

- Have students look at the picture on page 111 and then read each student's words aloud. Then ask students what question they think the woman is asking.
- Ask: *Who do you think the woman is? What is her job? How can you tell?* (Possible answers: researcher, reporter, interviewer)
- Invite each student to answer the interviewer's question. Record and tally their responses on the chalkboard. Ask: *Which instrument do you like the best?* Tally votes for each instrument on the board.

Unit 7 The Top Five

Read...

- Survey reports about what people like most, from *TIME For Kids* magazine. Kids share their favorite things with researchers.

Link to Literature

- A list poem written by a student.

Objectives:

Reading:
- A report: Understanding an information survey
- Strategies: Comparing information, noting surprising facts
- Literature: Reading a list poem

Writing:
- Writing a short research report that involves a survey
- Listing information in order
- Making a chart that presents data

Vocabulary:
- Recognizing word families: Nouns and verbs that are the same word
- Learning math vocabulary

Listening/Speaking:
- Listening for information
- Interviewing others (to take a survey)
- Giving a short oral report

Grammar:
- Forming present tense questions

Spelling and Phonics:
- Learning about digraphs

BEFORE YOU BEGIN

alk with your classmates.

1. Look at the picture. Read what each student says. What do you think the woman is asking?
2. Who could the woman be? What could her job be?
3. Imagine that you are in the picture. How would you answer the question?

A CONNECTING TO YOUR LIFE

Standard
- Share preferences

WARM UP

- Have students look again at their list of favorite musical instruments. According to your tally, which instrument is #1? #2? #3? Explain that this is an example of ranking, or putting things in order depending on how important or popular they are. Ask: *Which instrument is the least popular?*

TEACHING THE LESSON

1. Tuning In

- Tell students they will hear an interviewer asking kids some questions. Ask them to listen carefully to find out what the kids are talking about.
- Play the tape or CD, or read the script as students listen. Have students say what the interviewer is asking about.
- Have students listen a second time. This time, have them tell you which pizza topping nobody likes.

2. Talking It Over

- Conduct a round robin, having students take turns reading each ice cream flavor aloud.
- Now describe each flavor without naming it—randomly—as students guess and write the flavor. For example: *This ice cream has chocolate in it ... and nuts ... and little pieces of marshmallow ...* (rocky road).
- Ask students to imagine that they are visiting an ice cream factory. The owner wants to give each of them a free ice cream cone. Write the names of the nine flavors on the chalkboard. Ask a volunteer to play the factory owner and ask each student: *What's your favorite flavor of ice cream?* Students can respond with answers such as: *I like vanilla* or *My favorite flavor is vanilla.* Have a student keep a tally on the board. At the end, have a student point out the most popular flavor.
- Have students look again at the title of the unit. Have them use finger signals to tell you what they think the unit is about.

READING

A CONNECTING TO YOUR LIFE

1. Tuning In Listen to a woman interview a group of students. What are the students telling us?

- ☐ They are telling us what they like best for dinner.
- ☐ They are telling us their favorite pizza toppings.
- ☐ They are telling us how to make a good pizza.

2. Talking It Over
Imagine that your class is visiting an ice cream factory. Order your favorite flavor! Which flavor is at the top of your class list?

1. vanilla
2. chocolate
3. strawberry
4. neopolitan
5. butter pecan
6. black cherry
7. pepper-mint
8. chocolate chip
9. rocky road

Read the title of this unit. What do you think the unit is probably about? Check (✓) the correct answer.

_____ 1. It's about things people like best or most.
_____ 2. It's about ice cream toppings.
_____ 3. It's about things that cost less than five dollars.

112 Unit 7

✓ WRAP UP

- Have students look back at the tallies on the chalkboard and tell what the #2 favorite ice cream flavor of students in the class is. Which is the least popular flavor?

ANSWER KEY

Tuning In: They are telling us their favorite pizza toppings.

Talking It Over: 1.

B GETTING READY TO READ

. **Learning New Words** Read the sentences below. Try to figure .ıt the meanings of the underlined words.

1. Maria likes basketball better than other sports. Maria prefers basketball to other sports.
2. Out of 100 kids, 50 like vanilla ice cream best. That's 50 percent.
3. According to the TV weather report, it will be sunny tomorrow.
4. California is the most popular state to visit—it's number one!
5. Tran is asking kids what kind of pizza they like best. He is taking a survey about pizza.
6. I read in The New York Times that Graciela Pérez will run for president. The New York Times is the source of that story.

ow match the word or phrase on the left with its correct definition on e right.

1. prefer	a. the best or most important person or thing
2. percent (%)	b. to like something better than something else
3. according to	c. a person or book you get information from
4. number one	d. said or written by someone
5. survey	e. the amount in every hundred
6. source	f. a set of questions you ask other people to find out what they like or think

. **Talking It Over** Work in a group. Look Have everyone in the ·oup pick their five favorite ice cream flavors, then rank them below (the avor with the most votes is number one, etc.).

_________ Our #1 choice

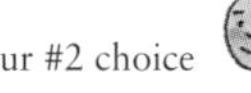

_________ Our #2 choice

_________ Our #3 choice

_________ Our #4 choice

_________ Our #5 choice

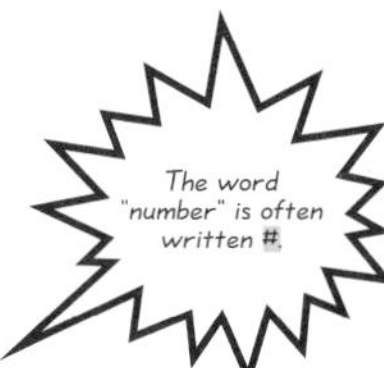
The word
"number" is often
written #.

B GETTING READY TO READ

Standards

- Use context to figure out the meaning of new words
- Share and discuss preferences

WARM UP

- Say: *If everyone in our class voted on their favorite pizza topping, which would be the top three? Guess. Write your guesses on a piece of paper.* Have them save their guesses for later.

TEACHING THE LESSON

1. Learning New Words

- Focus on the underlined word in each sentence and talk students through a situation that will help them understand what it means.

For item 1, say: *I like vanilla ice cream best. I like chocolate, too, but I like vanilla even more. I prefer vanilla ice cream to chocolate ice cream.* Have students read the sentences after you and say the underlined word: *prefer.* Ask: *What does prefer mean?* Have volunteers share their ideas, as you record. Do not provide the correct answer.

- Repeat this procedure with the rest of the new words.
- Now have groups complete the activity and share out. Confirm the correct answers.

2. Talking It Over

Team Talk Have students work in small groups. First, ask each person in the group to write down his or her five favorite flavors. Then have students go around the group reading off their list. Ask a volunteer write the names of the flavors on a large piece of chart paper and tally the total number of votes for each flavor.

- Next, have students count up the tallies and rank the top five flavors.

WRAP UP

- Now have students share their guesses about the top three pizza toppings. Have students share their actual favorites as you write them on the board. Rank the top three in order. Did anyone guess correctly?

Access for All Invite a student with strong logical-mathematical intelligence to make a graph that shows the top five ice cream flavors visually.

ANSWER KEY

Learning New Words: 1. b; 2. e; 3. d; 4. a; 5. f; 6. c.

C READING TO LEARN

Standards

- Read and understand a short survey report
- Identify the main idea and details in text

WARM UP

- Tell students that Activity 2 on page 113 was a survey. Discuss what a survey is and brainstorm with students the kinds of surveys they might see (most popular musical group, best movie of the year, strongest political candidate, etc.).

TEACHING THE LESSON

1. Before You Read

- Ask: *On a hot summer day, what do you eat or drink to stay cool?* Have students share with a partner.

2. Let's Read

- Tell students that they will be reading some information based on surveys. Ask students to compare the results of the first survey with their own top five favorite ice cream flavors. (Reading Strategy box). Explain that when you *compare,* you notice the similarities and differences between two things or ideas.

My Turn: Read Aloud/Think Aloud Read the first survey aloud. Comment on and paraphrase the information as you read:

Three point five percent is a very low percentage.

- Play the tape or CD for the first survey. Stop to make comments.

Our Turn: Interactive Reading Now have students help you read the beverage survey. Focus on the glossed words, ask questions, and make comments.

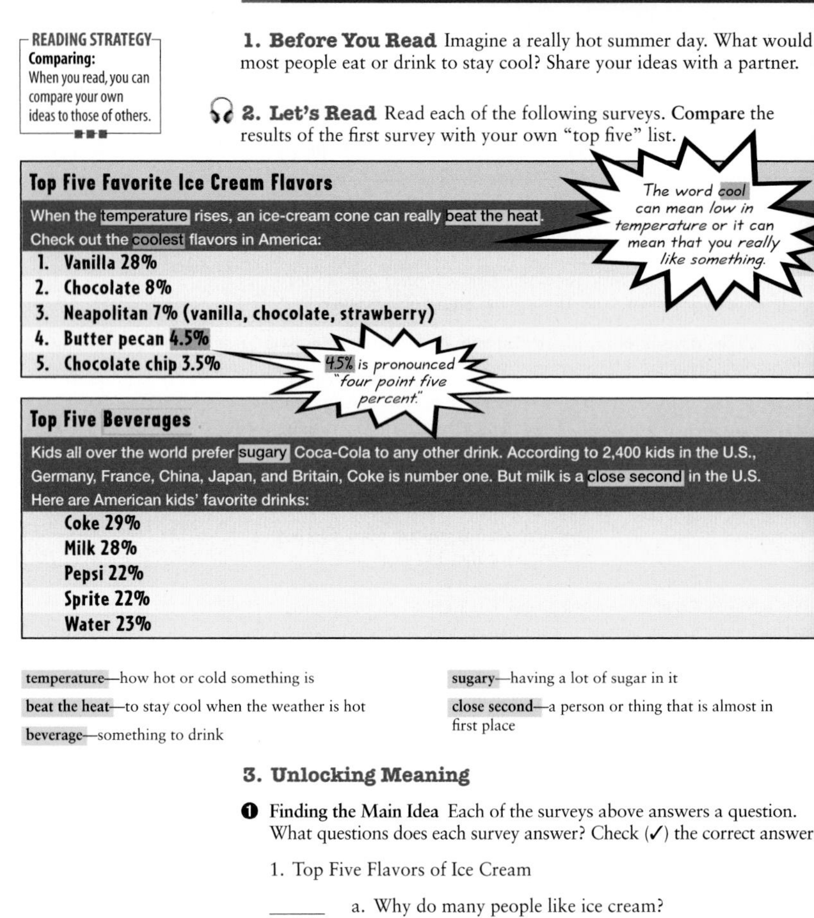

READING

C READING TO LEARN — Surveys

READING STRATEGY
Comparing: When you read, you can compare your own ideas to those of others.

1. Before You Read Imagine a really hot summer day. What would most people eat or drink to stay cool? Share your ideas with a partner.

2. Let's Read Read each of the following surveys. **Compare** the results of the first survey with your own "top five" list.

Top Five Favorite Ice Cream Flavors

When the temperature rises, an ice-cream cone can really beat the heat. Check out the coolest flavors in America:

1. Vanilla 28%
2. Chocolate 8%
3. Neapolitan 7% (vanilla, chocolate, strawberry)
4. Butter pecan 4.5%
5. Chocolate chip 3.5%

The word cool can mean low in temperature or it can mean that you really like something.
4.5% is pronounced "four point five percent."

Top Five Beverages

Kids all over the world prefer sugary Coca-Cola to any other drink. According to 2,400 kids in the U.S., Germany, France, China, Japan, and Britain, Coke is number one. But milk is a close second in the U.S. Here are American kids' favorite drinks:

Coke 29%
Milk 28%
Pepsi 22%
Sprite 22%
Water 23%

temperature—how hot or cold something is
beat the heat—to stay cool when the weather is hot
beverage—something to drink
sugary—having a lot of sugar in it
close second—a person or thing that is almost in first place

3. Unlocking Meaning

1 Finding the Main Idea Each of the surveys above answers a question. What questions does each survey answer? Check (✓) the correct answers.

1. Top Five Flavors of Ice Cream

_____ a. Why do many people like ice cream?

_____ b. What are the flavors of ice cream people like most?

_____ c. How do you make ice cream?

114 Unit 7

Question All-Write Play the tape or CD for the second survey. After reading the introduction to the beverage survey, have students write the answer to these questions: *What is the most popular soda worldwide?*

Which two beverages are tied for third place?

- **Build Fluency** Have students take turns reading parts of the survey aloud to each other.

Your Turn: Independent Reading Pose this question: *Which fact on each survey is the most surprising to you? Why?* Have students read the surveys, then share their ideas.

CULTURE NOTE

Ask different students to explain how the results of these surveys would be different if the interviewer asked only people from his or her home culture. Which ice cream flavors and beverages would probably win out? Which would be very low on the list?

2. Top Five Beverages

_____ a. Do American kids drink too many soft drinks?

_____ b. Who made Coke for the first time?

_____ c. What drinks do kids like best?

Finding Details Read each of the following sentences. Write *T* for True and *F* for False.

_____ 1. Many people like to eat ice cream on hot days.

_____ 2. Vanilla is everyone's favorite ice cream.

_____ 3. Chocolate ice cream is a close second to vanilla in the U.S.

_____ 4. More people like chocolate chip than butter pecan.

_____ 5. Coke is the favorite drink of kids around the world.

_____ 6. Milk is the second favorite drink of kids around the world.

_____ 7. American kids like orange juice better than Coke.

Think about It Look again at the first survey. The percentages add up to *less than 100%*. Choose the best reason for this. Check (✓) the correct answer.

_____ 1. A lot of people named other flavors.

_____ 2. The report is wrong.

_____ 3. The number 4.5% is wrong. It should be 45%.

Now look at the second survey. The percentages add up to *more than* 100%. Choose the best reason for this. Check (✓) the correct answer.

_____ 1. A lot of people can't tell the difference between Coke and Pepsi.

_____ 2. Many people probably named more than one favorite drink.

_____ 3. Water should not be on the list.

Before You Move On Work with a partner. Make an ad for your favorite drink. Share your ad with classmates.

Sources: "Top Five Ice Cream Flavors," *TIME For Kids*, Sept. 19, 2003, Vol. 9, No. 12, p. 3. Used with permission from TIME For Kids Magazine.
"Top Five Beverages," *TIME For Kids*, Sept. 26, 1997, Vol. 3, No. 3, p. 2. Used with permission from TIME For Kids Magazine.

3. Unlocking Meaning

FINDING THE MAIN IDEA

- Have students check the correct answers in their books. Have a volunteer explain why each answer is correct.

✓ FINDING DETAILS

- Have students do the activity by reading the statements and deciding whether they are true or false. Have them mark their answers and discuss them.

THINK ABOUT IT

Think Aloud Have a student read the instructions and possible answers aloud. Then guide students through the reasoning process. You might say something like this for the first survey:

#1 could be right. The numbers on the list add up to 51%. That could mean that a lot of ice cream flavors didn't make it into the top 5.

I think #2 is wrong. I think the report is right. Several people would have checked it carefully before "Time for Kids" published it.

The 4.5% in #3 couldn't be 45%. It would be at the top of the list if it were. Also, the total would be way over 100% if that number were really 45%. So that means #1 is the correct answer.

- Have students choose an answer for the second survey, then share their responses.

BEFORE YOU MOVE ON

Heads Together Have students work in pairs to make ads for their favorite drinks. Invite pairs to share their completed drink ads with the class.

WRAP UP

- Ask students if they think that surveys influence how people think. Ask: *Does knowing what other people think about a movie or a musical group affect what you think about it?*

PB PRACTICE BOOK ACTIVITY

See Activity A, Revisit and Retell, on Practice Book page 61.

ANSWER KEY

Before You Read: Answers will vary.

Finding the Main Idea: 1. b; 2. c

Finding Details: 1. T; 2. F; 3. F; 4. F; 5. T; 6. T; 7. F

Think about It: 1; 2.

D WORD WORK

Standards
- Identify parts of speech
- Identify sound/spelling relationships

WARM UP

- Write these sentences on the chalkboard, underlining the word *cook*:

  Jack is a cook. He loves to cook.

- Have students explain how the word *cook* has a different job in each sentence. (In the first sentence *cook* is a noun. It's the name of a job. In the second sentence *cook* is a verb form. It describes what someone does.)
- Write this sentence on the board and have students identify the noun and the verb: *A cook cooks.*

TEACHING THE LESSON

1. Word Detective

- Have students complete the activity and share responses.

2. Word Study

- Tell students that some words can be used as both nouns and verbs. Words like this make up a word family.
- Remind students that a noun is the name of a person, place, or thing. Ask for examples of nouns. Then ask another volunteer to explain what a verb is. Ask for examples.

3. Word Play

- Have students complete the activity and share out.

Spelling and Phonics

- Write the words *chocolate*, *dish*, and *pharmacy* on the board and circle the digraphs (*ch*, *sh*, *ph*). Then say the three words aloud. Ask students what they notice about the circled letters. (The two letters make one sound.)

D WORD WORK

1. Word Detective The same word in a word family can have two different jobs. Read the sentences below. Write *N* if the underlined word in the sentence is a noun. Write *V* if the word is a verb.

N 1. Many people dislike the desert. They hate the heat.

_____ 2. I'm hungry! Let's heat the oven and bake a pizza!

_____ 3. My favorite drink is milk.

_____ 4. I love to drink milk.

_____ 5. Juan's favorite drink is milk, too.

_____ 6. Do you know how to milk a cow?

_____ 7. That was a good guess!

_____ 8. Try to guess the answer.

2. Word Study Two (or more) words belong to the same "word family" when they have related meanings, but have different jobs in a sentence.

Nouns	Verbs
Ms. Yee always gives me good grades.	Ms. Yee grades hard. She hardly ever gives A's.
Ms. Yee lets us work in small groups.	Ms. Yee often groups the seventh graders together.

SPELLING AND PHONICS: To do this activity, go to page 185.

3. Word Play The underlined words below are *verbs*. Complete the second sentences with *nouns*.

1. Juan always salts his food. Too much salt isn't good for him.
2. Margaret always laughs at my jokes. She has a funny ___________.
3. Please slice the pie in eight pieces. Give each person a ___________.
4. Does your sandwich taste OK? My sandwich has a funny ___________.
5. Tran likes to cook. He wants to be a ___________ when he grows up.
6. Juana painted her bedroom walls purple. She put green ___________ on the ceiling!

- Have students complete the activity. Review the answers.

✓ WRAP UP

- Say sentences using word family words and have students tell you whether the word is a noun or a verb.

PB PRACTICE BOOK ACTIVITY

See Activity B, Word Work, on Practice Book page 62.

ANSWER KEY

Word Detective: 1. N; 2. V; 3. N; 4. V; 5. N; 6. V; 7. N; 8. V.

Word Play: 1. salt; 2. laugh; 3. slice; 4. taste; 5. cook; 6. paint

Spelling and Phonics: dish; pharmacy; think; chorus; what; cheese; either; who; weather; shoe; sing; thank; with; when; chicken; photo.

E GRAMMAR Present Tense Questions

. **Listen Up** Listen to the conversation. Hold up one finger if the sentence is a question. Hold up two fingers if the sentence is an answer.

1. Who is your favorite teacher?
2. I like Ms. Vasquez.
3. Who's your favorite teacher, Tran?
4. I like Mr. Gold...and Ms. Lee.

. **Learn the Rule** There are a few different ways to form a question. Read the following rules. Then do Activity 1 again.

PRESENT TENSE QUESTIONS				
	Question Word	Helping Verb	Subject	Main Verb + Rest of Sentence
When the answer to your question is *yes* or *no*, begin your question with **do** or **does.**		*Do* *Does*	*you/we/they* *he/she/it*	*like ice cream?*
When you are asking for information about a thing, use **what.**	*What*	*do*	*you*	*like to do after school?*
When you are asking about a person, use **who.**	*Who*	*does*	*Juan*	*like best?*
When you are asking about several different choices, you often use **which.**	*Which*	*do*	*you*	*like best—dogs or cats?*

. **Practice the Rule** Work with a partner. Write a question for each of the answers below. Practice asking and answering the questions.

_______________ 1. I eat burritos for lunch.
_______________ 2. I prefer Pepsi.
_______________ 3. I like PE best.
_______________ 4. I hang out with Stefan.
_______________ 5. I like to watch TV.
_______________ 6. I like ice cream for dessert.

E GRAMMAR

Standard

- Ask well-formed questions

WARM UP

- Ask students *What do you do after school? Who is your favorite singer?* After you get several responses, tell students they are about to learn how to make present tense questions.

TEACHING THE LESSON

1. Listen Up

- Play the tape or CD twice, or read the sentences aloud. Have students hold up one finger if the sentence is a question and two fingers if it is an answer.

2. Learn the Rule

- Write these sentences on the board: *He likes ice cream. They like ice cream.* Say: *These sentences are statements. A statement is a sentence that gives information.* Go over the chart.
- Help students form the questions: *Does he like ice cream?* and *Do they like ice cream?* Write them under the statements on the board. Circle the main verb in both statements and both questions. Ask students: *What happens to the main verb when you make a question?* (It doesn't change.) Now underline the helping verb in both questions. Ask: *What part of the verb changes when you ask a question?* (The helping verb.)
- Go over the differences between *what, who,* and *which.*
- Repeat the Listen Up activity, reteaching as needed.

3. Practice the Rule

Heads Together Have students work in pairs, taking turns giving the questions that go with each of the answers.

WRAP UP

- Have students ask you questions, using *what, which,* or *who.*

PB PRACTICE BOOK ACTIVITY

See Activity C, Grammar, on Practice Book page 63.

ANSWER KEY

Listen Up: The questions are: 1, 3.

Practice the Rule: Possible questions:
1. What do you eat for lunch? 2. Which do you prefer—Coke or Pepsi? 3. Which do you like best—PE or Math? 4. Who do you hang out with? 5. What do you do after school? 6. What do you like for dessert?

F BRIDGE TO WRITING

Standard

- Read and understand a short survey report

WARM UP

- Encourage volunteers to share their favorite book and tell the class why they like it.

TEACHING THE LESSON

1. Before You Read

Heads Together Have students tell each other what their favorite school subjects are.

2. Let's Read

- As you read and reread these surveys with students, ask them to look for surprising information and take notes (Reading Strategy box).

My Turn: Read Aloud/Think Aloud Read the first survey aloud. Comment on and paraphrase the information as you read:

In the first line, "recess doesn't count" means that students shouldn't consider recess a class.

They talked to over 1,000 kids. That's a lot!

Paraphrase *"More than 1 in 4 picked math"* as *More than one out of every four kids chose math* or *More than 25% of the kids liked math best.*

- Play the tape or CD for the first survey. Stop to make comments.

Our Turn: Interactive Reading Now have students help you read the favorite books survey. Focus on the glossed words, ask questions, and make comments:

F BRIDGE TO WRITING — Surveys

READING STRATEGY
Note Taking: When you read, you can write down facts or ideas that interest or surprise you.

1. Before You Read What is your favorite subject in school? Share the information with a partner.

2. Let's Read As you read, take notes on a separate piece of paper about any facts that surprise you. Be ready to share them later.

Top Five Favorite Subjects

Can you guess which school subjects kids like the best? (Recess doesn't count.) Researchers asked 1,016 students ages 10 to 17 this question. More than 1 in 4 picked math. Here are subjects that make the grade:

28% Math
21% Science
16% Art
15% History/Social Studies
13% English

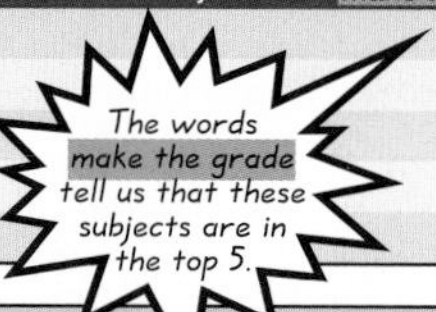

The words make the grade tell us that these subjects are in the top 5.

Top Five Favorite Kids Books of All Time

What's the best book you have ever read? That's the question the National Education Association asked in a recent survey of 1,800 students ages 7 to 15. Here are their top picks:

1. Harry Potter (series)–J.K.Rowling
2. Goosebumps (series)–R.L. Stine
3. Green Eggs and Ham–Dr. Seuss
4. The Cat in the Hat–Dr. Seuss
5. Arthur (series)–Marc Brown

recess—free time during the school day
researcher—someone who studies a subject
pick—the best thing out of a group
series—a set of things, like books, that come one after another

In the introduction, is the word "picks" a noun or a verb? What other word could you use in its place? (choices, preferences)

- **Build Fluency** Model how to read the series titles. For example: *The Harry Potter series by J. K. Rowling.* Have students take turns reading parts of the survey aloud to each other.
- Play the tape or CD before students read the second survey together.

Your Turn: Independent Reading Now have students read the favorite books survey on their own. As they read, ask them to take more notes about surprising facts. Have them share these with the class.

Making Content Connections Work with a partner. Discuss your ›rites for each of the following groups. Then complete the chart below.

What is your favorite...	You	Your partner
...ice cream flavor?		
Why?		
...drink?		
Why?		
...school subject?		
Why?		
...book?		
Why?		

Expanding Your Vocabulary Surveys often include numbers, h as fractions (½), decimals (.50), and percentages (50%). Complete chart below with the numbers from the box. Write the numbers that an the same thing. Practice saying the numbers aloud.

~~50~~	¾	33%	⅒	⅔	25%
7%	.10	~~50%~~	.33	¼	.75

raction	1/2			1/3		
ecimal	.50	.25			.67	
ercent	50%		75%			10%

ces: "Top Five Favorite Subjects," *TIME For Kids*, Nov. 26, 1997, Vol. 3, No. 9, p. 2. Used with ission from TIME For Kids Magazine.
Five Favorite Kids' Books of All Time," *TIME For Kids*, Sept. 12, 2003, Vol. 9, No. 11, p. 3. Used permission from TIME For Kids Magazine.

3. Making Content Connections

Heads Together Have students work in pairs. Ask them to discuss their favorite ice cream flavors, beverages, school subjects, and books. Then ask them to complete the chart, listing their own and their partner's choices.

4. Expanding Your Vocabulary

- Point to the decimals, fractions, and percentages in the box above the chart and model pronunciation. Ask students to repeat. For example: *Point five oh, three quarters* and *thirty-three percent.* Then ask a volunteer to read the first column of the chart aloud. Say: *These three numbers have the same value. They are different ways of saying the same thing.*

Heads Together Have students complete the activity by filling in the missing numbers in each column using the choices provided in the box. Ask them to practice saying the numbers aloud with a partner. For example: *Point 25 is the same as 25 percent. Seventy-five percent is the same as three fourths.*

✓ WRAP UP

Outcome Sentence Have students complete this sentence stem, then share:

It would be fun to survey ____________ *and find out* ______________________.

PB PRACTICE BOOK ACTIVITY

See Activity D, Test-Taking Practice, on Practice Book pages 64 and 65.

See Activity E, Using New Vocabulary, on Practice Book page 66.

ANSWER KEY

Before You Read: Answers will vary.

Making Content Connections: Answers will vary.

Expanding Your Vocabulary: ½, *.50, 50%;* ¼, .25, 25%; ¾, .75, 75%; ⅓, .33, 33%; 2/3, .67, 67%; 1/10, .10, 10%.

G WRITING CLINIC

Standards

- Identify the structural features of a survey report
- Use content-area vocabulary (mathematics)

WARM UP

- Ask students to look once again at the school subject survey and the favorite books survey. What is the same about the two surveys?

TEACHING THE LESSON

1. Think about It

- Remind students that surveys and reports use numbers to give exact information. Ask students: *Which of these three kinds of information does a survey contain?*

2. Focus on Organization

- Read aloud each annotation to the right of the survey in Part 1 and ask students to locate the related information within the survey. For example, read: *The title tells you what the survey report is about.* Then ask students to find the title. Repeat for *introduction, question, who was asked the question, results,* and *source.*

G WRITING CLINIC Surve

1. Think about It A survey is a type of report. What does a report usually tell you?

☐ facts you didn't know ☐ how to make something ☐ a story that is true

2. Focus on Organization

❶ Look again at the survey report on kids' favorite books.

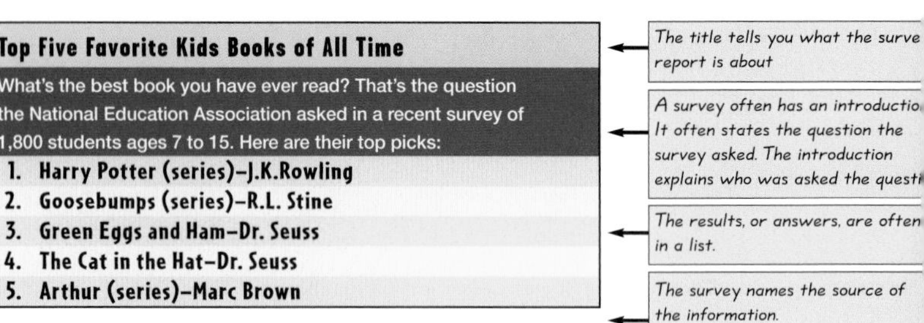

Top Five Favorite Kids Books of All Time

What's the best book you have ever read? That's the question the National Education Association asked in a recent survey of 1,800 students ages 7 to 15. Here are their top picks:

1. Harry Potter (series)–J.K.Rowling
2. Goosebumps (series)–R.L. Stine
3. Green Eggs and Ham–Dr. Seuss
4. The Cat in the Hat–Dr. Seuss
5. Arthur (series)–Marc Brown

The title tells you what the surve report is about
A survey often has an introductio It often states the question the survey asked. The introduction explains who was asked the questi
The results, or answers, are often in a list.
The survey names the source of the information.

Source: "Top Five Favorite Kids' Books of All Time," *TIME For Kids*, Sept. 12, 2003, Vol. 9, No. 11, p. 3. Used with permission from *TIME For Kids Magazine*.

Harry Potter
#1
J. K. ROWLING

HARRY POTTER and all related characters and elements are trademarks of and © Warner Bros. Entertainment Inc.

Now read the survey about school subjects one more time.

p Five Favorite Subjects

Can you guess which school subjects kids like the best? (Recess doesn't count.) [2]Researchers asked 016 students ages 10 to 17 this question. [3]More than 1 in 4 picked math. [4]Here are subjects that make the grade.

28% Math
21% Science
16% Art
15% History/Social Studies
13% English

Answer the following questions.

1. Which sentence asks the survey question? Sentence #______
2. Which sentence tells who was asked the survey question? Sentence #______
3. Which sentence tells you about the results of the survey? Sentence #______

What is missing from this survey? Check (✓) the correct answer.

______ title ______ introduction ______ source

Focus on Style Every report needs an introduction. Read both of se introductions.

We asked 2,400 kids around the world to name their favorite beverage. Here is what they told us:

b. What do kids prefer to drink when they are thirsty? We asked 2,400 kids around the world to name their favorite beverage. Here is what they told us:

What is the difference between the two introductions? Which one is more interesting? Why?

Asking a question is a good way to begin an introduction. Match each survey title on the left with an introductory question on the right.

1. Top 5 Film Actors
2. Top 5 Most Popular Desserts
3. Top 5 Kinds of Music
4. Top 5 School Subjects
5. Top 5 After-school Activities

a. What do kids like to do when school is over?
b. What classes do American students enjoy most?
c. Who are Americans' favorite stars?
d. What do music fans listen to on the radio?
e. How do Americans like to end a meal?

- Now have students look once again at the school subjects survey (Part 2).
- Have students answer the questions on their own (Part 3). Review the answers together in class.
- Ask students to say what is missing from the survey (Part 4).

PB PRACTICE BOOK ACTIVITY

See Activity F, Focus on Organization, on Practice Book page 67.

3. Focus on Style

- Have students read the two introductions to themselves and choose the more interesting one. Guide them to understand that the one on the right is more interesting because it engages our interest with a question.
- Have students match up the titles and introductory questions on their own, then share and explain.

✓ WRAP UP

- Read aloud the following survey introduction and ask students to think of a question to go at the beginning of the paragraph: *That's the question the National Sports Association asked 500 gym teachers in high schools across the U.S. It turned out that most of their schools had basketball teams but very few had soccer teams. Here are the results of the survey.*
- Ask students to write their questions and share out.

PB PRACTICE BOOK ACTIVITY

See Activity G, Focus on Style, on Practice Book page 68.

ANSWER KEY

Think about It: facts you didn't know.

Focus on Organization 3: 1. 1; 2. 2; 3. 3 or 4.

Focus on Organization 4: source.

Focus on Style 1: b. It contains a clearly stated survey question.

Focus on Style 2: 1. c; 2. e; 3. d; 4. b; 5. a.

H WRITER'S WORKSHOP

Standard

- Use the writing process: prewriting

1. Getting It Out

WARM UP

- Tell students that it's now time for them to become researchers—surveying others to learn what they like, then writing a short survey report.

TEACHING THE LESSON

- Tell students that they first need to decide what they want to find out (Part 1). Have them look at the pictures, then generate other ideas, as you record.
- Have students choose the question they will focus on.
- Now have students write their questions (Part 2). Remind them that questions need to be in the correct form. Have volunteers write their questions on the board.

H WRITER'S WORKSHOP Survey

What do other kids like? Find out for yourself and tell others! Write yo own survey report.

1. Getting It Out

❶ What do you want to learn? Look at the following survey ideas, or think of your own.

a.

Favorite TV shows

b.

Favorite music

c.

Favorite desserts

d.

Favorite pets

e.

Favorite sports

f.

You decide!

❷ Write the question you will ask.

EXAMPLE: *What is your favorite after-school activity?*

QUESTION: ______________________

Decide who you will interview, or talk to. Plan to interview 10 people or more.

Your classmates

Kids in other classes

Family members and neighbors

Conduct your interview. Write down each person's answer in a notebook while you are talking to them.

What is your favorite after-school activity?

Play sports	*Play soccer*
Play basketball	*Go to the sandwich shop*
Hang out with my friends	*Do homework*
Go over to my best friend's house	*Watch TV*
Be with my friends	*Play volleyball*
Get a pizza	*Play football*
Watch TV	

Organize and tally, or count, the results.

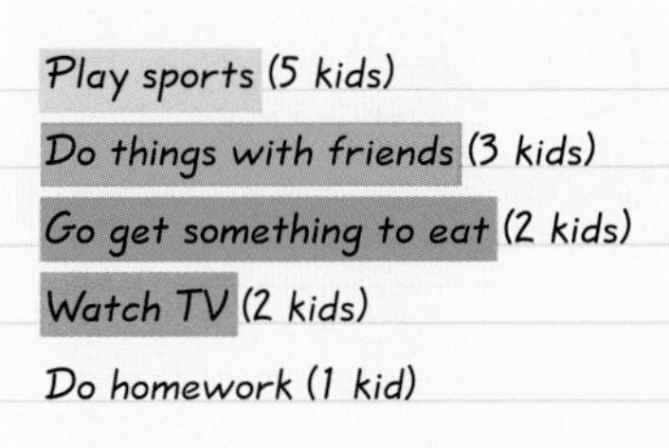
Play sports (5 kids)
Do things with friends (3 kids)
Go get something to eat (2 kids)
Watch TV (2 kids)
Do homework (1 kid)

MINI-LESSON
When you make a list that is in order of importance, number each item starting with "1."

- Next have students decide who they will interview (Part 3). Remind them that they need to interview at least ten people.

TEACHING TIP To avoid interview overload, and to broaden the age range and background of the respondents, encourage students to interview friends and family members outside the school community.

- Remind students that they need write down what each person says (Part 4). Ask students to take notes as they interview at least ten people.
- Walk students through the process of tallying the results (Part 5). Point out that in the example, some answers (sports, basketball, soccer, volleyball, football) overlap and can be included in a single category (sports).

Mini-Lesson on Conventions
Point out the Mini-Lesson box. Explain that when listing items in the order of their importance, they should put the most important one first and the least important one last.

WRAP UP

- Invite students to share any surprising facts they found out while doing their surveys.

H WRITER'S WORKSHOP

Standards

- Use the writing process: drafting, revising, and editing
- Use an outline to draft writing
- Give a short oral report

2. Getting It Down

WARM UP

- Ask students how people responded to being asked survey questions. Were they happy to take part? What questions of their own did they ask, if any?

TEACHING THE LESSON

- Copy the outline onto the board (Part 1). Use the information in Graciela's report to model the steps in this section. Invite volunteers to fill in the missing information on the model chart.
- Then ask students to make their own survey outlines. They can use the form on Practice Book page 69.
- Tell students that it's time to turn their outlines into reports (Part 2). Look again at Graciela's report, identifying each of its strengths.
- Give students time to turn their outlines into reports.
- Have students make simple charts headed *Top Five* _____________ to go with their reports (Part 3). Students will display the charts as they present their reports. Have them use chart paper and markers so that others will be able to see.

WRAP UP

- Tell students that they will have a chance to revise their work during the next session. Have them locate the ChecBric for this unit in the Student Book or Practice Book. Have them prepare for Getting It Right by reviewing the ChecBric on their own, underlining indicators they're not sure about.

WRITING

2. Getting It Down

❶ Make an outline to help you organize your survey results. Use a planner like the one below.

TITLE: Top Five ______________________

INTRODUCTION

My question: ______________________?

Who I talked to: ______________________

RESULTS

Here are the __________ *that kids like most:*

1. ______________ ______%
2. ______________ ______%
3. ______________ ______%
4. ______________ ______%
5. ______________ ______%

Figure out percentages if you interviewed a lot of kids.

SOURCE (Your name): ______________

❷ Now, turn your outline into a report on the survey you took. Here is what Graciela wrote in her survey. What do you think?

Graciela states the question in her introduction. She tells us how many kids she interviewed.

Top 5 After School Activities

What do kids like to do best after school? I asked 13 classmates. Here is what they said:

1. Play sports	*38%*
2. Do things with friends	*23%*
3. Go get something to eat	*15%*
4. Watch TV	*15%*
5. Do homework	*8%*

She lists the results in order.

Source: Graciela Alvarez, Kennedy Middle School

❸ Write a list of your results on a large piece of paper to use when you present your report.

124 Unit 7

PB PRACTICE BOOK ACTIVITY

See Activity H, Writer's Workshop, on Practice Book page 69.

Getting It Right

ke a careful look at your report. Use this guide to make it better.

Question to Ask	How to Check	How to Revise
1. Does my report have a good introduction?	Circle the question that your survey answers.	Begin your introduction with a question.
	Underline the sentence that explains who you interviewed.	Be specific. Explain who you interviewed, how many people there were, and how old they were.
2. Did I present the results accurately and clearly?	Check to see that the order of the items is correct.	Change the order if you need to.
3. Did I state the source?	Put a star (★) next to the source.	Add your own name as the source of the survey.

Presenting It Read your report to your classmates.

Begin by reading the title.

Next, read the introduction. Read slowly and speak clearly.

Show your classmates the list with your results. Read the list.

Ask for feedback.

You chose an interesting question to ask.

You talked to lots of kids.

Your chart is easy to read.

3. Getting It Right

WARM UP

- Guide students through the ChecBric for this unit. Explain that they will use the ChecBric to prepare a final draft of their writing.
- Have volunteers explain, in their own words, what each indicator in the ChecBric means.

TEACHING THE LESSON

- Have students use the chart and the ChecBric to revise their work.

Group Share Model how students will share their reports and give feedback. Have several volunteers practice giving feedback on a classmate's report.

WRAP UP

- Have volunteers share one surprising thing they learned as they conducted their surveys.

Help students fill out the ChecBric on Practice Book page 113. Ask them to attach it to their writing when they put it in their portfolios.

4. Presenting It

WARM UP

- Do a quick survey of the report topics. Tell students that you are excited to hear what they learned.
- As a class, develop a simple presentation checklist. Focus on content, organization, speaking skills (poise, expression, volume, posture, eye contact), enthusiasm, use of visuals, creativity, involvement of the audience, and length of presentation.

TEACHING THE LESSON

- Tell students that you want them to pay attention to these things as they present their work:
  1. Use a loud and clear voice.
  2. Read slowly.
  3. Show your audience your chart as you present.
  4. Ask for feedback.
- Have each presenter show his/her chart with the survey results on it and read the information to the class.
- Have each presenter ask for feedback.

WRAP UP

- Invite volunteers to tell one interesting or surprising thing they learned from someone else's survey report.

I BEYOND THE UNIT

Standards
- Understand and use graphs to express information
- Read and respond to poetry

1. On Assignment

WARM UP

- Have students look at the pie chart. Explain what the chart tells us.

TEACHING THE LESSON

- Help students gather the necessary materials (Part 1). Explain that they can use the compass to draw a pie chart circle, and that they can use the protractor to measure off the different sections of their pie charts.
- Ask students to draw a circle using a compass or some flat, round object like the lid of a jar that is the right size (Part 2).
- Ask students to convert the percentages on the chart into decimals (Part 3). Explain that they can do this by removing the % sign after the number and adding a decimal point in front of it.
- Now have students multiply the number of degrees in a circle (360) by the first decimal number (.40) (Part 4). Explain that the resulting number (144) shows how many degrees of the circle that decimal number represents.
- Point out the numbers that indicate various degrees on the protractor scale (Part 5). Then have students center the protractor on the circle and mark a zero-degree point on the circle. Ask them to draw a line from the center of the circle to the zero-degree point. Then show them how to mark off where 40 degrees falls on the circle and have them draw another line to that point. Elicit or explain that the section between the two lines is the part of the circle that represents 40% of the whole circle.
- Have students color in the various sections of the pie chart in different colors and then label each one (Part 6 and 7).
- Ask students to display their pie charts and explain how their survey results are represented on the chart (Part 8).

WRAP UP

- Invite volunteers to share something interesting or surprising they learned from looking at the pie charts of other students' survey results.

I BEYOND THE UNIT

1. On Assignment Make a pie chart that shows your survey resu

❶ Gather your materials. These are the things you will need.

- Large sheet of paper
- Pencil
- Black pen
- Colored markers
- Protractor
- Compass (or coffee can lid)

❷ Draw a circle on the sheet of paper. Use a compass, coffee can lid, or other round object as a guide. Use pencil to draw the circle.

❸ Turn each percentage on your chart into a decimal.

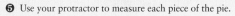

50% = .50
25% = .25

❹ Next, change the decimals into degrees. To do this, multiply eac decimal figure by 360° (degrees)

vanilla .50 X 360° = 180°
chocolate .25 X 360° = 90°
strawberry .10 X 360° = 36°

❺ Use your protractor to measure each piece of the pie.

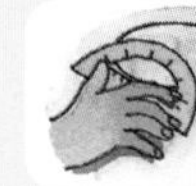

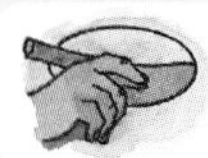

❻ Color each section of the pie a different color.

❼ Label each section of your pie chart.

❽ Share your pie chart and the results of your survey with your classm

126 Unit 7

Link to Literature 

SHARED READING Read this list poem written by a student.

LET'S TALK Answer the following questions.

1. Why is this kind of poem called a "list poem"?
2. What is the poem about?
3. Suppose you wanted to write a list poem about your "top five" favorites. What would you write about?

JUST FOR FUN Write your own "top five" list poem.

My locker has
dirty gym socks
last week's assignments
crumpled papers
broken pencils
dirty Kleenex
saxophone reeds
apple cores
rotten banana peels
overdue library books
and a lock that will not open.
Source: Love Me When I'm Most Unlovable
by Robert Ricken

assignment—a piece of schoolwork

crumpled—crushed into a ball

broken—cracked in pieces

reed—a thin piece of wood attached to the mouthpiece of an instrument to help it make a sound

core—the center of something, like an apple

rotten—going bad or decaying

overdue—late being returned to the library

2. Link to Literature

WARM UP

- Ask students to name one object you might find in their lockers. List objects as students share. Explain that they have just written a list poem!

TEACHING THE LESSON

Shared Reading Read the poem aloud as students follow along, or play the tape or CD. Model correct oral expression and use pauses that help clearly communicate the meaning of the phrases.

- **Build Fluency** Have volunteers read lines from the poem aloud. Encourage students to read with expression.

Let's Talk Use the questions to lead a discussion of the poem. Ask students why the poem is called a "list poem." Have a volunteer tell the class what the subject matter of the poem is. Ask students what they would include in a list poem entitled "My Top Five Favorites."

JUST FOR FUN

Ask students to write a list poem about their favorite things. They can use the form provided on Practice Book page 70. Have them draw a picture to accompany their list poem.

✓ WRAP UP

- Reread the autobiography poem from Unit 3. Ask students to think about this question: *How is this list poem similar to an autobiography poem and how is it different?* Invite students to share.

PB PRACTICE BOOK ACTIVITY

See Activity I, Responding to Literature, on Practice Book page 70.

✓ UNIT WRAP UP

- Have students make a list poem that tells what they did in Writer's Workshop.

Memories

Unit Overview

Section	At a Glance	Standards
Before You Begin	Students tell a story, based on a picture.	■ Derive meaning from visual information
A. Connecting to Your Life	Students share childhood memories.	■ Listen for details ■ Recount experiences in a logical sequence
B. Getting Ready to Read	Students share unforgettable experiences and learn useful vocabulary.	■ Use context to figure out the meaning of new words ■ Recount experiences in a logical sequence
C. Reading to Learn	Students read about childhood memories of famous athletes. PRACTICE BOOK: Students complete paragraphs that paraphrase memories in the Student Book.	■ Read and understand short personal narratives
D. Word Work	Students use synonyms to describe feelings. PRACTICE BOOK: Students read a sentence with an underlined word and complete a second sentence using a synonym for the underlined word.	■ Recognize synonyms ■ Identify sound/spelling relationships
E. Grammar	Students practice using the past tense. PRACTICE BOOK: Students complete paragraphs using correct past tense forms.	■ Express past actions: simple past tense
F. Bridge to Writing	Students read more memories of famous athletes. PRACTICE BOOK: Students practice taking Reading Vocabulary and Reading Comprehension tests. PRACTICE BOOK: Students practice using new vocabulary words.	■ Read and understand short personal narratives

Section	At a Glance	Standards
G. Writing Clinic	Students examine the organization of personal narratives and practice using descriptive adjectives. PRACTICE BOOK: Students identify the ways four different memories are organized. PRACTICE BOOK: Students rewrite stories to make them more exciting.	■ Identify the structural patterns of narrative text ■ Use descriptive words
H1. Writer's Workshop: Getting It Out	Students choose a time in their lives to write about and make a memory web of the experience. PRACTICE BOOK: Students use graphic organizers to record a memory and to make a memory web.	■ Use the writing process: prewriting
H2. Writer's Workshop: Getting It Down	Students turn their memory web into an outline and then use it to write a short memory.	■ Use the writing process: drafting ■ Use an outline to draft writing
H3. Writer's Workshop: Getting It Right	Students check and revise their memories.	■ Use the writing process: revising and editing
H4. Writer's Workshop: Presenting It	Students present their memories to their classmates.	■ Give a short oral presentation
I. Beyond the Unit	Students interview an adult about a memorable childhood experience and share the interviews with the class. Students also read a poem about feelings. PRACTICE BOOK: Students write their own memory poems.	■ Ask and answer questions ■ Interview others ■ Read and respond to poetry

BEFORE YOU BEGIN

Standard

- Derive meaning from visual information

- Have students look at the picture on page 129. Ask: *What can you tell about the boy? What is he doing? What is his name?*

Shared Writing Have students tell Ramon's story, based on the picture. Record what students say.

Unit 8 Memories

Read...

- Selections from "My First Sports Memory," from *Sports Illustrated for Kids*. Learn about star athletes and the highlights of their early, early, early careers!

Link to Literature

- A memory poem written by a student.

Objectives:

Reading:
- Responding to personal memories
- Strategy: Questioning the author
- Literature: Reading a memory poem

Writing:
- Writing a personal memory
- Expressing feelings
- Using adjectives to express emotion

Vocabulary:
- Recognizing synonyms
- Learning sports vocabulary

Listening/Speaking:
- Listening to a short narrative
- Presenting a personal memory to others
- Speaking with expression

Grammar:
- Understanding the simple past tense

Spelling and Phonics:
- Pronouncing words with silent consonants

Ramon Cisneros,
when he hit his first home run

BEFORE YOU BEGIN

alk with your classmates.

1. Look at the picture. What is the boy doing?
2. Read the caption. What is the boy's name?
3. What story does the picture tell? Help your teacher write several sentences about the picture.

A CONNECTING TO YOUR LIFE

Standards
- Listen for details
- Recount experiences in a logical sequence

WARM UP

- Have students write down a memory from a time when they were young. Invite volunteers to share. List student memories. Save for later.

TEACHING THE LESSON

1. Tuning In

- Tell students they are going to listen to an interview with Yankees star, Bernie Davis. Have them write down one fact they learn about Bernie. Play the tape or CD, or read the script, and elicit students' responses.
- Have students listen one more time. Why does Bernie remember the game?

2. Talking It Over

- Have the class look again at their list of memories. Note that some memories are happy, some make you laugh, and some may not be so happy.
- Ask different students to describe what is happening in the pictures. Which memories are happy? Which are not?

Heads Together Ask students to work in pairs. Have them share their memories with a partner, using the words in the captions.

- Read the unit title aloud. Have students use finger signals to tell what they think the unit might be about.

READING

A CONNECTING TO YOUR LIFE

1. Tuning In Listen to an interview with Bernie Davis, a star player for the New York Yankees. He started playing Little League baseball when he was young. What does he remember about that experience?

- ☐ He broke his bat.
- ☐ He won the game for his team.
- ☐ He learned he could run fast.

2. Talking It Over
Talk with a partner. Share one or more of your own childhood memories and the feelings that you remember from that time.

Something that . . .

. . . made me happy

. . . made me excited

. . . made me mad

. . . made me sad

Read the title of this unit. What do you think the unit is probably about? Check (✓) the correct answer.

_____ 1. It's about how to teach children.

_____ 2. It's about memories from childhood.

_____ 3. It's about how to play sports.

130 Unit 8

✓ WRAP UP

Outcome Sentence Have students look again at the picture of Ramon. Have them complete this sentence stem, then share:

Ramon remembers a time that ______________________.

TEACHING TIP Steer students away from any personal topics that should not be shared.

ANSWER KEY

Tuning In: He won the game for his team.

Talking It Over: 2.

B GETTING READY TO READ

Learning New Words Read the sentences below. Try to figure t the meanings of the underlined words.

1. Juan screams when he sees a spider. He is afraid of spiders.
2. We watched the All-Star Game on TV. Both teams had their best players.
3. The New York Yankees play in the American League. The Los Angeles Dodgers play in the National League. The two teams play in different baseball leagues.
4. Pele is still the world's most famous soccer player. He is a legend.
5. Ben didn't expect a call from Jennifer. He was surprised to hear her voice.
6. Our team scored more points than the other team. We won the game!
7. The other team lost the game. They scored fewer points than we did.

atch each word on the left with the correct definition on the right.

1. afraid of	a. a feeling you have when something happens that you don't expect
2. all-star	b. to be first in a game or contest
3. league	c. frightened by something
4. legend	d. involving only the top athletes
5. surprise	e. to come in last in a game or contest
6. win	f. a group of sports teams that play against each other
7. lose	g. someone who is famous for being very good at something

An experience is something that happens to you in life.

. **Talking It Over** Work in a small group. Talk about an experience om your life that you will never forget. Share your feelings about it. ook at the following examples for ideas.

A time you learned to do something

Something you did for the first time

Something you did with your family or friends

A special event you remember

B GETTING READY TO READ

Standards

- Use context to figure out the meaning of new words
- Recount experiences in a logical sequence

WARM UP

- Ask students to recall the Talking It Over activity on the previous page and see how many of their classmates' childhood memories they can remember.

TEACHING THE LESSON

1. Learning New Words

- Write the new words on the board. Have students work in trios, trying to write a definition for any three of the words or phrases.
- Have a volunteer read each item aloud. Ask: *What does the underlined word mean?* Do not correct or comment.
- Now have each trio complete the activity, then compare their original definitions with the definitions in the book. Have them correct their original definitions and then share out which words they originally defined incorrectly.

TEACHING TIP If students have difficulty understanding past tense verbs in this exercise, ask volunteers to explain what they mean.

2. Talking It Over

- Ask a different student to read each caption and describe what is happening in the picture. Then ask students to think back over their own lives about similar experiences they have had.

Team Talk Have students work in small groups. Have each student share an experience with the group, telling how it made him or her feel.

✓ WRAP UP

Outcome Sentence Have students complete this sentence stem and then share:

I'll never forget the time that ________.

Access for All Encourage students with limited oral skills to express their ideas using single words, groups of words, or sentence fragments. Restate their ideas in complete sentences. Ask them to repeat the full sentences.

ANSWER KEY

Learning New Words: 1. c; 2. d; 3. f; 4. g; 5. a; 6. b; 7. e.

C READING TO LEARN

Standard
- Read and understand short personal narratives

WARM UP

- Have students think of a time when they did something really well and then have them share the experience.

TEACHING THE LESSON

1. Before You Read

- Have students look at the pictures and source information and guess who these people are.

2. Let's Read

- **Note** Since sports stars frequently change teams, point out that some of the information in these passages may have changed since this book was published.

TEACHING TIP Ask volunteers to define past tense verbs as necessary and/or paraphrase the sentences they appear in.

My Turn: Read Aloud/Think Aloud Read the passages aloud. Model correct phrasing and fluent reading. As you read, focus on the use of the past tense verb forms, previewing the grammar lesson:

Most past tense verbs end in "-ed." In Jonny's memory, "skied" is one of those.

"Tore" is the past tense of "tear" but "tore" doesn't end in "-ed."

- Tell students that one way to understand what you read is to think of questions for the author (Reading Strategy box).
- Now play the tape or CD, or read the passages twice. As students listen, ask them to write one question they would like to ask each person and then share.

C READING TO LEARN Personal Memories

READING STRATEGY
Questioning the Author:
When you read, think of questions you might ask the author.

1. Before You Read Look at the pictures and the source information below. Who do you think these people are?

☐ athletes ☐ actors ☐ students like you

2. Let's Read A magazine asked some star athletes about their early sports memories. As you read, think of a question you would like to ask one of them.

I skied and tore ligaments in my knee when I was five. The next day, my brother tore his ligaments! We sledded the rest of the winter.
—**Jonny Moseley,** skier
Hometown: San Francisco, California

The first time I had a chance to carry the football as a running back was when I was seven years old. I scored five touchdowns in one game!
—**Terrell Davis,** running back, Denver Broncos
Hometown: San Diego, California

I was the first girl to play in the all-boys' summer basketball league. I ended up doing really well. Everybody was surprised, and it was a lot of fun.
—**Nykesha Sales,** guard, Orlando Miracle
Hometown: Bloomfield, Connecticut

Source: *Sports Illustrated for Kids*

tore—the past tense of the verb *tear*, which means to rip or split apart

ligament—one of the "bands" that hold your bones together

sled—to ride a vehicle that slides over snow

touchdown—the action of moving the football into the other team's end zone to score points

132 Unit 8

Our Turn: Interactive Reading Have students help you reread each memory. As students read, focus on the glossed words, ask questions, and make comments.

- **Build Fluency** Have different students read a sentence or two after you. Encourage them to copy your fluency and intonation.

Your Turn: Independent Reading Now have students read on their own, writing down one additional question they would ask each person. Ask students to share their questions.

Access for All Students who are interested in/skilled at athletics may enjoy reading about sports stars in *Sports Illustrated for Kids,* which is in many public libraries.

CULTURE NOTE

Invite students to comment on which sports are important to people from other cultures and countries and which are important to them.

Unlocking Meaning

Finding the Main Idea Choose the best ending for each of the following statements. Check (✓) the correct answer.

1. Jonny Moseley remembers the time...

_____ a. ...he fell down in the snow.

_____ b. ...he hurt his knee while he was skiing.

_____ c. ...he learned to ride a sled.

2. Terrell Davis remembers the time...

_____ a. ...he played quarterback on his team.

_____ b. ...he scored the most touchdowns in one season.

_____ c. ...he scored a lot of touchdowns in a single game.

3. Nykesha Sales remembers the time...

_____ a. ...she played in an all-boys' basketball league.

_____ b. ...she was the best player in the league.

_____ c. ...she learned how to play basketball.

Finding Details Read the sentences below. Write *T* for True or *F* for False.

_____ 1. Jonny hurt his knee while he was skiing.

_____ 2. Jonny's knee got better in a couple of days.

_____ 3. Terrell Davis grew up in San Diego, California.

_____ 4. Terrell was the star quarterback in the league.

_____ 5. Many people were amazed that Nykesha was so good at basketball.

_____ 6. Nykesha played basketball better than many of the boys.

Think about It Reread Nykesha's sports memory. Which of the following sentences explains how she felt about her experience?

1. She felt proud because she played so well.
2. She felt foolish playing on a boys' team.
3. She felt jealous of the boys because they played better.

Before You Move On Talk with a partner. Which sports memory was most interesting to read? Why?

3. Unlocking Meaning

✓ FINDING THE MAIN IDEA

Ask a different student to read each question and its possible answers aloud. Call on another student to give the correct answer and tell why he or she thinks it is correct.

✓ FINDING DETAILS

- Ask students to work individually as they read the sentences and mark them true or false. Review the correct answers with the whole class.

THINK ABOUT IT

- Review the meaning of the words *proud, foolish,* and *jealous* with the class. Write the words on the board and point to each as you define and explain it. Say:

  When you get 100% on a test, how do you feel? You think you have done well. You feel proud.

  When you think you didn't do well, or if you made a mistake, you don't feel proud—you feel foolish. You might feel foolish if you wore two different color socks to class.

  If you want what someone else has, you feel jealous. You might be jealous of a friend's new bike, or of your friend's talent at math or sports.

- Ask students to give examples from their own lives of times they have felt proud, foolish, and jealous. Then have them review the passage about Nykesha and use finger signals to show how she felt about her experience.

BEFORE YOU MOVE ON

Heads Together Have pairs of students share which memory they thought was the most interesting and explain why.

✓ WRAP UP

Outcome Sentence Have students complete this sentence stem, then share:

The story I liked best was _________ because _________________________.

PB PRACTICE BOOK ACTIVITY

See Activity A, Revisit and Retell, on Practice Book page 71.

ANSWER KEY

Before You Read: athletes.

Finding the Main Idea: 1. b; 2. c; 3. a.

Finding Details: 1. T; 2. F; 3. T; 4. F; 5. T; 6. F.

Think about It: 1.

D WORD WORK

Standards
- Recognize synonyms
- Identify sound/spelling relationships

WARM UP

- Write the following pairs of synonyms on the board and ask students what is special about each pair. (Both words in each pair mean the same thing.)

happy/glad *angry/mad*

TEACHING THE LESSON

1. Word Detective

- Read the directions and have students complete the activity.

2. Word Study

- Read the sentences aloud. Explain or elicit the difference between the word *fun* and the word *enjoyable*. *Fun* is used in the first sentence because the person is playing the game. *Enjoyable* is used in the second sentence because the person is sitting back and watching the game.

3. Word Play

Heads Together Ask students to complete the activity in pairs. Have them discuss the words in the box and look up any that they don't know. When they're finished, have them share their answers.

Spelling and Phonics

- Remind students that a consonant is any letter except the vowels, *a, e, i, o, u*. Explain that a consonant cluster is two or more consonants grouped together. Read the sample sentence aloud. Ask which consonant in the word *knee* is silent.
- Have students complete the activity and share their answers.

READING

D WORD WORK

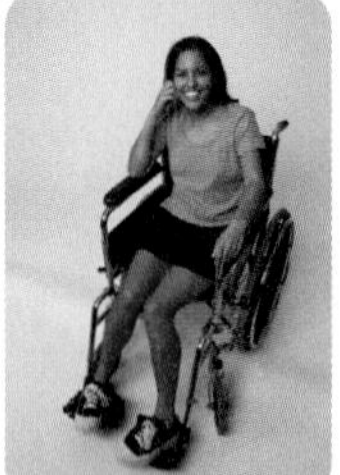
happy

1. Word Detective All these adjectives explain how people feel. Match each word on the left with the word on the right that means the same thing (or almost the same thing).

1. surprised	a. frightened
2. great	b. shocked
3. sad	c. angry
4. happy	d. glad
5. afraid	e. unhappy
6. mad	f. wonderful

2. Word Study Two words that mean almost the same thing are called synonyms. Knowing synonyms can help you choose just the right word for a sentence.

fun	Baseball is fun.
enjoyable	Monday Night Football is enjoyable.

3. Word Play Work with a partner. Rewrite each of the sentences below. Replace each underlined word with a word from the box. You ca use your dictionary.

~~furious~~	terrific	cheerful
scared	alone	terrible

1. My father was mad.
   My father was furious.
2. Juan feels lonely.
3. We had a great time at the game.
4. Michele is afraid of dogs.
5. Maria is a happy person.
6. Tran is sick. He feels very bad.

SPELLING AND PHONICS: To do this activity, go to page 185.

✓ WRAP UP

- Write three adjectives on the board and ask students to find at least two synonyms for each.

PB PRACTICE BOOK ACTIVITY

See Activity B, Word Work, on Practice Book page 72.

ANSWER KEY

Word Detective: 1. b; 2. f; 3. e; 4. d; 5. a; 6. c.

Word Play: 1. My father was furious. 2. Juan feels alone. 3. We had a terrific time at the game. 4. Michele is scared of dogs. 5. Maria is a cheerful person. 6. Tran is sick. He feels terrible.

Spelling and Phonics: know; eight; write; island; ghost; wrap; comb; spaghetti; listen; right; often; dumb; sign; knock; wreck; rhyme.

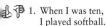

GRAMMAR — Simple Past Tense

Listen Up You usually use the simple past tense to talk about the st. Listen to each sentence. Point your thumb up if it sounds correct, down if it sounds wrong.

1. When I was ten, I played softball.
2. Jonny fall and hurted his knee.
3. We sledded over the snow.
4. The game yesterday is a lot of fun.
5. The team losed every game.
6. I was a ball boy for the Yankees when I was young.

Learn the Rule Use the past tense to talk about things that ppened to you in the past. Learn about the past tense by reading the es below. Then do Activity 1 again.

THE SIMPLE PAST TENSE
Jse the past tense to describe an action or event that took place at a specific time in the past.
1. *Regular* verbs add **–ed** or sometimes just **–d** to form the past tense.
*Ken plays baseball. When he was ten, he play**ed** on a Little League team.*
2. *Irregular* verbs have past tense forms that can be very different from the present tense. Check the Irregular Verbs List on page 200 in your book if you're not sure.
*Tony's soccer team usually wins. Last year, the team **won** every game!*

Practice the Rule Work with a partner. Write the past tense form each verb below. Underline the irregular verbs. Then choose three gular verbs and three irregular verbs and write sentences in the past tense.

have	listen	take
ski	run	play
be	go	walk
throw	lose	wear
speak	carry	jump

Memories 135

E GRAMMAR

Standard

- Express past actions: simple past tense

WARM UP

- Have students make a simple timeline, telling you what they have done since they got up this morning. Record student responses exactly. Do not correct verb forms. Save for later.

TEACHING THE LESSON

1. Listen Up

- Play the tape or CD twice, or read the sentences aloud. Have students point their thumbs up if the sentence sounds correct, and point them down if it sounds wrong.

2. Learn the Rule

- Read the rule for regular past tense forms, the ones that end in *–ed* or just *-d*. Explain that most past tense verbs are regular. List these pairs of verb forms on the board and help students make up present and past tense statements with them: *walk/walked; watch/watched; stay/stayed.*
- Now focus on irregular past tenses. Write these pairs of verb forms on the board and help students make present and past tense statements with them: *find/found; have/had; buy/bought.*
- Ask students to think about the things they do every morning before school. Elicit sentences in the present tense (I get up; I take a shower; I eat breakfast; etc.) as you record. Then help students change sentences to the past tense.
- Repeat the Listen Up activity, reteaching as needed.

3. Practice the Rule

Heads Together Have students complete the activity with a partner. Review the correct answers.

- Have students write six sentences and volunteer to read them aloud.

✓ WRAP UP

- Return to the timeline students made. Ask students to help you make sure that each past tense verb is correct.

PB PRACTICE BOOK ACTIVITY

See Activity C, Grammar, on Practice Book page 73.

ANSWER KEY

Listen Up: Correct sentences: 1, 3, 6.

F BRIDGE TO WRITING

Standard

- Read and understand short personal narratives

WARM UP

- Invite students to describe their favorite sport and tell why they like it.

TEACHING THE LESSON

1. Before You Read

- Ask students to look at the three pictures and the athletes' names and tell what sport each persons is involved in.

2. Let's Read

Remind students that a good way to understand what they are reading is to think of questions they would like to ask the author (Reading Strategy box).

My Turn: Read Aloud/Think Aloud Read the three passages aloud. Model correct phrasing and fluent reading. As you read, comment on words and ideas:

Here we see the past tense form of the verb "lose" in Jerry's memory. It's irregular. The past tense form is "lost."

A "ball boy" is in charge of providing extra balls during practice.

Pele is a "legend"—a very famous soccer player from Brazil.

Michele Timms was a "catcher." She crouched behind the batter and caught the ball.

- Now play the tape or CD, or read the passages twice. As students listen, ask them to notice how old each person was at the time of their experience.

Our Turn: Interactive Reading Have individual students help read. Focus on the glossed words, ask questions, and make comments:

WRITING

F BRIDGE TO WRITING — Personal Memori

READING STRATEGY
Questioning the Author:
When you read, think of questions you might ask the author.

1. Before You Read Look at the pictures of athletes below. What three sports are they talking about?

2. Let's Read Read three more sports memories. Think of a questio you would like to ask one of the athletes.

When I was nine years old, I played on a football team. I was an offensive guard. We lost every game. But it was fun being on the field and wearing a football uniform.
—**Jerry Stackhouse,** guard, Detroit Pistons
Hometown: Kinston, North Carolina

I was a ball boy for the New York Cosmos soccer team when I was six or seven. It was great. Soccer legend Pele was on the team. I had my picture taken with him.
—**Tony Meola,** goalkeeper, Kansas City Wizards
Hometown: Kearney, New Jersey

When I was ten years old, I played softball. I was the catcher, and I remember always being afraid of getting hit by the ball.
—**Michele Timms,** guard, Phoenix Mercury
Hometown: Melbourne, Australia

Source: *Sports Illustrated for Kids*

offensive guard—the person in a football game who plays guard when his or her team has the ball

uniform—clothing worn by team members

softball—a game like baseball except that a larger, softer ball is used

136 **Unit 8**

In the first passage, what is an offensive guard—does anyone know?

What did Jerry Stackhouse enjoy about these early games?

✓ **Question All-Write** Have students respond in writing to these questions:

What does Tony remember about being a ball boy?

What was Tony's memory of Pele?

What was Michele afraid of?

Your Turn: Independent Reading Have students read the passages on their own, listing at least one question that they would like to ask one of the athletes.

Access for All Pair students who don't know anything at all about sports with partners who do. The less knowledgeable students can learn things from their partners, and the more knowledgeable students can practice explaining things in English.

Making Content Connections Work with a partner. Choose two sports stars from the list who you think had the *most interesting* mories. Then complete the chart below.

☐ Michele Timms	☐ Terrell Davis	☐ Jerry Stackhouse
☐ Jonny Moseley	☐ Nykesha Sales	☐ Tony Meola

Name of the sports star:	What did the person remember?	Why did the person remember this experience?
1.		
2.		

Expanding Your Vocabulary Learn more about sports. Work :h a partner. In each row, circle the position that doesn't fit the sport.

Baseball

pitcher

batter

outfielder

goalkeeper

Football

forward

quarterback

running back

receiver

Basketball

guard

forward

catcher

center

PB PRACTICE BOOK ACTIVITY

See Activity D, Test-Taking Practice, on Practice Book pages 74 and 75.

See Activity E, Using New Vocabulary, on Practice Book page 76.

ANSWER KEY

Before You Read: football, soccer, softball.

Making Content Connections: Answers will vary.

Expanding Your Vocabulary: Row 1: goalkeeper; Row 2: forward; Row 3: catcher.

3. Making Content Connections

Heads Together Have pairs of students work together to choose the two sports stars with the most interesting memories from the list. Then have them fill in the chart with information about what each person did and why the person remembers his or her particular experience so well. Invite individuals to share their responses with the class.

4. Expanding Your Vocabulary

Heads Together Have pairs of students figure out which position doesn't match the sport shown in each row.

WRAP UP

- Invite students to share their fantasy of a meeting with a famous sports figure. Who would they like to meet? What would they like to ask this person?

G WRITING CLINIC

Standards

- Identify the structural patterns of narrative text
- Use descriptive words

WARM UP

- Ask students to tell which of the memories from this unit they remember best and why.

TEACHING THE LESSON

1. Think about It

Heads Together Ask students what kind of experiences people describe when they write memories—are they real experiences or imaginary ones?

2. Focus on Organization

- Read the annotations next to each memory aloud and ask volunteers to show the connection between the notes and the memory (Part 1). For example: *Jerry Stackhouse talks about his own experience. He tells about playing offensive guard when he was nine years old.*

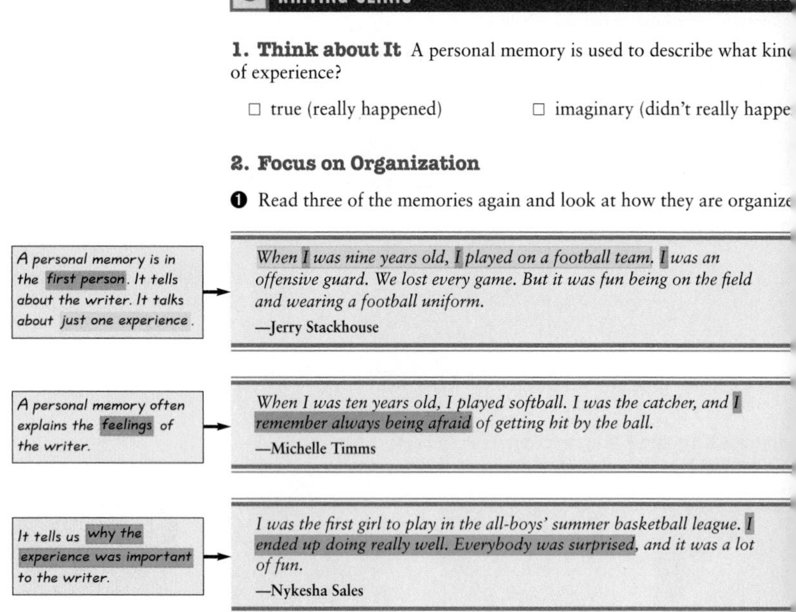

WRITING

G WRITING CLINIC — Personal Memori[e]

1. Think about It A personal memory is used to describe what kin[d] of experience?

☐ true (really happened) ☐ imaginary (didn't really happe[n])

2. Focus on Organization

❶ Read three of the memories again and look at how they are organize[d].

A personal memory is in the first person. It tells about the writer. It talks about just one experience. →

When I was nine years old, I played on a football team. I was an offensive guard. We lost every game. But it was fun being on the field and wearing a football uniform.
—Jerry Stackhouse

A personal memory often explains the feelings of the writer. →

When I was ten years old, I played softball. I was the catcher, and I remember always being afraid of getting hit by the ball.
—Michelle Timms

It tells us why the experience was important to the writer. →

I was the first girl to play in the all-boys' summer basketball league. I ended up doing really well. Everybody was surprised, and it was a lot of fun.
—Nykesha Sales

138 **Unit 8**

Look again at these personal memories. Talk about them with your classmates. Answer the questions that follow each personal memory.

[1] I was a ball boy for the New York Cosmos soccer team when I was six or seven. [2] It was great. [3] Soccer legend Pele was on the team. [4] I had my picture taken with him.
—Tony Meola

1. Which sentence describes Tony's experience? Sentence # ______
2. Which sentence explains why Tony remembers the experience? Sentence # ______
3. Which sentence tells us how Tony felt? Sentence # ______

[1] When I was nine years old, I played on a football team. [2] I was an offensive guard. [3] We lost every game. [4] But it was fun being on the field and wearing a football uniform.
—Jerry Stackhouse

1. Which sentence describes Jerry's experience? Sentence # ______
2. Which sentence explains why Jerry remembers the experience? Sentence # ______
3. Which sentence tells us how Jerry felt? Sentence # ______

Focus on Style Adjectives can help you describe how you felt ›ut something. Which person below liked the game the most?

Michele

Tony

Juan

ınk of something you liked a lot (a movie, a book, a party). Write three tences about how you felt about it. Use different adjectives. You can the adjectives in the box or think of some other adjectives.

antastic	terrific	super	tremendous
ɾonderful	fabulous	astounding	excellent

XAMPLE: *"The Lord of the Rings" was a fantastic movie.*

- Have students locate the sentence in each memory that describes the experience, the sentence that tells why the person remembers the experience, and the sentence that tells how the person felt (Part 2). Have students share their answers.

PB PRACTICE BOOK ACTIVITY

See Activity F, Focus on Organization, on Practice Book page 77.

3. Focus on Style

- Ask a volunteer to read the speech bubbles aloud to the class. Ask: *What are the differences in meaning?* Then ask students to rate the words *nice, great,* and *awesome,* telling which is the weakest (nice), which is medium (great), and which is strong (awesome).
- Read the boxed words aloud with expression (as if each had an exclamation point after it) and ask students to repeat. Ask students what the words have in common. (They mean almost the same thing.)

Team Talk Ask students to write their sentences and share them in small groups. Have the groups choose the two best sentences from their group and write them on the board.

✓ WRAP UP

Outcome Sentence Have students complete this sentence stem and then share:

A personal memory tells ___________.

PB PRACTICE BOOK ACTIVITY

See Activity G, Focus on Style, on Practice Book page 78.

ANSWER KEY

Think about It: true.

Focus on Organization 2: Tony Meola: 1. 1; 2. 3 or 4; 3. 2. **Jerry Stackhouse:** 1. 1; 2. 3 or 4; 3. 4.

Focus on Style: Juan liked the game the most.

H WRITER'S WORKSHOP

Standards
- Use the writing process: prewriting, drafting
- Use an outline to draft writing

1. Getting It Out

WARM UP

- Tell students that they are going to write a class book of memories—similar to the memories they have read. Ask: *Who might be interested in reading your book of memories?*

TEACHING THE LESSON

- Have students make a memory chart (Part 1). Have them fold the paper into four parts and then copy the heading in each quadrant. Next have them list things they remember in each of the four squares. Then ask them to circle the most important memory and share with classmates.
- You can have students use the forms on Practice Book page 79 for Parts 1 and 2.
- Tell students that they now need to think more about the experience, remembering all of the details. Explain that they are going to make a memory web (Part 2).
- Walk students through Ramon's memory web. Ask them to identify the experience (First time I played baseball), then the details (seven years old, hit home run, want to be a baseball player one day). Ask students to look for the feelings words (proud, happy) and point out that they grew out of the memory of hitting the home run.
- Give students time to complete their own memory webs.

WRITING

H WRITER'S WORKSHOP Personal Memori

Help make a class book of short memories. Write your own memory fo the book.

1. Getting It Out

❶ Make a chart like the one below. Fold a sheet of paper in half and then in half again to create four parts. Put a title in each part. Make list of things you remember in each part. Circle the memory that is most important to you.

1. The first time you did something	2. A time you learned how to do something
played baseball	*rode a bicycle*
3. Something you did with your family or friends	4. A special event you remember
went on a camping trip	*went to my older sister's wedding*

❷ What do you remember about the experience you circled? Make a memory web of your experience. Here is Ramon's memory web. Wh do you think?

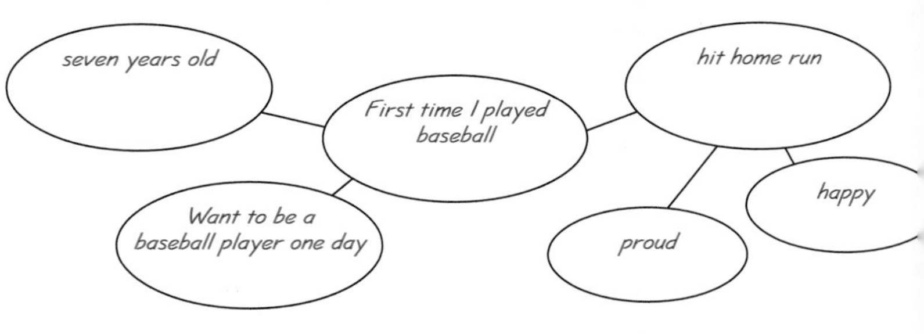

140 Unit 8

✓ WRAP UP

Outcome Sentence Have students complete this sentence stem and then share:

When I ______________, I felt really ____________________.

PB PRACTICE BOOK ACTIVITY

See Activity H, Writer's Workshop, on Practice Book page 79.

Getting It Down

Turn your memory web into an outline. Use a planner like the one below.

What I did: ______
How I felt: ______
The reason I remember the experience: ______

Now turn your outline into a short memory. Here is what Ramon wrote about his memorable experience.

I remember the first time I played baseball! My first time at bat, I hit a home run! Everyone cheered. I felt happy!

Ramon describes the experience.

He explains the reason he remembers the experience so well.

He tells us how he felt.

MINI-LESSON

Capitalizing Pronouns:
Always capitalize the pronoun *I*. Do not capitalize other pronouns unless they begin the sentence.

My first time at bat, I hit a home run.
Ramon's first time at bat, he hit a home run.
He hit a home run his first time at bat.

2. Getting It Down

WARM UP

- Tell students that they will now turn their memory webs into an outline and then a written memory.

TEACHING THE LESSON

- Copy the planner on the board. Ask students to help you complete the planner based on Ramon's chart and memory web. Write the information on the board. Then have students make their own planners and complete them using information from their own charts and memory webs (Part 1).
- It's time for students to create their own short memories (Part 2). Point out how Ramon turned his notes into complete sentences. Have students use the information in their planners to write complete sentences that tell what they did, how they felt, and why they remember the experience.

Mini-Lesson on Conventions
Point out the Mini-Lesson box. Explain the meaning of *capitalize* and use the words *capital letters* and *capitalize* in several sentences.

WRAP UP

- Tell students that they will have a chance to revise their work during the next session. Have them locate the ChecBric for this unit in the Student Book or Practice Book. Have them prepare for Getting It Right by reviewing the ChecBric on their own, underlining indicators they're not sure about.

H WRITER'S WORKSHOP

Standards

- Use the writing process: revising and editing
- Give a short oral presentation

3. Getting It Right

WARM UP

- Guide students through the ChecBric for this unit. Explain that they will use the ChecBric to prepare a final draft of their writing.
- Have volunteers explain, in their own words, what each indicator in the ChecBric means.

TEACHING THE LESSON

- Ask students to use the chart and the ChecBric to look for changes they might want to make to their memories. Suggest that they go through the chart and the ChecBric, section by section, and follow each set of instructions.

Group Share Model how students will present their memories to their classmates. Have several volunteers practice giving feedback on a classmate's memory.

WRAP UP

- Ask students to compare their first drafts and second drafts and share with the class one change they made.

Help students fill out the ChecBric on Practice Book page 115. Ask them to attach it to their writing when they put it in their portfolios.

3. Getting It Right

❶ Take a careful look at what you have written. Use this guide to revise your story.

Question to Ask	How to Check	How to Revise
1. Did I describe the experience?	Underline the sentence that describes the experience.	Add details so that the reader knows what you did.
2. Did I tell why I remember the experience?	Put a check mark (✓) in front of the sentence that tells why the experience was important.	Add a sentence that helps others understand why you remember the experience.
3. Did I use adjectives that tell how I felt?	Circle the adjective(s) that tell how you felt.	Add a sentence with an adjective that tells how you felt.

❷ Share your memory in a small group. Ask for feedback from your classmates.

❸ Revise your memory using the feedback from your classmates. Write final draft of your memory.

I remember the first time I played baseball! My first time at bat, I hit a home run! Everyone cheered. I felt happy and proud!

Presenting It Share your memory with your classmates.

Practice reading your personal memory aloud. Read it several times to a partner before you read to the class.

• Read your memory aloud to your classmates. Read slowly and speak clearly.

• Use your voice to help tell the class how you felt.

• Ask if anyone has any questions.

How old were you?
Would you like to be a baseball player one day?
Do you still like baseball?

4. Presenting It

WARM UP

- Do a quick survey of memory topics. Tell students that you are excited to hear about their experiences.
- As a class, develop a simple presentation checklist. Focus on content, organization, speaking skills (poise, expression, volume, posture, eye contact), enthusiasm, use of visuals, creativity, involvement of the audience, and length of presentation.

TEACHING TIP Decide whether students will present to the whole class or in smaller groups. Form groups if necessary to provide balance.

TEACHING THE LESSON

- Tell students that you want them to pay attention to four things as they present their memories:
  1. Use a loud and clear voice.
  2. Read slowly.
  3. Use expression in your voice.
  4. Ask if anyone has any questions.
- Review with students the kinds of questions they might ask—referring to the speech bubbles.

Heads Together Have students rehearse reading their memories to a partner.

- Ask students to present their memories.
- Have students invite their classmates to ask questions about the memory they just heard.

WRAP UP

Outcome Sentence Invite students to think about the memories they just heard and tell one interesting fact they learned about a classmate. Have them complete this sentence stem:

I learned that ____________________.

I BEYOND THE UNIT

Standards
- Ask and answer questions
- Read and respond to poetry
- Interview others

1. On Assignment

WARM UP

- Brainstorm with students a list of adults they know that they think might have interesting memories to share.

TEACHING THE LESSON

- Have students decide who they will interview. Invite them to share with the class (Part 1).

> TEACHING TIP You may wish to guide students as they choose who they will interview in order to obtain an interesting variety of ages and types of people.

- Have students write their interview questions (Part 2). They can start with the examples shown. Encourage them to think of other interesting questions to ask.
- As they do their interviews, have students copy down the person's exact words (Part 3). Some students may wish to tape record their interviews and then write out their interviewees' exact words later.
- Have students read their interviews to the class (Part 4). Encourage them to ask questions and give each other positive feedback.

I BEYOND THE UNIT

1. On Assignment Interview an adult about a memorable childhood experience. Share what you learned from the interview with your classmat

❶ Choose someone to interview.

A family member

A teacher

Someone in your community

❷ Plan the questions you will ask. Write them on a piece of paper before the interview.

1. What do you remember?
2. Why do you still remember the event?
3. How did you feel at the time?

❸ Interview the person. Write down their exact words as they speak.

What do you remember?

I remember my first job. I delivered papers.

❹ Share the interview with your classmates.

144 Unit 8

WRAP UP

- Ask students to vote to select the most interesting person interviewed. Consider inviting that person to class and having students prepare further questions to ask him or her.

Link to Literature

SHARED READING Sometimes people write poems about memories. Read the memory poem that a student wrote.

LET'S TALK Answer the following questions.

1. What memory does the writer share with us?
2. Find the words that explain how the writer *feels*.

JUST FOR FUN Write your own memory poem.

1. Choose a memory to write about. What happened?
2. Think about how you felt when this happened.
3. Think about why you remember this event.
4. Write four or five sentences about the memory. Include information about what happened, how you felt, and why you remember the event.

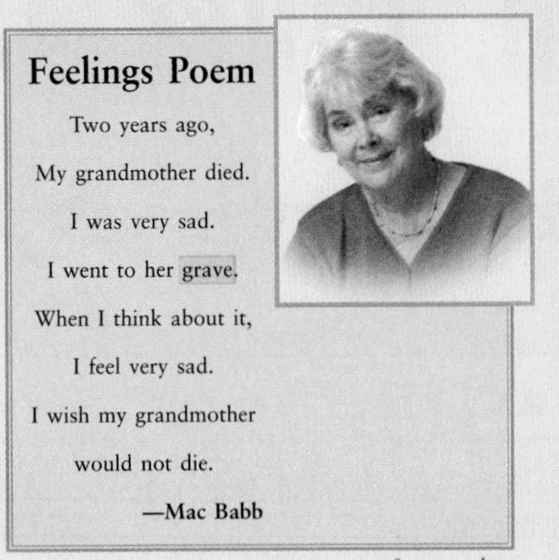

Feelings Poem

Two years ago,
My grandmother died.
I was very sad.
I went to her grave.
When I think about it,
I feel very sad.
I wish my grandmother
would not die.

—Mac Babb

Source: ascd.org

grave—the place where a dead body is buried

2. Link to Literature

WARM UP

- Have students look back at their memories. Ask volunteers to share some of the words they used that describe feelings. List the words on the board.

TEACHING THE LESSON

Shared Reading Read "Feelings Poem" aloud or play the tape or CD as students follow along. Use your tone of voice and pauses to help clearly communicate the meaning of each line.

- Have volunteers read lines from the poem aloud. Encourage students to read with expression.

Let's Talk Ask a student to explain what Mac's memory is all about. Have students say the words that describe how Mac is feeling. As you discuss the second question, ask students to paraphrase lines from the poem using synonyms for the word *sad*.

JUST FOR FUN

Have students choose a memory to write about. They can borrow ideas from their memories, or focus on an entirely different memory. Ask them to think about how they felt while the event was happening. Have them reflect on why they remember the event so well. Then ask them to write four or five lines including what happened, how they felt, and why they remember the event.

PB PRACTICE BOOK ACTIVITY

See Activity I, Responding to Literature, on Practice Book page 80.

WRAP UP

- Invite volunteers to read their poems to the class. Encourage other students to give positive feedback.

UNIT WRAP UP

Outcome Sentence Have students complete this sentence stem:

One thing I learned about myself in this unit was ___________.

Tall, Taller, Tallest

Unit Overview

Section	At a Glance	Standards
Before You Begin	Students talk about Mt. Everest, the world's tallest mountain.	▪ Derive meaning from visual information ▪ Share information and ideas
A. Connecting to Your Life	Students explore examples of the most extreme places on earth.	▪ Listen for details ▪ Share information and ideas
B. Getting Ready to Read	Students share what they know about the world's geography and learn content-area vocabulary.	▪ Use context to figure out the meaning of new words ▪ Use content-area vocabulary (geography) ▪ Share information and ideas
C. Reading to Learn	Students read a passage about some of the longest rivers in the world. PRACTICE BOOK: Students answer factual questions about rivers, using complete sentences.	▪ Read and understand informational text ▪ Use complete sentences ▪ Identify main idea and details in text
D. Word Work	Students use ordinal numbers. PRACTICE BOOK: Students complete sentences using the correct ordinal numbers.	▪ Use cardinal and ordinal numbers ▪ Identify sound/spelling relationships
E. Grammar	Students use comparative and superlative adjectives. PRACTICE BOOK: Students complete sentences with correct comparative and superlative forms.	▪ Express comparison
F. Bridge to Writing	Students read a passage about the highest mountains in the world and learn content-area vocabulary. PRACTICE BOOK: Students practice taking Reading Vocabulary and Reading Comprehension tests. PRACTICE BOOK: Students practice new vocabulary.	▪ Read and understand informational text ▪ Use content-area vocabulary (geography)

Section	At a Glance	Standards
G. Writing Clinic	Students match topic sentences with specific facts. Then they make an outline with a topic sentence and corresponding facts. PRACTICE BOOK: Students practice organizing paragraphs using topic sentences and facts. PRACTICE BOOK: Students practice combining sentences as they rewrite paragraphs.	■ Identify the structural features of informational text ■ Identify topic sentences and supporting details
H1. Writer's Workshop: Getting It Out	Students prepare to write a page for a class atlas showing "Wonders of the World." They select a place to write about and start reading about it. PRACTICE BOOK: Students research a place to write about and use a form to take notes.	■ Use the writing process: prewriting
H2. Writer's Workshop: Getting It Down	Students turn their notes into an outline, and then draft their pages.	■ Use the writing process: drafting ■ Use an outline to draft writing
H3. Writer's Workshop: Getting It Right	Students check and revise their own atlas pages.	■ Use the writing process: revising and editing
H4. Writer's Workshop: Presenting It	Students present their pages to classmates.	■ Give a short oral presentation
I. Beyond the Unit	Students make picture graphs comparing things at school or at home. Students also read a diamante poem, "The Earth." PRACTICE BOOK: Students write their own diamante poems.	■ Use graphic tools to express information ■ Read and respond to poetry

BEFORE YOU BEGIN

Standards
- Derive meaning from visual information
- Share information and ideas

- Have students look at the picture on page 147. Ask them to describe what they see in the photograph.
- Have students read the caption.

Shared Writing What do students know about Mt. Everest? Record their ideas.

- **Build Background** Explain that Sir Edmund Hillary and Tenzing Norgay were the first to climb Mt. Everest, in 1953. Hillary was from New Zealand and Norgay was from Nepal, the country where Mt. Everest is located. Since then, over 1300 people have climbed Everest. Many others have died trying. It takes about three weeks to reach the top.

Unit 9 Tall, Taller, Tallest

Read...
- Selections from *Hottest, Coldest, Highest, Deepest* by Steve Jenkins. Climb the tallest mountain and swim in the deepest lake in this book about the earth!

Link to Literature
- A diamante poem written by a student.

Objectives:

Reading:
- Reading information about our world
- Understanding maps and picture graphs
- Strategy: Using maps and other visuals to understand meaning
- Using information in charts
- Literature: Reading a poem

Writing:
- Writing an informational paragraph
- Writing paragraphs with a topic sentence and facts/details
- Combining sentences

Vocabulary:
- Learning geography terms: Landforms
- Learning ordinal numbers

Listening/Speaking:
- Listening to information for facts
- Comparing two places
- Giving feedback

Grammar:
- Forming comparative and superlative adjectives with *-er, -est*

Spelling and Phonics:
- Pronouncing words with the pattern *i* + consonant + e

146 Unit 9

Mount Everest

FORE YOU BEGIN

k with your classmates.

1. Look at the picture. What do you see? Help your teacher make a list.
2. Read the caption. What is the name of the mountain?
3. What do you know about Mount Everest?

A CONNECTING TO YOUR LIFE

Standards
- Listen for details
- Share information and ideas

WARM UP

- Ask students to name a well-known mountain (other than Everest), river, lake, or other place on earth. Why is it famous?

TEACHING THE LESSON

1. Tuning In

- Ask students to listen carefully. Play the tape or CD or read the script.
- Have students listen again. Have them point their thumbs up if a statement is true and point their thumbs down if it is not.

2. Talking It Over

Heads Together Have students work in pairs to complete each caption. Have them share out.

- Have students look at the title of the unit and mark their answers. Have them use finger signals to tell you what they think the unit is about.

WRAP UP

- Have students think about their own community, city, or state. Have them write a sentence about the tallest, longest, widest, or shortest "X," and then share—for example: *Los Angeles is the largest city in California.*

READING

A CONNECTING TO YOUR LIFE

1. Tuning In Listen to the sentences about land and water. Point your thumb up if the statement is true. Point your thumb down if it is false.

2. Talking It Over Work with a partner. Complete the captions for the pictures below with the phrases in the box.

a. ...the hottest place in the U.S.
b. ...the biggest lake in North America.
c. ...the longest bridge in the world.
d. ...the tallest volcano in the world.
e. ...the largest island in the world.
f. ...the coldest city in the U.S.

1. Island

Greenland is *the largest island in the world*

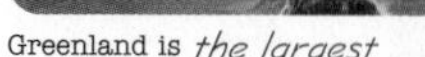

2. Lake

Lake Superior is... ____________

3. Desert

Death Valley is... ____________

4. Bridge

Akashi Kaikyo is... ____________

5. City

6. Volcano

Fairbanks, Alaska, is... ____________

Mauna Kea is... ____________

Read the title of this unit. What do you think the unit is probably about? Check (✓) the correct answer.

_____ 1. It's about places in the world that are fun to visit.
_____ 2. It's about places in the world that are "one of a kind."
_____ 3. It's about places in the world that are in Asia.

148 Unit 9

TEACHING TIP To check facts during class discussions, and to encourage students to do extra reading, have copies of world almanacs and other fact books available in the classroom. Students can also find information by going to http://www.guinnessworldrecords.com/ and entering phrases such as "longest river" or "highest mountain."

ANSWER KEY

Tuning In: Correct sentences: 1. A mountain is higher than a hill. 4. An ocean is deeper than a lake. 5. A river is longer than a stream.

Talking It Over: 1. e; 2. b; 3. a; 4. c; 5. f; 6. d.

Talking It Over: 2.

GETTING READY TO READ

Learning New Words Read the sentences below. Try to figure the meanings of the underlined words.

1. A foot is a measure of length or height. Mr. Valdez is six feet tall.
2. In many countries, people use kilometers to measure distance. In the U.S., we use miles, or 5,280 feet.
3. Mt. Whitney is 14,491 feet high. It takes a week to climb to the top, or the summit!
4. When you are standing on the beach, you are at sea level.
5. North America is a continent, or great area of land. The continental U.S. stretches from the Atlantic Ocean to the Pacific Ocean.

tch each word with the correct part of the picture below.

d	1. continental	____	4. mile
____	2. sea level	____	5. feet
____	3. summit		

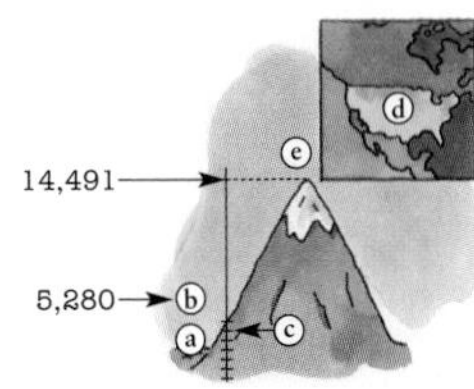

Talking It Over Work with a partner. How much do you know out the world? Complete the chart below. You can use an atlas.

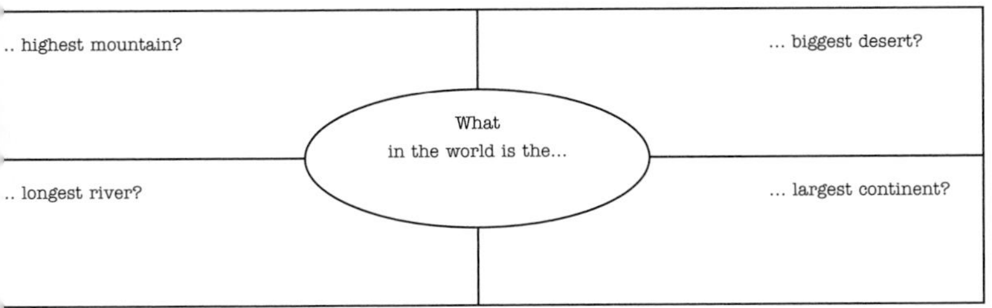

... highest mountain?
... biggest desert?
What in the world is the...
... longest river?
... largest continent?

B GETTING READY TO READ

Standards

- Use context to figure out the meaning of new words
- Use content area vocabulary (geography)
- Share information and ideas

WARM UP

- Brainstorm with the class a list of words used to measure distance, or that tell "how high, how tall, how far" something is. Record on the board, arranging the words from shortest to longest.

TEACHING THE LESSON

1. Learning New Words

- Write the new words on the board and point to each as you define and explain it. Say:

  A foot is a measure of length. (Show "one foot" and "two feet" on a yardstick.)

- Repeat with the remaining words.
- Have students complete the activity.

2. Talking It Over

- Read the words in the chart. Then write these landforms on the board:

Mt. McKinley	*Mojave Desert*
Amazon River	*Africa*
Mt. Everest	*Death Valley*
Ganges River	*Australia*
Mt. Fuji	*Sahara Desert*
Nile River	*Asia*

Heads Together Ask students to copy the chart. Have them decide which landform of its type is biggest and complete the chart. Encourage them to use an atlas or other resources.

- Have volunteers share their answers with the class.

✓ WRAP UP

Outcome Sentence Have students complete this sentence stem, then share out:

Something new I learned is that ________.

ANSWER KEY

Learning New Words: 1. d; 2. a; 3. e; 4. b; 5. c

Talking It Over: Mt. Everest, Sahara Desert, Nile River, Asia.

C READING TO LEARN

Standards

- Read and understand informational text
- Use complete sentences
- Identify main ideas and details in text

WARM UP

- Have students name important rivers they have heard of—other than the Nile, the Amazon, and the Ganges.

TEACHING THE LESSON

1. Before You Read

- Point out the picture of the Nile River on the map. Invite a volunteer to say where the Nile is located, pointing out clues if necessary. Allow the student to refer to a wall map or globe.

2. Let's Read

- Point to the visuals on the page—without reading any words. Explain that maps and other visuals can help you understand what you are reading (Reading Strategy box). Suggest that students look at the maps and visuals at three different points: before they read the passage to get an overview, while they are reading to help them understand specific sentences, and after they finish in order to double-check that they have understood correctly.

My Turn: Read Aloud/Think Aloud Read the selection aloud. Comment on words and ideas and paraphrase as you read:

The word "longest" means longer than any other. We use "-est" at the end of most adjectives to show something is one of a kind.

Notice the "-er" at the end of the word "mightier." We use "-er" at the end of most adjectives to compare two things.

READING

C READING TO LEARN

Short Reports: Our W

READING STRATEGY
Using Visuals:
Use maps and other visuals to understand what you are reading.

1. Before You Read Look at the picture below. Where is this rive

☐ in the United States ☐ in Japan ☐ in Egypt

2. Let's Read Read the following selection. It gives important information about the longest rivers in the world. As you read, make a list of facts you didn't know.

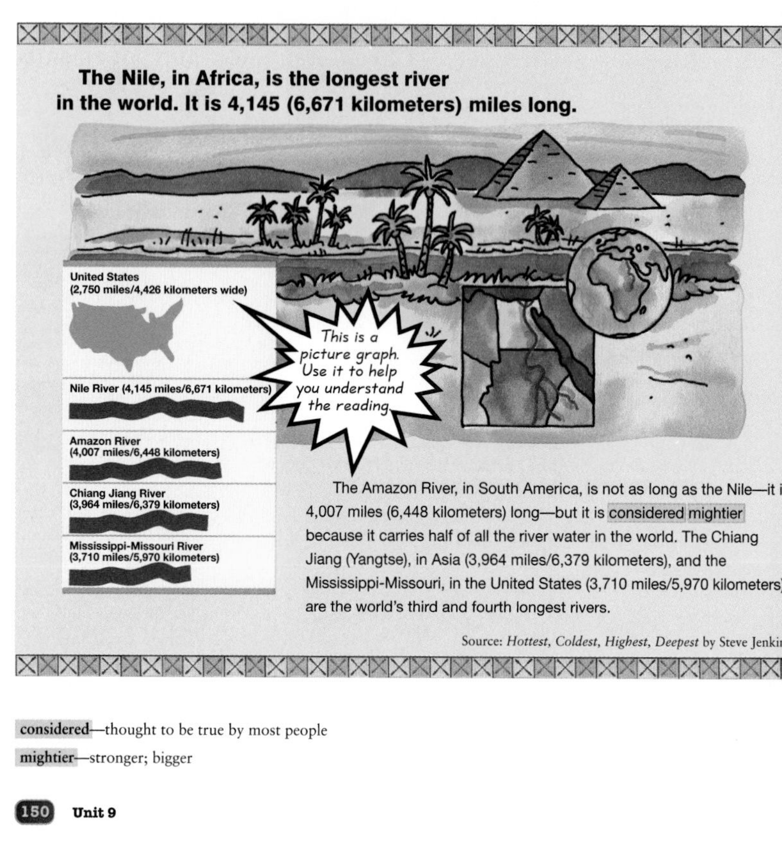
The Nile, in Africa, is the longest river in the world. It is 4,145 (6,671 kilometers) miles long.
United States (2,750 miles/4,426 kilometers wide)
Nile River (4,145 miles/6,671 kilometers)
Amazon River (4,007 miles/6,448 kilometers)
Chiang Jiang River (3,964 miles/6,379 kilometers)
Mississippi-Missouri River (3,710 miles/5,970 kilometers)
This is a picture graph. Use it to help you understand the reading.
The Amazon River, in South America, is not as long as the Nile—it is 4,007 miles (6,448 kilometers) long—but it is considered mightier because it carries half of all the river water in the world. The Chiang Jiang (Yangtse), in Asia (3,964 miles/6,379 kilometers), and the Mississippi-Missouri, in the United States (3,710 miles/5,970 kilometers) are the world's third and fourth longest rivers.
Source: *Hottest, Coldest, Highest, Deepest* by Steve Jenkin

considered—thought to be true by most people
mightier—stronger; bigger

150 Unit 9

The Amazon is just a little bit shorter than the Nile.

- Now play the tape or CD, or read the passage twice. As students listen, ask them to find out why the Amazon is considered "mightier" than the Nile. (The Amazon carries almost half the river water in the world.)

Our Turn: Interactive Reading Have individual students take turns reading aloud. As they read, focus on the glossed words, ask questions, and make comments:

Do you know what countries the Nile flows through? How about the Chiang Jiang? What states does the Mississippi-Missouri flow through?

Your Turn: Independent Reading Have students read the selection on their own. Ask students to look for new facts they didn't know as they read. Have them list these facts on a separate piece of paper.

Unlocking Meaning

Finding the Main Idea Which sentence tells the most important idea in the selection you just read. Check (✓) the correct answer.

_____ 1. The Nile is a river.

_____ 2. The Nile is the longest river on earth.

_____ 3. The Nile is 4,145 miles long.

Here's how you say long numbers:

The Nile is four thousand, one hundred forty-five miles long.

Finding Details Work with a partner. Reread the selection on major rivers. Then complete the chart below.

Name of the River	Continent/Country	Length in Miles
Nile	*Africa*	*4,145 miles*

Think about It Complete the "Top Ten" list below. Put the following rivers in order from the longest to the shortest.

Mekong (2,600 miles) Paraná (2,796 miles) Congo (2,900 miles)
~~Ob-Irtysh (3,362 miles)~~ Lena (2,734 miles) Huang (3,395 miles)

The Ten Longest Rivers

1. Nile (4,145 miles)
2. Amazon (4,007 miles)
3. Chiang Jiang (3,964 miles)
4. Mississippi-Missouri (3,710 miles)
5. *Ob-Irtysh (3,362 miles)*
6. ______
7. ______
8. ______
9. ______
10. ______

Before You Move On Think about your own community. Write answers to the following questions.

1. What is the tallest building in your community?
2. What is the longest street or road?
3. What is the largest park?

Tall, Taller, Tallest 151

3. Unlocking Meaning

✓ FINDING THE MAIN IDEA

- Ask students to check the correct answer in their books and compare answers with a partner. Have students use finger signals to tell what the most important idea in the selection was.
- Point out the note in the starburst that shows how to say long numbers using the words *thousand* and *hundred*. Write several four-digit numbers on the board and help students read them aloud. For example: *3,127; 5,439; 6,122; 47,855.*

✓ FINDING DETAILS

Heads Together Ask students to work in pairs to read the selection on major rivers again and complete the chart together. Review the completed chart with the class.

THINK ABOUT IT

- Ask students to work individually. Have them study the information about the six longest rivers. Then have them complete the list of the ten longest rivers by listing the remaining five, from longest to shortest, after the numbers 6–10 in their Student Books. Review the answers orally with the class.

BEFORE YOU MOVE ON

- Ask students to list the tallest building, the longest street or road, and the largest park in their community. Have them check maps or other sources of information if possible. Ask students to share their answers with the class.

✓ WRAP UP

Outcome Sentence Have students complete this sentence stem, then share:

The biggest __________ *in my community is* __________.

PB PRACTICE BOOK ACTIVITY

See Activity A, Revisit and Retell, on Practice Book page 81.

ANSWER KEY

Before You Read: in Egypt.

Finding the Main Idea: 2.

Finding Details: Nile, Africa, 4,145 miles; Amazon, South America, 4,007 miles; Chiang Jiang, Asia, 3,964 miles; Mississippi-Missouri, North America, 3,710 miles.

Think about It: 5. Ob-Irtysh (3,362 miles); 6. Huang (3,395 miles); 7. Congo (2,900 miles); 8. Paraná (2,796 miles); 9. Lena (2,734 miles); 10. Mekong (2,600 miles).

READING

D WORD WORK

1. Word Detective Look at these people in line. Match the descriptions on the left with the positions on the right.

1. man in the orange cap — a. first
2. girl in the blue cap — b. second
3. boy in the purple cap — c. third
4. boy in the green cap — d. fourth
5. girl in the pink cap — e. fifth
6. girl in the brown cap — f. seventh
7. woman in the black cap — g. eighth
8. boy in the red cap — h. tenth

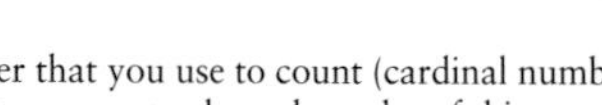

2. Word Study Each number that you use to count (cardinal numbe like *one*) also has a number that you use to show the order of things (ordinal numbers, like *first*). Most ordinal numbers end in *–th* or *–eth*.

SPECIAL WORDS FOR ORDER	MOST ORDINAL NUMBERS END IN *–TH*	SOMETIMES THE ORIGINA SPELLING CHANGES
one → first	four → fourth	nine → ninth
two → second	six → sixth	five → fifth
three → third	thirteen → thirteenth	twenty → twentieth

Beginning with twenty-one/ twenty-first, put a hyphen between the words.

Write the cardinal number for each ordinal number below.

fortieth *forty*	seventeenth ______	ninth ______	sixty-fifth ______
fifty-first ______	eightieth ______	eleventh ______	sixth ______

SPELLING AND PHONICS: To do this activity, go to page 186.

3. Word Play Work with a partner. Write the ordinal number for ea cardinal number below.

seven *seventh*	fifty ______	one ______
three ______	five ______	ten ______

152 Unit 9

D WORD WORK

Standards
- Use cardinal and ordinal numbers
- Identify sound/spelling relationships

WARM UP

- Ask students to tell you what grade they are in. Record responses, using ordinal numbers. Ask students if they have brothers or sisters. Ask what grades they're in. Explain that we use special numbers when we are counting things in order.

TEACHING THE LESSON

1. Word Detective

- Read the directions and explain the activity. For example, say: *The man in the orange cap is* (count off in ordinals) *seventh in the line.* Have students complete the activity.

2. Word Study

- Point out the three columns in the chart. Say: *The pairs of numbers in the first column sound very different from each other. The pairs of numbers in the second column are exactly the same except that the ordinal number has a "-th" added at the end. The pairs of numbers in the third column use "-th" but the spelling changes. For example you drop the "e" when you add the "-th" to the word "nine."*
- Have students complete the activity and share answers.

3. Word Play

Heads Together Have students complete the activity in pairs and share answers.

Spelling and Phonics

- Have students listen to the words and tell you what they notice about them. (The letter *i* is pronounced three different ways—like in the words *eye*, *if*, and *see*.)
- Have students complete the chart and share answers.

WRAP UP

- Have students make up sentences using the ordinal numbers *first* through *tenth*. For example: *The Yankees are in first place.*

PB PRACTICE BOOK ACTIVITY

See Activity B, Word Work, on Practice Book page 82.

ANSWER KEY

Word Detective: 1. f; 2. g; 3. d; 4. c; 5. h; 6. b; 7. e; 8. a.

Word Study: forty, fifty-one, seventeen, eighty, nine, eleven, sixty-five, six.

Word Play: seventh, third, fiftieth, fifth, first, tenth.

Spelling and Phonics: Nile: smile, line, five, time, like, prize, bike; **river:** give, fifth, shiver; **magazine:** gasoline, tangerine.

GRAMMAR — Comparatives and Superlatives: *-er, -est*

Listen Up Listen to each sentence. Point your thumb up if it
nds correct. Point your thumb down if it sounds wrong.

1. Mt. Everest is more tall than Mt. Whitney.
2. The Nile is longer than the Amazon.
3. The Amazon is more shorter than the Nile.
4. Fairbanks is more cold than Los Angeles.
5. Rome is warmer than London.
6. Lake Superior is more bigger than Lake Michigan.

Learn the Rule To compare things, you need to use comparative
superlative adjectives. Read and learn the following rules. Then do
ivity 1 again.

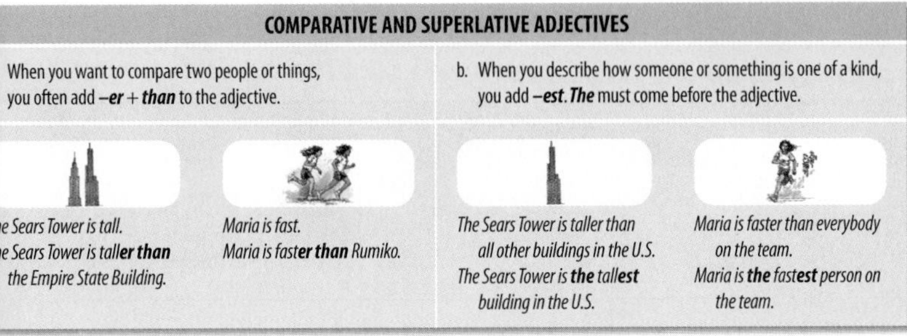

COMPARATIVE AND SUPERLATIVE ADJECTIVES
When you want to compare two people or things, you often add *–er + than* to the adjective.
b. When you describe how someone or something is one of a kind, you add *–est*. *The* must come before the adjective.
he Sears Tower is tall.
he Sears Tower is **taller than** the Empire State Building.
Maria is fast.
Maria is fast**er than** Rumiko.
The Sears Tower is taller than all other buildings in the U.S.
The Sears Tower is **the** tall**est** building in the U.S.
Maria is faster than everybody on the team.
Maria is **the** fast**est** person on the team.

Practice the Rule Work with a partner. Look around for items or
ple you can compare. Then write five sentences using comparative and
erlative adjectives.

XAMPLE: *Marco is the tallest person in class.*

1. __________
2. __________
3. __________
4. __________
5. __________

E GRAMMAR

Standard

- Express comparison

WARM UP

- Ask questions about students in the class that use comparative and superlative adjectives. For example: *Who is the fastest runner in the class? Who is older, Maria or Tran?*

TEACHING THE LESSON

1. Listen Up

- Play the tape or CD twice, or read the sentences. Have students point their thumbs up if the sentence sounds correct, and down if it sounds wrong.

2. Learn the Rule

- Review what adjectives are. (They are words that describe people, places, and things.) Ask students to give examples of adjectives that describe the size of rivers and mountains (long, wide, tall, high).
- Go over the chart. Point to the pictures and read the explanation of comparative adjectives. Have volunteers read the examples aloud. Then have two students stand next to each other and make a true statement: *"A" is taller than "B."*
- Repeat these steps with the explanation of superlative adjectives. Help students to identify the tallest person in the class.
- Repeat the Listen Up activity, reteaching as needed.

3. Practice the Rule

Heads Together Have students complete the activity with a partner. Have volunteers read sentences aloud.

✓ WRAP UP

- Write some other comparative and superlative forms on the board and challenge students to make up true sentences. For example: *big, bigger, biggest* and *new, newer, newest.*

PB PRACTICE BOOK ACTIVITY

See Activity C, Grammar, on Practice Book page 83.

ANSWER KEY

Listen Up: Correct sentences: 2, 5.

F BRIDGE TO WRITING

Standards

- Read and understand informational text
- Use content area vocabulary (geography)

WARM UP

- Brainstorm with the class a list of words used to describe geographical features like rivers, mountains, and lakes (long, wide, high, tall, dangerous, deep). Record on the board, arranging the words in columns under the headings *Water* and *Land*.

TEACHING THE LESSON

1. Before You Read

- Ask students to compare the names of the highest mountains they know of with a partner.

Suggest again that students look at the map and visuals at three different points: before they read to get an overview, while they are reading to help them understand specific details, and after they read to check their understanding (Reading Strategy box).

2. Let's Read

My Turn: Read Aloud/Think Aloud Read the introduction at the top and the paragraph at the bottom aloud. As you read, comment on words and ideas:

Look at the word "highest." This is an example of a superlative adjective.

Mount McKinley has another name—Denali.

- Now play the tape or CD twice, or read the title and paragraph. The second time students listen, ask them to look at the maps and the pictographs instead of reading along.

F BRIDGE TO WRITING

READING STRATEGY
Using Visuals:
Use maps and other visuals to understand what you are reading.

1. Before You Read Write the name of the highest mountain you c think of. Compare your idea with a partner's.

Highest mountain: ____________________

2. Let's Read Read about Mount Everest. Be ready to identify and share with the class one fact you didn't know before the reading.

Mount Everest is the highest mountain in the world. Its peak is 29,028 feet (8,848 meters) above sea level.

The highest mountain in North America is Mount McKinley (also called Denali), in Alaska, at 20,320 feet (6,194 meters). Mount Whitney, in California, is the highest peak in the continental United States. Its summit is 14,491 feet (4,417 meters) above sea level.

Source: *Hottest, Coldest, Highest, Deepest* by Steve Jenkins

peak—the top of a very tall mountain

Our Turn: Interactive Reading Have students read. Focus on glossed words, ask questions, and make comments:

As of 2004, 1,373 mountain climbers have reached the summit of Mount Everest.

Mt. McKinley got its name from the 25th president of the United States. Today, many people call it Denali, which is a Native American word that means "high one."

Your Turn: Independent Reading Have students read the passage on their own. Ask students to pick out one fact they didn't know before doing the reading and share it with the class.

Making Content Connections You have read about two places the world that are *unique* (one of a kind). Work with a partner. mplete the chart below. Use complete sentences.

	The Nile	Mt. Everest
Why is it unique?	It is the longest river in the world.	
Where is it located?		
What is one important fact about it?		

Expanding Your Vocabulary Learn the names of more dforms. Work with a partner. Match each word with a picture.

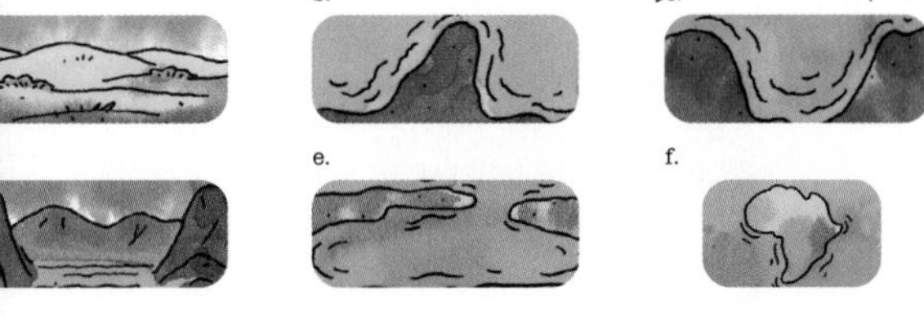

c 1. bay: an area of water with land around most of it (smaller than a gulf)

____ 2. continent: one of the seven great areas of land: Africa, Antarctica, Asia, Australia, Europe, North America, and South America

____ 3. gulf: an area of ocean with land around most of it (larger than a bay)

____ 4. peninsula: land with water on three sides

____ 5. prairie: a large area of flat land with tall grasses and few trees

____ 6. valley: a low place between two mountains

WRAP UP

- See how many proper names students can think of relating to the nine landforms they have studied. For example: *San Francisco Bay; continent of North America.*

PB PRACTICE BOOK ACTIVITY

See Activity D, Test-Taking Practice, on Practice Book pages 84 and 85.

See Activity E, Using New Vocabulary, on Practice Book page 86.

ANSWER KEY

Making Content Connections: Possible answers: **Nile:** It is the longest river in the world. It is in Egypt. It is 4,145 miles long. **Mt. Everest:** It is the tallest mountain in the world. It is in Asia. It is over 29,000 feet tall.

Expanding Your Vocabulary: 1. c; 2. f; 3. e; 4. b; 5. a; 6. d.

3. Making Content Connections

Heads Together Have pairs of students work together as they look back at the information about the Nile and Mount Everest and use this information to complete the chart.

Interactive Writing Copy the chart on the board or on an overhead transparency. Invite volunteers to fill in their responses.

4. Expanding Your Vocabulary

- Point to the pictures and say: *These are pictures of landforms. A landform is part of the earth's surface that has a special shape. A mountain is a landform. It has a pointed shape. A river is a landform. The water in a river makes a groove in the earth's surface.*

Heads Together Ask students to complete the activity in pairs. Have them read and discuss together each definition and then locate the picture that matches the description. Ask them to write the letter of the correct picture in front of each definition. Review the correct answers with the class.

G WRITING CLINIC

Standards
- Identify the structural features of informational text
- Identify topic sentences and supporting details

WARM UP

- Display a world map or a globe and ask students to take turns pointing out locations of the *longest, biggest, tallest, coldest,* and *hottest* places they have learned about in this unit.

TEACHING THE LESSON

1. Think about It

Heads Together Ask students to tell a partner which answers they think are correct and why. Review the correct answers with the class.

2. Focus on Organization

- Have students reread the paragraph about Mt. Everest and work with a partner to determine the main idea (Part 1). Have them share. Point out the starburst and read the information aloud. Say: *Look at the sentence in green. It's the topic sentence. A topic sentence introduces the subject of the paragraph and tells us what the whole paragraph is going to be about. Now look at the sentence in yellow. It gives a specific fact about the topic. This supporting sentence doesn't summarize the whole paragraph the way the topic sentence does.*
- Explain what a main idea is: *It's a statement that gives a general idea of what the paragraph is about. A main idea summarizes the content of the paragraph. Sometimes, the main idea is the same as the topic sentence.*

WRITING

G WRITING CLINIC Short Reports: Our Wor

1. Think about It Read the information about the Nile again.

The Nile, in Africa, is the longest river in the world. It is 4,145 miles (6,671 kilometers) long.

Where would you find information like this? Check (✓) all of the correct answers.

_____	1. in a magazine	_____	4. in an encycloped
_____	2. in a textbook	_____	5. in a book of poe
_____	3. in a story	_____	6. in your student handbook

2. Focus on Organization

The sentence in green is the topic sentence. The sentence in yellow is a fact. It supports the topic sentence.

❶ Read the short paragraph about Mt. Everest again. What is the main idea? Tell a partner what you think.

Mount Everest is the highest mountain in the world. Its peak is 29,028 feet (8,848 meters) above sea level.

❷ Match each topic sentence on the left with the correct fact on the rig

1. Denali is the highest mountain in North America.	a. Over 400 inches of rain fall every year.
2. Tutunendo, Colombia, is the wettest place on earth.	b. One year, more tha 1,200 feet of snow fell there.
3. The deepest place in the ocean is the Mariana Trench.	c. It is 20,320 feet hig
4. The snowiest place on earth is Mount Rainier, in Washington State.	d. It is over 4,000 mi in length.
5. The Amazon is the second longest river in the world.	e. It hasn't rained the in 400 years.
6. The Atacama Desert, in Chile, is the driest spot on earth.	f. It is 36,202 feet de

156 Unit 9

- Have students complete Part 2 by matching each topic sentence with its supporting fact. Review correct answers.
- Have students complete Part 3. Have one or two students write their outlines on the board and invite others to comment on it.

Technology Tip Invite interested students to research more extreme places and things using Web sites such as http://www.guinnessworldrecords.com/ and http://www.infoplease.com/homework/superlativesfaq.html. They can find information about world and U.S. geographical extremes as well as information about the tallest buildings, fastest animals, etc. Invite them to collect some interesting facts and share them with the class.

PB PRACTICE BOOK ACTIVITY

See Activity F, Focus on Organization, on Practice Book page 87.

Pretend you wanted to write a paragraph with these three sentences in it.

Mount Washington is in New Hampshire.

Mount Washington is the windiest place in North America.

Winds sometimes blow over 200 miles per hour there.

mplete the outline with the sentences from above. Write the sentence it would be a good topic sentence on the top line. Write sentences that e facts about the topic on the remaining two lines.

Topic sentence:

Fact:

Fact:

Focus on Style

Two sentences can often be combined (put together) to make an expanded sentence. Sometimes an expanded sentence is easier to read than two shorter sentences that repeat information.

The Nile is the longest river in the world.
The Nile is in Africa.
The Nile, *in Africa*, is the longest river in the world.

Combine each of the following pairs of sentences. Write each of the new combined sentences on a separate sheet of paper.

1. Mount Everest is the tallest mountain in the world. Mount Everest is in Nepal.
2. Tokyo is the largest city in the world. Tokyo is in Japan.
3. Greenland is the largest island in the world. Greenland is in the Atlantic Ocean.
4. Mauna Loa is the largest volcano in the world. Mauna Loa is in Hawaii.
5. The Sears Tower is the tallest building in the U.S. The Sears Tower is in Chicago.
6. The Amazon is the widest river in the world. The Amazon is in South America.

3. Focus on Style

- Write the three sentences on the board. Circle the words "in Africa" in the second and third sentences. Draw an arrow from these words in the second sentence to the same words in the third. Explain: *We can combine the first two sentences by inserting the words "in Africa" into the final sentence. The new sentence sounds better and is easier to understand than the two separate sentences.*
- Point out the commas before and after the words "in Africa" in the third sentence. Say: *When we add information, we sometimes put commas around it.*
- Write another set of sentences that can be combined on the board. For example: *McDonald's now serves veggie burgers. McDonald's is on Main Street.* Repeat the steps above and ask a volunteer to write the combined sentence under the other two. (McDonald's, on Main Street, now serves veggie burgers.)

Heads Together Have students complete the activity on their own and then compare answers with a partner.

WRAP UP

- Write a topic sentence on the board and invite students to suggest supporting facts to go with it. For example: *Our community is a good place to live.* (There are six movie theaters and two shopping malls. There are three big parks, etc.)

PB PRACTICE BOOK ACTIVITY

See Activity G, Focus on Style, on Practice Book page 88.

ANSWER KEY

Think about It: in a magazine, in an encyclopedia, in a textbook

Focus on Organization 1: Mount Everest is the highest mountain in the world.

Focus on Organization 2: 1. c; 2. a; 3. f; 4. b; 5. d; 6. e

Focus on Organization 3: Topic sentence: Mount Washington is the windiest place in North America.

Focus on Style: 2: 1. Mount Everest, in Nepal, is the tallest mountain in the world. 2. Tokyo, in Japan, is the largest city in the world. 3. Greenland, in the Atlantic Ocean, is the largest island in the world. 4. Mauna Loa, in Hawaii, is the largest volcano in the world. 5. The Sears Tower, in Chicago, is the tallest building in the U.S. 6. The Amazon, in South America, is the widest river in the world.

H WRITER'S WORKSHOP Short Reports: Our Wor

Help your class write an atlas, called "Wonders of the World." Make a page for the atlas. Your page should include each of the following items

- ☐ a drawing of the place you choose
- ☐ a short paragraph (two or three sentences) that tells why the place one of a kind
- ☐ a map or a picture graph that helps your reader understand the information even better

1. Getting It Out

❶ Choose a place to write about. Look at the pictures below for ideas choose another place you know about.

The hottest place on earth

Al Aziziyah

The coldest place on earth

Vostok

The world's highest waterfall

Angel Falls

The world's deepest lake

Lake Baikal

H WRITER'S WORKSHOP

Standard

- Use the writing process: prewriting

1. Getting It Out

WARM UP

- Display a world atlas and pass it around so that students can examine it. Ask students what is special about atlases. (They often contain different types of maps that show specific types of information including things such as rainfall and population, as well as geographical borders.)
- Tell students that they are going to write a class atlas. Each student will research information and contribute a page to the atlas.
- Say: *Each page will have three parts: a drawing of the place you decide to write about, a paragraph telling what is special about the place, and a map or picture graph to make the information easier to understand.*

TEACHING THE LESSON

- Help students choose a place to write about. Point out the ideas pictured in the book. Help students generate additional ideas for topics for their atlas pages. Have each student choose a topic.

Access for All More advanced learners may benefit from reading full encyclopedia or Internet articles about some of the places mentioned in this unit. Encourage them to choose a place that interests them.

- Have students use the chart in the book to do research if they chose one of the topics on the previous page. Otherwise, have them use other sources to do their research. Point out the ALA "Great Web Sites for Kids" note on page 159 and encourage students doing original research to use that site.
- Students can make notes on the form on Practice Book page 89.

WRAP UP

- Ask students to share with the class the topics they've decided to write about.

PB PRACTICE BOOK ACTIVITY

See Activity H, Writer's Workshop, on Practice Book page 89.

Learn more about the place you have chosen. Use this chart or do your own research on a different place.

Place	Country/Continent	Important Facts
Al Aziziyah	Libya (Africa)	Town in the Sahara Desert Hottest place on earth Shade temperature of 141° F (61°C) once recorded there Even hotter than the Mojave Desert in California
Vostok	Antarctica	Near the South Pole Coldest place on earth Temperature of 129° below zero (−129° F/−89° C) once recorded there Average temperature at the South Pole is −58° F (−50° C)
Angel Falls	Venezuela (South America)	World's highest waterfall 3,212 feet (979 meters) high Higher than Niagara Falls in the U.S. (180 feet/55 meters high) Discovered in 1935 by explorer James C. Angel
Lake Baikal	Russia (Asia)	World's deepest lake Deepest spot: 5,134 feet (1,565 meters) Over 25 million years old (the world's oldest lake) Contains 20% of the earth's fresh water

CONNECT TO THE WEB. CHECK IT OUT:

'or links to Web sites in different subject areas, go to the American ibrary Association's "Great Web Sites for Kids:" **www.ala.org/parentspage/greatsites**

H WRITER'S WORKSHOP

Standards

- Use the writing process: drafting, revising, and editing
- Use an outline to draft writing
- Give a short oral presentation

2. Getting It Down

WARM UP

- Ask students to look back at the pictures, maps, and pictographs featured earlier in this unit. Ask them to describe possible ways they could use similar visual materials on their own atlas pages.

TEACHING THE LESSON

- Have students draw an illustration showing the place they plan to write about (Part 1).
- Ask students to look at Rosita's paragraph. Read the statements in the speech bubbles aloud. Ask: *What does Rosita's topic sentence do?* (It gives the main idea of her paragraph.) Ask: *How many factual sentences are there?* (There are two factual sentences relating to the topic sentence.) Ask: *What does the third speech bubble do?* (It points out a grammar error.)
- Ask students to complete the outline (Part 2).

Mini-Lesson on Conventions
Point out the box and ask students to give other examples of sentences that could use an exclamation point at the end.

- Have students turn their outlines into paragraphs using Rosita's paragraph as a model (Part 3). Ask them to be sure that their topic sentence contains the main idea and that their factual sentences contain facts that support the topic sentence.
- Ask students to add maps and/or picture graphs to their pages (Part 4).

WRITING

MINI-LESSON
Using Exclamation Points:
When a sentence is especially interesting or really amazing, use an exclamation point.

It's even hotter than the Mojave Desert!

2. Getting It Down

1. Draw a picture of the place you have chosen.
2. Add words to explain and describe the picture. Complete the outline below.

Topic sentence:
Fact:
Fact:

3. Turn your outline into a paragraph. Here is what Rosita wrote. What do you think?

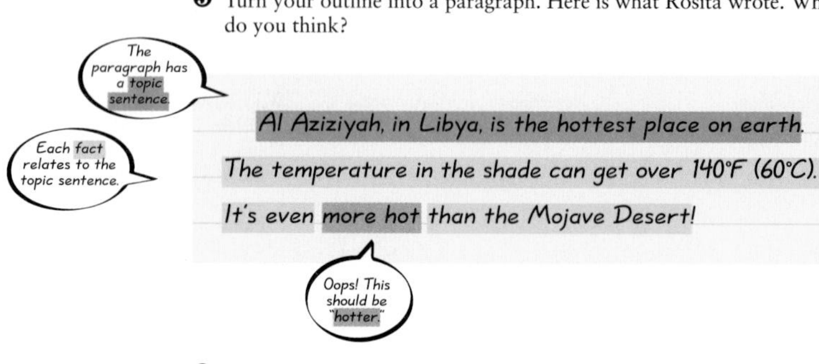

4. Add a map or a picture graph to help your reader understand what you have written.

160 Unit 9

WRAP UP

- Tell students that they will have a chance to revise their work during the next session. Have them locate the ChecBric for this unit in the Student Book or Practice Book. Have them prepare for Getting It Right by reviewing the ChecBric on their own, underlining indicators they're not sure about.

Getting It Right Look carefully at what you have written. Use this ide to revise your paragraph.

Question to Ask	How to Check	How to Revise
1. Does my paragraph have a topic sentence?	Underline your topic sentence.	Add a sentence that tells the main idea.
2. Do the facts relate to the topic sentence?	Put a check mark (✓) in front of each sentence that gives a fact.	Add sentences that give facts. Take out sentences that do not.
3. Do I use expanded sentences to avoid repeating information?	Look at the examples on page 157. Are there any sentences I can combine?	Try putting two sentences together to make one.

Presenting It Share the page you have written with your classmates.

Begin by showing the picture of the place you chose and naming it.

- Read your paragraph aloud. Read slowly and speak clearly.

- Ask for feedback from your classmates.

I learned a lot about the hottest place on earth.

The map is easy to read!

You spoke slowly and clearly. Your presentation was easy to listen to.

3. Getting It Right

WARM UP

- Guide students through the ChecBric for this unit. Explain that they will use the ChecBric to prepare a final draft of their writing.
- Have volunteers explain, in their own words, what each indicator in the ChecBric means.

TEACHING THE LESSON

- Ask students to use the chart and the ChecBric to look for changes they might want to make in their pages. Suggest that they go through the chart and the ChecBric, section by section, and follow each set of instructions.

Group Share Model how students will present their pages to their classmates. Have several volunteers practice giving feedback on a classmate's atlas page.

WRAP UP

- Congratulate students on a job well done. Ask students to compare their first and second drafts and share with the class one change they made.

Remind students to fill out the ChecBric on Practice Book page 117. Ask them to attach it to their writing when they put it in their showcase portfolios.

4. Presenting It

WARM UP

- Do a quick survey of the paragraph topics. Tell students that you are excited to hear what they learned.
- As a class, develop a simple presentation checklist.

TEACHING THE LESSON

- Tell students that you want them to pay attention to four things as they present their atlas pages:
  1. Use a loud and clear voice.
  2. Read slowly.
  3. Show your audience your picture, map, or graph as you present.
  4. Ask for feedback.
- Ask students to read their presentations to the class, then ask for feedback.

✓ WRAP UP

Outcome Sentence Have students complete this sentence stem, then share:

The most interesting thing I learned during this activity was that ________.

I BEYOND THE UNIT

Standards

- Use graphic tools to express information
- Read and respond to poetry

1. On Assignment

WARM UP

- Have students look at the picture graph. Explain that this is a type of graph. What makes it different or interesting? (It uses pictures to present information.)

TEACHING THE LESSON

- Have students review the pictograph in the book and then choose two or more items from their home or school setting to compare (Part 1).
- Ask them to take careful notes as they measure all the objects they plan to compare (Part 2).
- Have them make graphs and mark off inches or feet along one axis on their graphs (Part 3).
- Then have them draw the objects on the graph making sure that the size of the object takes into account the measurements they marked off along the axis (Part 4).
- Under each item on the picture graph, ask students to write the name of the object along with a short explanation of what it is (Part 5).

TEACHING TIP This activity will be easier and students' graphs will be more accurate if you can supply them with graph paper.

I BEYOND THE UNIT

1. On Assignment A picture graph uses pictures and numbers to compare two or more similar things. The picture graph below compares three of the world's tallest buildings.

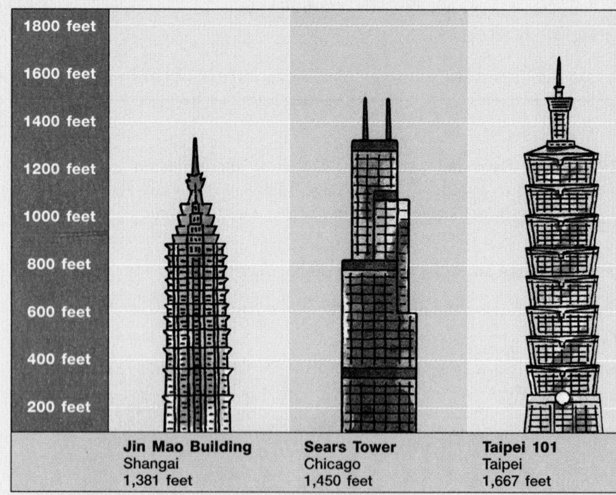

Make a picture graph that compares two or more things at your school or home.

❶ Decide what you will compare.

How high?

How long?

How wide?

How deep?

❷ Measure each object.

❸ Make a graph with inches or feet along one axis.

❹ Draw each object in your graph.

❺ Add a caption under each object explaining what it is.

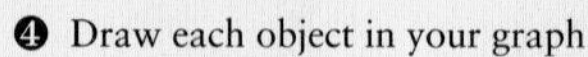

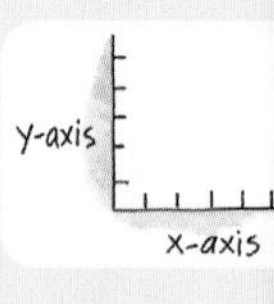

162 Unit 9

WRAP UP

- Ask students to move around the room sharing their picture graphs with several other students.

Link to Literature

SHARED READING Read the diamante poem written by an ESL student. A diamante poem is shaped like a diamond and has seven lines.

LET'S TALK Answer the following questions and do the activity.

1. How many lines does the poem have? How many words are in each line?
2. For each line, write the letter of the type of word that is used in that line.

__a__	Line 1	a. Noun
_____	Line 2	b. Adjective
_____	Line 3	c. Verb + *-ing*
_____	Line 4	
_____	Line 5	
_____	Line 6	
_____	Line 7	

3. How are line 1 and line 7 connected to each other?
4. Why is the title of the poem, "The Earth"?

The Earth

By Ivan

1 Mountain
2 High, rocky
3 Flying, looking, killing
4 Eagle, power, fear, rabbit
5 Living, moving, making noise
6 Deep, beautiful
7 Valley

Source: darkwing.uoregon.edu

Tall, Taller, Tallest 163

2. Link to Literature

WARM UP

- Focus students on the diamond shape of the poem. Point out how the lines get longer in the middle and then get shorter through the end.

TEACHING THE LESSON

Shared Reading Play the tape or CD, or read the poem aloud. Then have students read the poem to themselves.

Let's Talk Use the questions to lead a discussion of the poem. Ask students how many lines there are in the poem. (7) Then ask them to look a how many words or phrases there are in each line. (The pattern is 1 word in line 1, 2 in line 2, 3 in line 3, 4 in line 4, 3 or 4 in line 5, 2 in line 6, and 1 in line 7. Point out how this forms a diamond shape. Note that although line 5 has four words, it has three of the same kind of word: Verb + *ing*.

- If students are unsure of the parts of speech, review them briefly: *A noun is the name of a person, place, or thing; an adjective is a word that describes a person, place, or thing; a verb is a word that describes an action.* Then have students write the letter of the part of speech in front of each line number.
- Ask students how lines 1 and 7 relate to each other. (They represent the top and the bottom of the picture created by the poem.)
- Ask students why the title of the poem is "The Earth." (Possible answer: It's called "The Earth" because it includes lots of images of what life is like on earth.)

✓ WRAP UP

- Make this outline on the board and have students help you complete a diamante poem about a house.

Attic.

____

____

cooking, eating, laughing, sleeping

____

____

Cellar

PB PRACTICE BOOK ACTIVITY

See Activity I, Responding to Literature, on Practice Book page 90.

✓ UNIT WRAP UP

Outcome Sentence Have students complete this sentence stem, then share:

The most surprising thing I learned in this unit is that _______________.

ANSWER KEY

Let's Talk 2: 1. a; 2. b; 3. c; 4. a; 5. c; 6. b; 7.a.

What Do You Think?

Unit Overview

Section	At a Glance	Standards
Before You Begin	Students tackle a hot topic: Should a boy play on a girls' team—and vice versa?	■ Use visual information to derive meaning ■ Express an opinion
A. Connecting to Your Life	Students take a stand on a variety of issues.	■ Listen for details ■ Give reasons to support an opinion
B. Getting Ready to Read	Students defend their positions on various issues and learn useful vocabulary.	■ Use context to figure out the meaning of new words ■ Participate in discussion with classmates
C. Reading to Learn	Students read kids' opinions about whether baseball is still America's favorite sport. PRACTICE BOOK: Students paraphrase other kids' opinions.	■ Read and understand opinion statements ■ Identify main idea and details in text
D. Word Work	Students examine words that have common roots but have different jobs in a sentence. PRACTICE BOOK: Students practice using nouns and adjectives.	■ Identify the members of word families ■ Identify sound/spelling relationships
E. Grammar	Students make comparisons using *as...as, more...than,* and *–er...than.* PRACTICE BOOK: Students complete sentences using the three forms for comparison.	■ Express comparison
F. Bridge to Writing	Students read kids' opinions about whether or not boys and girls should play on the same sports teams. PRACTICE BOOK: Students practice taking Reading Vocabulary and Reading Comprehension tests. PRACTICE BOOK: Students practice using phrases that introduce opinions.	■ Read and understand opinion statements ■ Express opinions

Section	At a Glance	Standards
G. Writing Clinic	Students examine the organization of an opinion column. PRACTICE BOOK: Students make a list of opinions in a reading passage along with a reason for each opinion. PRACTICE BOOK: Students use quotation marks with direct quotes.	■ Identify the structural features of an opinion column ■ Use direct and indirect speech in writing
H1. Writer's Workshop: Getting It Out	Students interview other students for an opinion column, "The Question Kid." PRACTICE BOOK: Students interview other people.	■ Use the writing process: prewriting ■ Conduct an interview ■ Listen for information
H2. Writer's Workshop: Getting It Down	Students turn their notes into an outline, and then turn the outline into a first draft of an opinion column.	■ Use the writing process: drafting ■ Use an outline to draft writing
H3. Writer's Workshop: Getting It Right	Students revise and edit their own work.	■ Use the writing process: revising and editing
H4. Writer's Workshop: Presenting It	Students present their opinion columns to classmates.	■ Organize and give a short oral presentation
I. Beyond the Unit	Students write a letter to the editor and read a humorous poem, "Point of View," by Shel Silverstein. PRACTICE BOOK: Students write a letter, arguing that turkeys should be protected from holiday dinners.	■ Read and respond to poetry ■ Write an opinion letter

BEFORE YOU BEGIN

Standards

- Use visual information to derive meaning
- Express an opinion

- Ask a volunteer to describe what is happening in the pictures on page 165.
- Ask the boys: *Should a girl be allowed to play on a boys' sports team? Is this a good idea?* Have them circle their answers.
- Ask the girls: *Should a boy be allowed to play on a girls' sports team? What do you think?* Ask them to circle their answers.
- Tally the results for boys and girls. Have volunteers offer reasons for their opinions.

Unit 10

What Do You Think?

Read...

- Selections from opinion columns published by *Sports Illustrated for Kids*. Read students' opinions on interesting issues!

Link to Literature

- "Point of View," a poem by Shel Silverstein.

Objectives:

Reading:
- Evaluating students' opinions on various issues
- Strategy: Evaluating ideas as you read
- Literature: Responding to a poem

Writing:
- Writing an opinion column based on interviews
- Using complete sentences
- Using quoted words

Vocabulary:
- Recognizing word families: Related nouns and adjectives
- Learning language that expresses opinion

Listening/Speaking:
- Listening and responding to two sides of an issue
- Interviewing: Asking others about their opinions
- Sharing opinions and giving reasons to support an opinion

Grammar:
- Making comparisons: *as...as, more...than*

Spelling and Phonics:
- Spelling the /ī/ sound as in *my* and *high*

164 Unit 10

Yes or no?

ORE YOU BEGIN

: with your classmates.

1. Look at the two pictures. What do you think is happening?
2. If you are a **boy**: Should a girl play on a boys' sports team? Circle *Yes* or *No*.
   If you are a **girl**: Should a boy play on a girls' team? Circle *Yes* or *No*.
3. Help your teacher tally, or count, the boys' answers and the girls' answers.

A CONNECTING TO YOUR LIFE

Standards

- Listen for details
- Give reasons to support an opinion

WARM UP

- Ask for a show of hands indicating how much TV students watch. Have them raise their hands if they watch more than five hours a week; more than ten hours a week; more than 15 hours a week.

TEACHING THE LESSON

1. Tuning In

- Tell students they are going to listen to a conversation between Juan and Lori. Play the tape or CD, or read the script. Ask students to listen for information that will help them answer this question: *Do Juan and Lori agree with each other or do they disagree?* Go over student responses.
- Now have students listen a second time. Have them tell you whom they agree with, Juan or Lori. Ask them to tell you why.

2. Talking It Over

- Have students complete the chart.
- Have students choose one of the questions and write a sentence explaining why they chose the answer they did. Then call on volunteers to share out.
- Have students look again at the title of the unit and mark their answers in the book. Have them use finger signals to tell you what they think the unit is about.

READING

A CONNECTING TO YOUR LIFE

1. Tuning In Listen to Juan and Lori talk about TV. Who do you agree with, Juan or Lori?

2. Talking It Over Read the questions below. Check (✓) *Yes* or N for each question.

	Yes	No
1. Is watching a lot of TV bad for you?		
2. Are girls smarter than boys?		
3. Does school get out too early?		
4. Do kids have too much homework?		
5. Should kids have to take PE?		

Choose one of the questions above. Write the reason you answered *Ye* *No*. Share your reason with your classmates.

Question: ______________________________

Answer: ______________________________

Reason: ______________________________

____

____

____

Read the title. What do you think the unit is probably about? Check (the correct answer.

_____ 1. It's about interesting facts about the world.

_____ 2. It's about issues, or questions, students have ideas abo

_____ 3. It's about learning how to think better.

166 Unit 10

✓ WRAP UP

Outcome Sentence Write these sentence stems on the board. Have students complete one of the sentences and then share out.

My parents and I agree that ______________________________.

My parents and I disagree about ______________________________.

ANSWER KEY

Tuning In: Answers will vary.

Talking It Over: 2.

GETTING READY TO READ

Learning New Words Read the vocabulary words and r definitions.

action—exciting things that happen	**skill**—the ability to do something very well
different—not like something or someone else	**challenge**—something new or difficult that requires skill
allowed—having permission to do something	**out of style**—not in fashion or popular anymore

mplete the sentences with the vocabulary words above.

1. Susanna came to the U.S. from Germany two weeks ago. It is a ___________ for her to speak English.
2. Maria is the best player on the soccer team. She has a lot of ___________.
3. When students are taking a test, they are not ___________ to talk.
4. Sonia has bright blue hair. She looks ___________ from most other kids.
5. Mr. Johnson wears old-fashioned clothes. His clothing is ___________.
6. Tran likes movies with car chases and fighting. He likes movies with a lot of ___________.

Talking It Over Work in a small group. Talk about reasons for swering "yes" and reasons for answering "no" for each question in the rt below. Then complete the chart.

uestion	Reasons for answering "yes"	Reasons for answering "no"
. Is watching a lot of TV bad for you?	*You don't have time to do your homework.*	*You can learn a lot from TV.*
. Are girls smarter than boys?		
. Does school get out too early?		
. Do kids have too much homework?		
. Should kids have to take PE?		

B GETTING READY TO READ

Standards

- Use context to figure out the meaning of new words
- Participate in discussion with classmates

WARM UP

- Ask students how they go about learning new words.

TEACHING THE LESSON

1. Learning New Words

- Write the new words and phrases on the board and point to each as you define and explain it. Say:

  When I watch TV, I like shows with car chases. I like shows with a lot of action.

  Julio wears a different pair of shoes every day of the week. He never wears the same shoes twice.

  No one is allowed to smoke in the school building. It's against the rules.

  Maria has all the skills a soccer player needs: she is a fast runner, she can think quickly, and she knows how to kick a ball.

  For me, math is a real challenge. I study a lot, but I still can't understand it.

  Last year long skirts were popular, but this year they're out of style. This year everyone is wearing short skirts.

Heads Together Ask students to work in groups of three to complete the sentences. Then have different groups share their answers with the class.

2. Talking It Over

- Copy the chart on the board and point out the columns where students will list reasons for their "yes" and "no" answers. Then have students look back at the answers they checked in the Talking It Over exercise in Lesson A.

Team Talk Have students work in small groups as they talk over their "yes" and "no" responses and give reasons for their answers. Ask students to complete the chart with reasons for their own answers and share out.

✓ WRAP UP

- Have students write true sentences using three of the new words. Have them share their sentences with the class.

ANSWER KEY

Learning New Words: 1. challenge; 2. skill; 3. allowed; 4. different; 5. out of style; 6. action.

C READING TO LEARN

Standards

- Read and understand opinion statements.
- Identify main idea and details in text.

WARM UP

- Ask students about their favorite sports. Who likes baseball best? Why?

TEACHING THE LESSON

1. Before You Read

Heads Together Ask partners to tell each other what they think is the most popular sport in the U.S.

- **Build Background** Americans began playing baseball in the early 1800s. By 1900, professional baseball players had formed two leagues, the American League and the National League which still exist today. Every October millions of Americans watch the "World Series," a competition between the top teams from each of these leagues.

2. Let's Read

- Ask students to think about whether they agree or disagree as they read each opinion (Reading Strategy box).

My Turn: Read Aloud/Think Aloud Read the pro and con arguments aloud. Comment on and paraphrase information as you read.

- Now play the tape or CD, or read the passage twice. As students listen, ask them to choose the one statement that is the closest to their opinion of baseball.

Our Turn: Interactive Reading Call on a different student to read each opinion. After each student reads, focus on glossed words, ask questions, and make comments:

READING

READING STRATEGY
Evaluating Ideas: When you evaluate ideas, you decide whether you agree with them or not.

C READING TO LEARN

Opinion Colum

1. Before You Read What do you think is most Americans' favorit sport? Tell a partner.

2. Let's Read Read this opinion column. Kids shared their opinions or ideas, on baseball. As you read, decide what *your own* opinion is. Be ready to share your ideas.

The Cincinnati Red Stockings were the first professional baseball team. The team began playing in 1869.

Is Baseball Still America's Favorite Sport?

YES!	NO!
"Baseball is so good, you can't even begin to describe it. There's nothing like the crack of the bat or the smell of hot dogs." —**Nick,** *sent by e-mail*	"Americans are more interested in seei someone dunk than hit a home run. Th is especially true for kids." —**Kelsey J.,** *Sioux City, Io*
"In every city, kids are playing baseball. It's all over the newspapers, TV, magazines, and books." —**Brett R.,** *Bakersfield, California*	"People want to watch fast-paced sports, like football and basketball. Baseball is out of style." —**Jeff V.,** *Bartlesville, Oklahor*
"Baseball is like rock 'n' roll: It will never die." —**Chance C.,** *Grapevine, Texas*	"In baseball, 95 percent of the time the is no action. Only a few people want to watch that." —**Talia S.,** *Merion, Pennsylvar*
"It doesn't matter how old the game is, people still like baseball a lot." —**Yegor D.,** *Cleveland, Ohio*	

Source: *Sports Illustrated for Kid*

'n' is short for "and."

crack—a loud noise that sounds like something breaking
bat—a long wooden stick used for hitting a baseball
all over—everywhere you look
still—continuing until now or until a particular time
dunk—to push a basketball through the hoop at close range
home run—a long hit in baseball in which the hitter is able to run around all the bases and score a point
fast-paced—having lots of action

168 Unit 10

What does "the crack of the bat" sound like? Make the sound.

What sports do you think are "out of style?"

Your Turn: Independent Reading Have students read the passage on their own. Have them complete this sentence stem:

I think/don't think baseball is America's favorite sport because ______________________.

Access for All More advanced readers may enjoy reading articles about baseball in *Sports Illustrated for Kids,* and then reporting back to the class on anything interesting they learn.

CULTURE NOTE

Baseball is popular all over the world. In Japan, it is second only to sumo wrestling, the official national sport. Latin Americans love baseball as well, and they have produced such famous American baseball stars as Juan Marichal and Roberto Clemente.

Unlocking Meaning

Finding the Main Idea In this selection, what is each writer talking about? Check (✓) the correct answer.

_____ 1. reasons that baseball is so popular

_____ 2. his or her own opinion about baseball

_____ 3. reasons that most people like fast-paced sports like football

Finding Details Listen as your teacher reads each statement below. Point your thumb up if it supports the "YES!" opinion in the reading on the previous page. Point your thumb down if it supports the "NO!" opinion.

1. Read the sports page, and all you will find are stories about baseball.
2. Baseball will always be Number 1 for most people.
3. Most Americans, especially kids, like basketball more than baseball.
4. Baseball is a boring game because it is so slow.
5. Even though it is an old game, baseball is still popular.
6. Baseball is a game that mostly old people like to watch.

Think about It Talk with a partner. In the reading, which kid gives the best reason for his or her opinion? Why?

Before You Move On Think of one more reason for answering *Yes* or *No* to the question about baseball.

3. Unlocking Meaning

✓ FINDING THE MAIN IDEA

- Ask students to check the correct answer and compare answers with a partner. Have students use finger signals to indicate what the writers in the selection are explaining.

✓ FINDING DETAILS

- As you read the statements aloud, ask students to use thumbs up and thumbs down signals to show whether statements support the "Yes" opinion in the reading or the "No" opinion.

THINK ABOUT IT

Heads Together Have pairs of students take turns explaining to each other which person in the reading they think gives the strongest reasons for his or her opinion.

BEFORE YOU MOVE ON

- Invite volunteers to share one additional reason for saying baseball is or isn't still America's favorite sport.

WRAP UP

- Have students write copy for a "billboard" promoting a favorite sport.

PB PRACTICE BOOK ACTIVITY

See Activity A, Revisit and Retell, on Practice Book page 91.

ANSWER KEY

Finding the Main Idea: 2.

Finding Details: Yes: 1, 2, 5; **No:** 3, 4, 6.

D WORD WORK

Standards

- Identify the members of word families.
- Identify sound/spelling relationships

WARM UP

- Write these sentence frames on the board and ask students to complete them. *I put a lot of salt on my fries. The fries tasted _________.* (salty) *Three inches of _________ fell yesterday. It was a rainy day.* (rain)

TEACHING THE LESSON

1. Word Detective

- Have pairs complete the activity and share out.

2. Word Study

- Read and discuss the explanation and directions. Ask students to write two sentences using a pair from the matching activity. Invite volunteers to share out.

3. Word Play

Heads Together Ask pairs of students to complete the activity and share out. Have students choose three pairs and write a sentence for each word.

Spelling and Phonics

- Have students listen to the words and tell you what they notice about the vowel sounds. (They are all pronounced like the word *eye*.) Say the words again and have students repeat.
- Have students complete the activity and share answers. Encourage them to use their dictionaries to check their work.

D WORD WORK

1. Word Detective Words that look alike, or almost alike, often belong to the same word family. Match the noun on the left with its correct adjective form on the right.

1. difference	a. skillful
2. interest	b. long
3. skill	c. different
4. length	d. beautiful
5. beauty	e. friendly
6. friend	f. high
7. height	g. interesting

2. Word Study Words in the same word family look alike, but they have different meanings and different jobs in a sentence. Work with a partner. Choose one noun/adjective pair from above and write a senten for each word in the pair.

EXAMPLE: *interest/interesting*
Juan has many interests.
Juan is an interesting person.

3. Word Play Work with a partner. Write the missing nouns and adjectives. You can use your dictionary.

SPELLING AND PHONICS: To do this activity, go to page 186.

	Noun	Adjective
1.	_________	loveable
2.	music	_________
3.	salt	_________
4.	_________	colorful
5.	width	_________
6.	_________	dangerous
7.	_________	legendary

Now choose three noun/adjective pairs and write a sentence for each wo

1. noun: ____________________
   adjective: ____________________
2. noun: ____________________
   adjective: ____________________
3. noun: ____________________
   adjective: ____________________

WRAP UP

- Ask students to look back at the Word Play words and spell out some of the endings that are used to change a noun into an adjective (*-able, -al, -y, -ful, -ous, -ary*).

PB PRACTICE BOOK ACTIVITY

See Activity B, Word Work, on Practice Book page 92.

ANSWER KEY

Word Detective: 1. c; 2. g; 3. a; 4. b; 5. d; 6. e; 7. f.

Word Play: 1. love; 2. musical; 3. salty; 4. color; 5. wide; 6. danger; 7. legend.

Spelling and Phonics: a. style; b. nine; c. tie; d. pie; e. July; f. might; g. white; h. nice; i. night.

E GRAMMAR — Comparisons: *As...As, More...Than*

. Listen Up Listen to each sentence. Point your thumb up if it ounds correct. Point your thumb down if it sounds wrong.

1. Juan is as intelligent as Carlos.
2. Carlos is more better at sports than Juan.
3. The Nile is longer than the Amazon.
4. A lion is ferociouser than a tiger.

. Learn the Rule Certain words in a sentence show that two things re being compared. Read the following rules. Then do Activity 1 again.

COMPARISONS: *AS...AS, MORE...THAN*	
a. When you compare two things that are equal, or the same, use *as...as*.	
Girls' sports are important. Boys' sports are important.	*Girls' sports are **as** important **as** boys' sports.*
b. When you compare two things that are different, use *than*. Add *–er* to most adjectives to make them comparative. Irregular comparative adjectives have their own special form.	
*Mt. Whitney is tall. Mt. Everest is tall**er**.* *Sausage pizza is good. Pepperoni pizza is **better**.*	*Mt. Everest is tall**er than** Mt. Whitney.* *Pepperoni pizza is **better than** sausage pizza.*
c. For adjectives that have three or more syllables, use *more...than* to compare two things that are different.	
Senator Smith is important. President Chan is more important.	*President Chan is **more** important **than** Senator Smith.*

. Practice the Rule Complete the sentences below using the djectives in parentheses.

1. Juan and Carlos are both 6 feet tall. Juan is (tall) ___as tall as___ Carlos.
2. I like chocolate ice cream and vanilla ice cream. Chocolate ice cream is (good) ______________ vanilla.
3. Lori is 13. Maria is 15. Lori is (young) ______________ Maria.
4. English is easy for me, but math is difficult. Math is (difficult) ______________ English.
5. My mother and father are 37 years old. My mother is (old) ______________ my father.

GRAMMAR

Standard

- Express comparison

WARM UP

- Ask questions that use the comparatives *as...as* and *more...than*. For example: *Are you as tall as I am? Is the chalkboard bigger than the bulletin board?*

TEACHING THE LESSON

1. Listen Up

- Play the tape or CD, or read the sentences aloud twice. Have students point their thumbs up if the sentence sounds correct, and point them down if it sounds wrong.

2. Learn the Rule

- Compare things that are the same using *as...as*. For example: *Hilda is 15 and Rosa is 15. Hilda is as old as Rosa.* Ask students to repeat. Then read rule a and the example aloud and ask a volunteer to explain the rule in his or her own words.
- Ask several volunteers to write their names and ages on the board. Follow the same procedure for rule b that you used for rule a.
- Read the *good/better* examples aloud. Explain that some comparative adjectives have irregular forms.
- Brainstorm some adjectives with three or more syllables and list them on the board (expensive, difficult, exciting). Read rule c and the examples aloud.
- Repeat the Listen Up activity, reteaching as needed.

3. Practice the Rule

- Have students complete the activity. Review the correct answers.

WRAP UP

- Elicit the names of some extreme sports and write them on the board. For example, *mountain climbing, car racing*. Then challenge students to compare the sports using words such as *fun, safe, dangerous*.

PB PRACTICE BOOK ACTIVITY

See Activity C, Grammar, on Practice Book page 93.

ANSWER KEY

Listen Up: Correct sentences: 1, 3.

Practice the Rule: 1. as tall as; 2. as good as; 3. younger than; 4. more difficult than; 5. as old as.

F BRIDGE TO WRITING

Standards
- Read and understand opinion statements
- Express opinions

WARM UP

- Brainstorm with students a list of sports in which boys and girls are on the same team, although they may compete in different races or matches (cross-country, track, fencing, swimming, diving). Ask students how they would feel about being on a team with members of the opposite sex.

TEACHING THE LESSON

1. Before You Read

Heads Together Ask students to discuss with a partner what things, if any, boys should do only with other boys and girls with other girls. Invite volunteers to share their opinions.

2. Let's Read

Ask students to think about whether they agree or disagree as they read each opinion (Reading Strategy box).

My Turn: Read Aloud/Think Aloud Read the question and the opinions in the article aloud. As you read, comment on words and ideas. Point out the speech bubble and say: *Avery uses the word "would" because he's talking about a situation that isn't real.*

- Now play the tape or CD, or read the passage twice. As students listen, ask them to decide what the best reason is for allowing boys on girls' sports teams.

Our Turn: Interactive Reading Take turns having individual students read the quotes. As they read, focus on the glossed words, ask questions, and make comments:

F BRIDGE TO WRITING — Opinion Columns

READING STRATEGY
Evaluating Ideas: When you evaluate ideas, you decide whether you agree with them or not.

1. Before You Read Are there things that boys should do only with boys and girls should do only with girls? Talk with a partner.

2. Let's Read As you read, write each person's name on a piece of paper. Then draw a face next to the name showing how you feel about their opinion.

☺ = Good point! 😐 = Not sure ☹ = Silly idea

Avery uses "would" instead of "will" because boys don't really play on girls' teams. Use "would" for imaginary situations.

Should boys be allowed to play on girls' sports teams?

YES!	NO!
"Girls' sports take as much skill as boys' sports. So what difference does it make if a boy plays on a girls' team?" —**Annie B.**, *Cleveland Heights, Ohio*	"The girls would not feel comfortable playing with one boy, and the one boy would not feel comfortable playing with the girls." —**Thomas P.**, *Eugene, Orego*
"If boys played with girls' teams, it would make the games more interesting." —**Avery M.**, *Iowa City, Iowa*	"Boys play too hard and rough. Also, they wouldn't be allowed in the girls' locker room." —**Karissa E.**, *Billings, Montan*
"Boys and girls can help each other learn different sports." —**Ryan G.**, *Reno, Nevada*	"A boy would feel embarrassed in front of his friends if he was on a team with girls." —**Vince M.**, *Kenosha, Wisconsi*
"A boy can be on a girls' sports team—if he can handle the challenge." —**Annie S.**, *Oakton, Virginia*	"Girls don't need boys' help. Anything boys can do, girls can do better." —**Whitney-Ann S.**, *New Bedfor Massachusett*

Source: *Sports Illustrated for Kids*

comfortable—at ease and relaxed
embarrassed—feeling shy or ashamed in front of other people

Do you agree with Annie B. that girls' sports are just as hard as boys' sports? Why or why not?

Karissa thinks that boys play too rough. What other reason does she give for her "No" opinion?

Vince thinks boys would feel weird being on a girls' team. Do you think the boys in your class would feel this way?

- **Build Fluency** Have pairs of students take turns reading the opinions to each other. Encourage them to read fluently and with expression.

Your Turn: Independent Reading Have students read the article to themselves. Have them write down all the names from the article and draw a face next to each one showing how they feel about the person's opinion. Ask them to notice which opinions most closely match their own.

. **Making Content Connections** You have read kids' opinions bout two questions. Work with a partner. Think about the opinions you ave read and complete the chart below.

	Baseball still Number 1?	Boys on girls' teams?
What is the best "Yes" reason?		
What is the best "No" reason?		

. **Expanding Your Vocabulary** Give your opinion on one of the ssues you have read about. Role play with a partner. You can start with ne of the phrases below.

In my opinion, . . .
I believe that . . .
I feel that . . .
I think that . . .
It's my opinion that . . .
Kim

3. Making Content Connections

Heads Together Ask students to work in pairs. First have them look back at the opinion columns and the reasons people gave for their opinions. Ask the pairs to discuss which reasons they think are the strongest. Then have them complete the chart. Invite several volunteers to share their ideas with the class.

4. Expanding Your Vocabulary

Heads Together Have pairs of students practice giving their opinions on issues. Ask them to choose an issue from the previous readings and then choose opposite sides of the issue to defend. Then ask them to have a discussion in which each person practices using the target phrases to express their opinions.

Access for All Consider pairing a fluent reader with a less-fluent reader and having them go through the reading a line at a time. The less fluent reader can point out words or phrases that aren't clear, and the more fluent reader can paraphrase and/or explain them in simple English.

WRAP UP

- Ask students what they think will happen concerning mixed sex teams, both in school and in professional sports, in the next ten years.

PB PRACTICE BOOK ACTIVITY

See Activity D, Test-Taking Practice, on Practice Book pages 94 and 95.

See Activity E, Using New Vocabulary, on Practice Book page 96.

ANSWER KEY

Making Content Connections: Answers will vary.

G WRITING CLINIC

Standards

- Identify the structural features of an opinion column
- Use direct and indirect speech in writing

WARM UP

- Make the following pro and con statements. Then ask students to figure out what the question is. Pro: *Students would have a chance to learn more.* Con: *Students need a long summer vacation to rest up.* (Should summer vacation from school be shortened? Should schools be in session year-round?)

TEACHING THE LESSON

1. Think about It

- Say: *Which section of a newspaper would contain an opinion column?* Read the four choices aloud. Then ask students to check their choice and share with a partner. Ask a volunteer to give the correct answer and explain.

2. Focus on Organization

- Read each annotation aloud and ask a student to read the corresponding line from the article (Part 1). Discuss and clarify each annotation.
- Ask students to review the "No" opinions (Part 2). Then have them list three reasons that kids gave for their opinions. They should write the opinions in their own words. Check the answers by having volunteers read some of the reasons to the class.

PB PRACTICE BOOK ACTIVITY

See Activity F, Focus on Organization, on Practice Book page 97.

G WRITING CLINIC — Opinion Columns

1. Think about It In which part of a newspaper or magazine would you usually find an opinion column?

- ☐ sports section
- ☐ world and national news
- ☐ editorial page/letters from reader
- ☐ want ads

2. Focus on Organization

❶ Read again what kids said about boys playing on girls' teams.

The column begins with a question. → **Should boys be allowed to play on girls' sports teams?**

Yes opinions come first. → **YES!**

"Girls' sports take as much skill as boys' sports. So what difference does it make if a boy plays on a girls' team?"
—**Annie B.**, *Cleveland Heights, Ohio*

The person often gives a reason for his or her opinion. → "If boys played with girls' teams, it would make the games more interesting."
—**Avery M.**, *Iowa City, Iowa*

Quotation marks go around a person's actual words. → "Boys and girls can help each other learn different sports."
—**Ryan G.**, *Reno, Nevada*

Sometimes the person's opinion makes you laugh. → "A boy can be on a girls' sports team—if he can handle the challenge."
—**Annie S.**, *Oakton, Virginia*

Reread the *No* opinions. List three reasons kids give for their
inions. Use your own words.

IO!

The girls would not feel comfortable playing with one boy, and the one boy would ot feel comfortable playing with the girls."
—Thomas P., *Eugene, Oregon*

Boys play too hard and rough. Also, they wouldn't be allowed in the girls' ocker room."
—Karissa E., *Billings, Montana*

A boy would feel embarrassed in front of his friends if he was on a team ith girls."
—Vince M., *Kenosha, Wisconsin*

Girls don't need boys' help. Anything boys can do, girls can do better."
—Whitney-Ann S., *New Bedford, Massachusetts*

Focus on Style

People's actual words are interesting to read. Quotation marks tell you that you are reading exactly what a person said.

"If a boy plays on a girls' team, it's like cheating on a test. Boys are stronger and faster. Only girls' scores should count."
–Steven H., Florida

Practice using quotation marks. Rewrite each person's actual words.

Sara Dubois

2.

Mr. Torres, parent

3.

Ms. Fields, teacher

Kids have too much homework.

Lori Chang

5.

Kids shouldn't have to take PE.

Stefan Kopec

6.

The school day is too short.

Ms. Chan, school principal

PB PRACTICE BOOK ACTIVITY

See Activity G, Focus on Style, on Practice Book page 98.

ANSWER KEY

Think about It: editorial page/letters from readers.

Focus on Organization 2: Answers will vary.

Focus on Style 2: "Girls are smarter than boys." —Sara Dubois; "Kids don't have enough homework." —Mr. Torres, parent; "Watching a lot of TV is bad for you!" —Ms. Fields, teacher; "Kids have too much homework." —Lori Chang; "Kids shouldn't have to take PE." —Stefan Kopec; "The school day is too short." —Ms. Chan, school principal.

3. Focus on Style

- Read the explanation aloud and have students locate the quotation marks at the beginning and end of the sentence (Part 1). Point out that the quotation marks surround the exact words that Steven H. wrote or said. Then write this sentence on the board: *Steven says that having boys play on a girls' team isn't fair because boys are stronger and faster.* Ask: *Should we use quotation marks with this sentence?* (No.) *Why not?* (Those aren't Steven H.'s exact words.)
- Have students work independently as they rewrite the sentences using quotation marks (Part 2). When they finish, have pairs of students check each other's work.

✓ WRAP UP

- Have students think of one more reason that boys should or should not be allowed to play on girls' teams. Ask them to quote their own words, in writing, using correct punctuation. Have volunteers write their sentences on the board.

H WRITER'S WORKSHOP

Standards
- Use the writing process: prewriting
- Conduct an interview
- Listen for information

1. Getting It Out

WARM UP

- Show students an opinion column from the newspaper. Tell them that they are going to write a "Question Kid" column that might appear in a school newspaper.

TEACHING THE LESSON

- After they look at the examples in the book, have students decide on an interesting question to ask their classmates (Part 1). Remind them that their questions must have a "yes" or "no" answer.

H WRITER'S WORKSHOP Opinion Column

Imagine that you are a reporter for your school newspaper. Your job is to interview other students for "The Question Kid," a weekly opinion column.

1. Getting It Out

1. Choose an interesting question to ask students. Use one of the following questions, or think of your own. Your question should:
   - be interesting.
   - have a "yes" or "no" answer.

1.

Does school get out too early?

2.

Do students have too much homework?

3.

Is watching a lot of TV bad for you?

4.

Are girls smarter than boys?

5.

Should students have to take PE?

6.

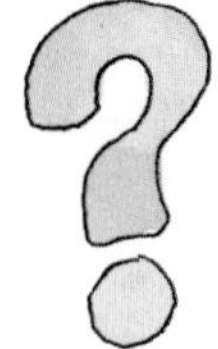

Make your own question!

Make a note-taking sheet like the one below.

Question: Should students have to take PE?

YES:

NO:

Interview six to eight classmates or other friends and family members. Write down each person's *exact words*!

Question: Should students have to take PE?

YES:
Yes. Students should exercise every day.

NO:

Put the person's name and grade, or position if it is a teacher or the principal, in parentheses next to his or her words.

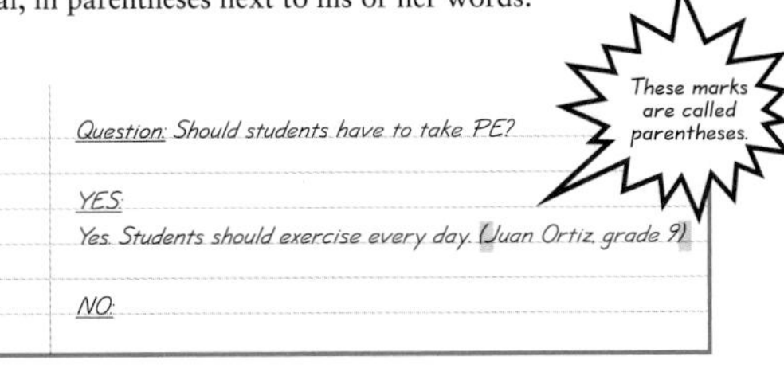

Question: Should students have to take PE?

YES:
Yes. Students should exercise every day. (Juan Ortiz, grade 9)

NO:

Listen to the tape or CD. Write down each person's answers. Write their *exact* words.

- Ask students to prepare a note-taking sheet like the sample in the book (Part 2).

Play the tape or CD, or read the script twice. As students listen, ask them to write down the exact words they hear on their note-taking sheets (Part 5). Invite students to write the different statements on the chalkboard. Check the work on the board and then have students check their own papers.

- Have students prepare another note-taking sheet or use the form on Practice Book page 99 (Part 3). Then have them interview several friends or family members and write down the exact words people say.
- Ask students to add names and grades of the people they interview in parentheses (Part 4). If they interview a teacher or principal, they should put the person's position in parentheses.

WRAP UP

- Ask students to share how they felt while they were interviewing people. Did they feel relaxed? Did anyone feel nervous or uncomfortable asking questions? Did they think the people gave good answers?

PB PRACTICE BOOK ACTIVITY

See Activity H, Writer's Workshop, on Practice Book page 99.

H WRITER'S WORKSHOP

Standards
- Use the writing process: drafting, revising, and editing
- Use an outline to draft writing
- Organize and give a short oral presentation

2. Getting It Down

WARM UP

- Tell students they are now going to turn their interview notes into an outline, and then use the outline to write an opinion column.

TEACHING THE LESSON

- Have students make their outlines based on their interview notes (Part 1).
- Ask students to look at Lori's interview at the bottom of the page. Ask:

  What is her question? (Should kids have to take PE?)

  Where does it appear on the outline? (At the very top.)

  How did she divide up the opinions she got? (She put the "Yes" opinions first and then the "No" opinions.)

Mini-Lesson on Conventions
Have students read the information on their own. Then ask: *What is special about the way Lori writes the people's opinions?* (She puts quotation marks around them.) Point out the Mini-Lesson box with the reminder that the period goes inside the quotation marks, not outside. Ask: *Did Lori make any errors? (She left out some periods.)*

What does she put in front of the name of each person she interviewed? (She puts a long dash before each name.)

WRITING

2. Getting It Down

❶ Make an outline like the one below.

Question: *Should students have to take PE?*	
YES:	NO:
Name: *Juan Ortiz, grade 9* Opinion: *Students should exercise every day.*	Name: ______ Opinion: ______
Name: ______ Opinion: ______	Name: ______ Opinion: ______
Name: ______ Opinion: ______	Name: ______ Opinion: ______

MINI-LESSON
Using Periods with Quotation Marks:

Put periods inside quotation marks:

"PE teaches you to play by the rules."

❷ Draft your opinion column. Put quotation marks around each person's words. Here is part of what Lori wrote. What do you think

Lori repeats the question.

The Question Kid: Should kids have to take PE?

YES!	*NO!*
"Students should exercise every day" *–Juan Ortiz, Grade 9* *"PE teaches you to play by the rules."* *–Lourdes Aguiao, Grade 9* *"PE helps build strong muscles"* *–Arnulf Schwarz, Grade 8*	*"Taking showers with others is embarrassing"* *–Paris Valdez, Grade*

She puts quotation marks around each student's words. She names each student and tells the grade.

178 **Unit 10**

What does she put after each person's name? (She puts a comma and then the grade the person is in.)

- Have students draft their opinion columns (Part 2).

WRAP UP

- Tell students that they will have a chance to revise their work during the next session. Have them locate the ChecBric for this unit in the Student Book or Practice Book. Have them prepare for Getting It Right by reviewing the ChecBric on their own, underlining indicators they're not sure about.

TEACHING TIP Some students may benefit from tape recording their interviews. This allows those who have trouble writing fast to replay the words as necessary. It also allows them to check that their facts are correct.

3. Getting It Right Look carefully at your opinion column. Use this guide to revise your work.

Question to Ask	How to Check	How to Revise
Do I restate the question at the top of the column?	Put a star (★) next to the question.	Make sure that the word order is right and that you use a question mark.
Did I report at least three "yes" opinions and three "no" opinions?	Put a number next to each opinion.	Interview more people.
Did I report each person's exact words?	Show each person the words you wrote down.	Change the words to get them right.
Did I put quotation marks around each person's words?	Check to see that quotation marks begin and end each quotation and that the period is inside.	Add quotation marks. Change the location of the period.

resenting It Share your opinion column with your classmates.

orm a group with other students who asked the same question. ecide who will read first, then second, then third, and so forth.

ead all of the *Yes* opinions to the class. Be sure that everybody has a hance to give a report.

hen read the *No* opinions.

sk if anyone wants to add another idea or opinion.

3. Getting It Right

WARM UP

- Guide students through the ChecBric for this unit. Explain that they will use the ChecBric to prepare a final draft of their writing.
- Have volunteers explain, in their own words, what each indicator in the ChecBric means.

TEACHING THE LESSON

- Ask students to use the chart and the ChecBric to revise their work.

Group Share Model how students will present their opinion columns to their classmates. Have several volunteers practice giving feedback on a classmate's column.

WRAP UP

- Ask students to look back at their first and second drafts. Invite volunteers to share specific changes and corrections they made.

Remind students to fill out the ChecBric on Practice Book page 119. Ask them to attach it to their writing when they put it in their portfolios.

4. Presenting It

WARM UP

- Do a quick survey of the questions students asked.
- As a class, develop a simple presentation checklist.

TEACHING THE LESSON

- Tell students that you want them to pay attention to three things as they present their work:

  1. Use a loud and clear voice.
  2. Read slowly.
  3. Ask for feedback.

- Have students who chose the same topic present their findings as a group. Have group members take turns reading all of their "Yes" opinions, then all of the "No" opinions. Have students invite classmates to add their own ideas or opinions.

✓ WRAP UP

Outcome Sentences Write these sentence stems on the board. Have students complete them and share what they have written:

One opinion I agree with is ________________.

One opinion I disagree with is ________________.

I BEYOND THE UNIT

Standards

- Read and respond to poetry
- Write an opinion letter

WARM UP

- Tell students that many magazines have a "letters to the editor" column. Explain that anyone who wants to can write a letter expressing an opinion about something they read in the magazine. Magazines usually print both pro and con letters about a given situation.

TEACHING TIP You might wish to give students photocopies of some letters to the editor from a local newspaper or a magazine and ask students to summarize the opposing opinions in their own words.

TEACHING THE LESSON

1. On Assignment

- Read the first letter to the editor aloud (Part 1). Then say:

  Is this letter for or against year-round school? Why does Kasey feel this way?

  During what part of the day do you feel most "on the ball?"

- Ask a volunteer to read the second letter aloud. Then say:

  Stress and pressure make us nervous and can even make us sick. What kinds of things create stress and pressure?

  What opinion is expressed in the second letter? Do you agree?

  What do you do during summer vacation?

Heads Together Have students work in pairs as they extract lists of "Yes" and "No" reasons from the letters to the editor (Part 2). Ask them to restate the reasons in their own words.

- Have students write a letter to the editor of their own school newspaper and have volunteers read their letters to the class (Part 3).

WRAP UP

- Ask several volunteers to say whether they agree with Kasey or Michelle about the need for year-round school and give one new reason for their answer.

I BEYOND THE UNIT

1. On Assignment Read the following letters that students wrot
Junior Scholastic Magazine.

❶ *Junior Scholastic* asked its readers for their opinions about year-r
school. Read letters from two students:

Dear Editor:
I think the new school year would be a good change. We would still get our vacations, but we would get it at different times of the year. It would also keep us fresh and on the ball because during summer vacation we just stop thinking of school.

Kasey Jasper

Dear Editor:
Summer is a time fo kids to relax and clear minds of the stress and pressure of the school world. It also gives us t to maybe take a vacatio and have more outdoor experiences. We can als spend more time with o families.

Michelle Walter

Source: Letters written by students at Broad Meadows Middle School in Quincy, Massa

year-round school—schools that are open all year. Students have more short vacations rather than a long summer vacation.

on the ball—able to think quickly

stress—worries that keep you from relaxing

pressure—a feeling that you have too much work a other things to do

outdoor experiences—activities like camping and fi

❷ Work with a partner. Make a list of the reasons kids give for their opinions about year-round schools. Use your own words.

❸ Now think of an issue you have an opinion about. Write a short l to the editor of your school newspaper. Use the form below to he with your letter.

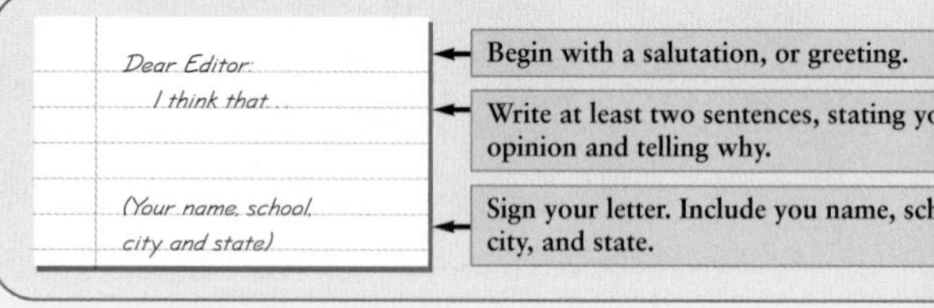

Dear Editor:
I think that...
(Your name, school, city and state)
Begin with a salutation, or greeting.
Write at least two sentences, stating yo opinion and telling why.
Sign your letter. Include you name, sch city, and state.

Unit 10

ink to Literature

ARED READING Read this poem about point of ew. It's by Shel Silverstein.

'S TALK

1. What is the turkey's "point of view" about Thanksgiving dinner?
2. Why is it a good idea to look at things from another point of view?
3. Why is the poem clever and funny?

ST FOR FUN Think of a situation from your aily life. Imagine it from the point of ew of an object or a thing. Write a poem bout it.

OUT THE AUTHOR

Shel Silverstein was born in Chicago and died in 1999. He wrote nearly twenty-five books, published in 30 different languages. *Where the Sidewalk Ends*, *A Light in the Attic*, and *Falling Up* are three of his most famous collections of poetry and drawings.

POINT OF VIEW

Thanksgiving dinner's sad and thankless
Christmas dinner's dark and blue
When you stop and try to see it
From the turkey's point of view.

Sunday dinner isn't sunny
Easter feasts are just bad luck
When you see it from the viewpoint
Of a chicken or a duck.

Oh how I once loved tuna salad
Pork and lobsters, lamb chops too
Till I stopped and looked at dinner
From the dinner's point of view.

Source: *Where the Sidewalk Ends*, by Shel Silverstein

thankless—unpleasant and without thankful feelings

blue—sad

sunny—happy

feast—a large meal, often for many people

viewpoint—what someone believes or thinks

lobster—an ocean shellfish with large claws

chop—a piece of meat

till—until

What Do You Think? 181

2. Link to Literature

WARM UP

- Explain that some schools have a "backwards day" where students teach some of the classes and do some of the work in the main office, and the teachers and the principal sit in on classes taught by students. Ask students what they would want to do if their school had a backwards day.

TEACHING THE LESSON

Shared Reading Read the poem aloud. Pause after each stanza to answer any questions students may have.

Let's Talk Discuss the poem with students, using the discussion questions as a guide. Ask students what they think the best idea in the poem is. Invite students to take turns pointing out examples of rhyming words. Ask them what they would change if they were in charge of the school.

JUST FOR FUN

Ask students to imagine a situation from the point of view of something or someone else. Have them write poems about these situations.

WRAP UP

- Have students read their poems to the class.

PB PRACTICE BOOK ACTIVITY

See Activity I, Responding to Literature, on Practice Book page 100.

✓ UNIT WRAP UP

Outcome Sentence Have students complete this sentence stem, then share:

I think the best way to change someone's mind is to _____________.

Spelling and Phonics Activities

UNIT 1

Spelling and Phonics The letter *i* can sound different, depending on the word it is in. Listen to these words.

pride winner

Complete the chart below. Put each word from the box in the correct column.

like	wild	picture	nice
stupid	in	I'm	live

/ī/ as in *pride*	/i/ as in *winner*
like	

UNIT 2

Spelling and Phonics The letter *a* can sound different depending on the word it is in. Listen to these words.

walk candy man lawn

Complete the chart below. Put each word from the box in the correct column.

draw	paw	eyeball
glass	swan	hat
wall	avalanche	talk

/a/ as in *candy*	/ô/ as in *walk*
	draw

UNIT 3

Spelling and Phonics The letter *o* can be pronounced in different ways when a consonant + *e* follows it. Listen to the following words.

role   come

Complete the chart below. Put each word from the box in the correct column.

home	love	some	stove
shove	Coke	go	rope
done	close	none	one

/ō/ as in *role*	/ŭ/ as in *come*
home	

UNIT 4

Spelling and Phonics The consonant sound /s/ can be spelled in many ways. Listen to the following words.

house   city   kiss   listen

Supply the missing letters for each of the following incomplete words. Use your dictionary to check your work.

a. Eeek! I see a mou_s_e!

b. Do you mi__ me?

c. I live in San Fran__isco.

d. I am taking five cla__es.

e. Juan blew the whi__le.

f. Do you celebrate Chri__mas?

g. Five __ents equals a nickel.

h. What's your addre__?

i. I see my fa__e in the mirror.

UNIT 5

Spelling and Phonics The letter *a* can sound different depending on the word it is in. Listen to these words.

cat snake yawn

Complete the chart below. Put each word from the box in the correct column.

have	mantis	male	Africa
swallow	alligator	talk	small
praying	Asia	gigantic	anaconda

/a/ as in *cat*	/ā/ as in *snake*	/ô/ as in *yawn*
have		

UNIT 6

Spelling and Phonics The consonant sound /k/ can be spelled in many ways. Listen to these words.

cool school kid kick quick

Supply the missing letters for each of the following incomplete words. Use your dictionary to check your work.

a. Juan loves to _c_ook.

b. My stoma__ hurts.

c. The paper costs a __uarter.

d. Can you __eep a secret?

e. I feel si__!

f. Do you have a __uestion?

g. I feel lu__y.

h. __ould you help me?

i. What's the s__edule?

UNIT 7

Spelling and Phonics *Digraphs* are two consonants that we put together to make just one sound. Listen to the following sentence. Look at the circled digraph in the underlined word.

My favorite ice cream is chocolate.

Each of the following words has a digraph. Say each word, and then circle the digraph.

dish	what	weather	with
pharmacy	cheese	shoe	when
think	either	sing	chicken
chorus	who	thank	photo

UNIT 8

Spelling and Phonics Sometimes a consonant (or consonant cluster) is silent. Listen to the sentence. Which consonant is silent in the underlined word?

Johnny tore ligaments in his knee.

Each of the following words has a silent consonant or consonants. Say each word, and then circle the silent consonant or consonants.

know	ghost	listen	sign
eight	wrap	right	knock
write	comb	often	wreck
island	spaghetti	dumb	rhyme

UNIT 9

Spelling and Phonics The letter *i* can be pronounced in different ways when a consonant + *e* follows it. Listen to the following words.

Nile river magazine

Copy the chart below on a separate piece of paper. Put all the words in the following table with the same *i* sound together in the chart.

gasoline	line	time	prize
smile	five	like	tangerine
give	fifth	shiver	bike

/ī/ as in *Nile*	/i/ as in *river*	/ē/ as in *magazine*
smile		

UNIT 10

Spelling and Phonics The sound /ī/ can be spelled many ways. Listen to the following words.

line die my high

Supply the missing letters for each of the following incomplete words. Use your dictionary to check your work.

a. Baseball is out of st_y_le.

b. Tim has n__ne brothers!

c. I have to t__ my shoe.

d. Do you like apple p__?

e. Juan was born in Jul__.

f. Maria m__t go with us.

g. Snow is usually wh__te.

h. Tran is a n__ce guy.

i. I go to bed at n__t.

ChecBrics*

UNIT 1

ChecBric for "Me" Collage

Focus	Overall rating
Organization ____ I used both words and pictures. ____ I placed my pictures in an interesting way.	____ 4 = Wow! ____ 3 = Strong ____ 2 = Some strengths ____ 1 = Needs work
Content My collage tells about... ____ me. ____ my family and friends. ____ what I like. ____ what I like to do.	____ 4 = Wow! ____ 3 = Strong ____ 2 = Some strengths ____ 1 = Needs work
Style ____ I used pictures and photos. ____ I used words to tell about me. ____ I used different sizes of letters and words. ____ My collage is nice to look at.	____ 4 = Wow! ____ 3 = Strong ____ 2 = Some strengths ____ 1 = Needs work
Grammar and mechanics ____ I spelled the words correctly. ____ I capitalized people's names.	____ 4 = Wow! ____ 3 = Strong ____ 2 = Some strengths ____ 1 = Needs work

**ChecBric name and concept created by Larry Lewin.*

ChecBric for Signs

Focus	Overall rating
Organization ____ The signs on each page have the same job. ____ I used pictures with my signs. ____ Each page has a caption.	____ 4 = Wow! ____ 3 = Strong ____ 2 = Some strengths ____ 1 = Needs work
Content You see my signs— ____ in towns and cities. ____ in the country. ____ along streets and highways. ____ in schools and libraries. My signs tell about— ____ things to do (or not do). ____ places. ____ things people like or want.	____ 4 = Wow! ____ 3 = Strong ____ 2 = Some strengths ____ 1 = Needs work
Style ____ Each sign looks real. ____ I used different types of letters. ____ I used pictures with my signs.	____ 4 = Wow! ____ 3 = Strong ____ 2 = Some strengths ____ 1 = Needs work
Grammar and mechanics ____ I spelled words correctly. ____ I used commands correctly. ____ I capitalized the names of places.	____ 4 = Wow! ____ 3 = Strong ____ 2 = Some strengths ____ 1 = Needs work

ChecBric for Personal Web Page

Focus	Overall rating
Organization ____ My Web page gives information in groups (me, my friends, my family, etc.). ____ I used sentences to give information.	____ 4 = Wow! ____ 3 = Strong ____ 2 = Some strengths ____ 1 = Needs work
Content The Web page tells others about... ____ me. ____ my family and friends. ____ my school. ____ my favorite things.	____ 4 = Wow! ____ 3 = Strong ____ 2 = Some strengths ____ 1 = Needs work
Style ____ My Web page has a welcome and a logo. ____ My Web page includes photos or art that tell about me.	____ 4 = Wow! ____ 3 = Strong ____ 2 = Some strengths ____ 1 = Needs work
Grammar and mechanics ____ I used complete sentences. ____ I made sure that *be* verbs agree with their subjects. ____ I capitalized all proper nouns.	____ 4 = Wow! ____ 3 = Strong ____ 2 = Some strengths ____ 1 = Needs work

ChecBric for Map

Focus	Overall rating
Organization ____ My map has a title. ____ My map uses symbols and has a legend. ____ I labeled landmarks and routes. ____ My map has a one-sentence caption.	____ 4 = Wow! ____ 3 = Strong ____ 2 = Some strengths ____ 1 = Needs work
Content ____ I drew my map to scale. ____ I put landmarks in the right location. ____ I used the correct names of landmarks and routes. ____ The map is easy to read and use.	____ 4 = Wow! ____ 3 = Strong ____ 2 = Some strengths ____ 1 = Needs work
Style ____ I drew my map neatly. ____ I printed landmarks and routes clearly. ____ I used color in my map.	____ 4 = Wow! ____ 3 = Strong ____ 2 = Some strengths ____ 1 = Needs work
Grammar and mechanics ____ I used a complete sentence for my caption. ____ I used a capital letter for each noun in the title. ____ All names begin with capitals.	____ 4 = Wow! ____ 3 = Strong ____ 2 = Some strengths ____ 1 = Needs work

ChecBric for Field Guide

Focus	Overall rating
Organization ____ My title names the animal. ____ My page gives information about the animal. ____ My page has a map.	____ 4 = Wow! ____ 3 = Strong ____ 2 = Some strengths ____ 1 = Needs work
Content The information tells... ____ where the animal lives. ____ the animal's size. ____ the animal's weight. ____ what the animal eats. ____ My page also tells one amazing fact about the animal.	____ 4 = Wow! ____ 3 = Strong ____ 2 = Some strengths ____ 1 = Needs work
Style ____ My writing is easy to understand. ____ I used at least one adjective. ____ I included a picture of the animal.	____ 4 = Wow! ____ 3 = Strong ____ 2 = Some strengths ____ 1 = Needs work
Grammar and mechanics ____ I used complete sentences. ____ I made sure that all verbs agree with their subjects. ____ I used a capital letter to begin each sentence and a period to end each one.	____ 4 = Wow! ____ 3 = Strong ____ 2 = Some strengths ____ 1 = Needs work

ChecBric for How-to Instructions: Recipe

Focus	Overall rating
Organization ____ I gave my recipe a name. ____ I wrote a short introduction for my recipe. ____ I listed the utensils you will need. ____ I listed the ingredients you will need. ____ I put the steps in time order.	____ 4 = Wow! ____ 3 = Strong ____ 2 = Some strengths ____ 1 = Needs work
Content ____ I explained how much or how many of each ingredient you need. ____ Each step is accurate. ____ My recipe is "as easy as 1-2-3" to follow.	____ 4 = Wow! ____ 3 = Strong ____ 2 = Some strengths ____ 1 = Needs work
Style ____ I gave my recipe an interesting name. ____ Each sentence is short and simple.	____ 4 = Wow! ____ 3 = Strong ____ 2 = Some strengths ____ 1 = Needs work
Grammar and mechanics ____ Each instruction is complete. ____ I used the right prepositions.	____ 4 = Wow! ____ 3 = Strong ____ 2 = Some strengths ____ 1 = Needs work

ChecBric for Report: Survey

Focus	Overall rating
Organization ____ I gave my report a title. ____ My report has an introduction that asks my survey question. ____ I listed the result answers in order from the largest to the smallest number of people. ____ I named my source at the end of the survey.	____ 4 = Wow! ____ 3 = Strong ____ 2 = Some strengths ____ 1 = Needs work
Content ____ I asked an interesting question. ____ I explained who and how many people I asked. ____ I gave accurate numbers or percentages. ____ My source is accurate.	____ 4 = Wow! ____ 3 = Strong ____ 2 = Some strengths ____ 1 = Needs work
Style ____ My survey has an introduction. ____ I pose an interesting question that hooks the reader.	____ 4 = Wow! ____ 3 = Strong ____ 2 = Some strengths ____ 1 = Needs work
Grammar and mechanics ____ I used complete sentences in my introduction. ____ I numbered the results in my list.	____ 4 = Wow! ____ 3 = Strong ____ 2 = Some strengths ____ 1 = Needs work

ChecBric for Personal Memory

Focus	Overall rating
Organization ____ I wrote my memory in the first person, using "I." ____ I described events the way they happened.	____ 4 = Wow! ____ 3 = Strong ____ 2 = Some strengths ____ 1 = Needs work
Content ____ My memory describes the event or experience that is important to me. ____ I told how I felt about the event. ____ I explained why I remember the experience.	____ 4 = Wow! ____ 3 = Strong ____ 2 = Some strengths ____ 1 = Needs work
Style ____ I wrote like I was talking to the reader. ____ I used adjectives that describe my feelings.	____ 4 = Wow! ____ 3 = Strong ____ 2 = Some strengths ____ 1 = Needs work
Grammar and mechanics ____ I used complete sentences. ____ I used the right forms of past tense verbs. ____ I used a capital letter for the pronoun *I*.	____ 4 = Wow! ____ 3 = Strong ____ 2 = Some strengths ____ 1 = Needs work

ChecBric for Short Report: Our World

Focus	Overall rating
Organization ____ My title names the place. ____ My paragraph has a topic sentence. ____ I gave at least one fact to support my topic sentence.	____ 4 = Wow! ____ 3 = Strong ____ 2 = Some strengths ____ 1 = Needs work
Content ____ I told about a place that is special, or one of a kind. ____ I gave interesting facts. ____ I included a picture of the place and a map.	____ 4 = Wow! ____ 3 = Strong ____ 2 = Some strengths ____ 1 = Needs work
Style ____ My writing is easy to understand. ____ I put two sentences together into one to make my writing "flow" for the reader.	____ 4 = Wow! ____ 3 = Strong ____ 2 = Some strengths ____ 1 = Needs work
Grammar and mechanics ____ I used complete sentences. ____ I used the correct comparative and superlative adjectives. ____ I used a capital letter for the names of places and buildings.	____ 4 = Wow! ____ 3 = Strong ____ 2 = Some strengths ____ 1 = Needs work

ChecBric for Opinion Column

Focus	Overall rating
Organization ____ My title is the same as the question I asked. ____ I wrote "yes" answers first, then "no" answers. ____ I named each person who answered my question.	____ 4 = Wow! ____ 3 = Strong ____ 2 = Some strengths ____ 1 = Needs work
Content ____ I asked an interesting question. ____ I chose the most interesting answers to report.	____ 4 = Wow! ____ 3 = Strong ____ 2 = Some strengths ____ 1 = Needs work
Style ____ I used people's real words. ____ Each quote is accurate.	____ 4 = Wow! ____ 3 = Strong ____ 2 = Some strengths ____ 1 = Needs work
Grammar and mechanics ____ I used the right word order for my question. ____ I used complete sentences for each answer. ____ I put quotation marks around each person's words.	____ 4 = Wow! ____ 3 = Strong ____ 2 = Some strengths ____ 1 = Needs work

Glossary

UNIT 1

athletic—good at sports
awesome—really, really great
best—better than anyone or anything else
brat—a bad, difficult child
friend—someone you like and who likes you
hip-hop—a type of music lots of kids like
Hotmail—an Internet e-mail service
innocent—sweet or nice
loveable (*also* **lovable**)—easy for other people to love
popular—having a lot of friends
sleep in—to get up later than you usually do
special—different from most other people or things
sports—games people or teams play against each other
wow—what you say when something surprises you

UNIT 2

area—a part of a building, park, office, etc., for doing something
avalanche—snow, ice, and rocks that fall off a mountain side
crossing—a place where you can go from one side of the street to the other
danger—a harmful situation
deposit—to put something into something else
detour—a different way of going from one place to another
diner—a restaurant with simple food and low prices
fly rod caster—someone who fishes with a special type of fishing pole
frisbee heaver—someone who throws a Frisbee
recycle—to use things again that people throw away
special treat—something good to eat
spray can sprayer—someone who uses a spray can to paint on a wall

UNIT 3

attend—to go to class or school regularly
auto wholesaler—someone who sells cars
brand—the name of the company that makes something
chorus—a group of people who sing together
enjoy—to like doing something
exercising—doing activities that make you strong and healthy
favorite—liked better than anything else
future—any time after right now
future plans—what you want to do when you are older
goal—something you hope to do one day
graduate— to finish high school, college, or some other educational program
heights—high places
hobby—an activity you do for fun, usually by yourself
hometown—the place you come from
honor roll—a list recognizing students who get all A's and B's
nickname—a name your friends call you
personal living—a class that teaches you skills for everyday life
role model—a person you want to be like
size—how big or small something is
successful—good at what you do
Super Bowl—the championship football game played every year in January
Vikings—Minnesota's football team
welcome—a friendly greeting

UNIT 4

curve—to move like part of a circle
direction—the way someone or something is facing, moving, or located in relation to you
Earth—the planet we live on
enter—to go in
equal—to be the same as
flat—without any high or low areas
foot—a unit for measuring length (= 12 inches or 30.5 centimeters)
imaginary—not real
inch—a unit for measuring short lengths (= 1/12 of a foot or 2.54 centimeters)
lamplight—the light from a lamp
mile—a U.S./English unit used to measure long distances (= 5,280 feet or 1.6 kilometers)
round—shaped like a ball or the letter "o"
travel—to go places
wrap around—to go all the way around

UNIT 5

address—the street name and number where someone lives or works
blazing—very hot
breed—a type of animal
caiman—a type of crocodile
clover—a grasslike plant with three round leaves
cud—food already eaten once, then brought back into the mouth
dandelion—a plant with tiny yellow flowers
domestic—used to describe an animal that lives with people or works on a farm
gigantic—very large
grain—crops like corn, wheat, or rice
greater than—more than
hare—a wild rabbit
herb—a plant used for flavor in cooking
hug—to use arms or legs to squeeze
mate—the partner of an animal
nectar—sweet liquid in flowers
pasture—grassland where cattle feed
pop—to break
poultry—birds like chickens and turkeys
pound—a unit used to measure weight (= 16 ounces or 454 grams)
savannah—grassland
size—how big or how small something is
submerged—under water
sunburned—used to describe skin that is burned by the sun
swallow—to make food go down your throat
swamplands—land that is covered with water
tapir—an animal with a heavy body and short legs
weight—how heavy or how light something is
wild boar—a type of wild pig
yawn—to open your mouth wide when you are sleepy

UNIT 6

add—to put something else in with other things
adventurous—willing to try new and different things
baking pan—a metal pan used to cook or bake food in the oven
baloney—something silly or not true
Big Apple—a nickname for New York City
bread knife—a tool you use to slice bread
can opener—a tool you use to open cans
chicken—afraid
crashing—making a sudden loud noise
crumb—a very small piece of bread or cake
difficulty—how easy or hard it is to do something
eat your words—to admit being wrong
feather—one of the light, soft things that cover a bird
glass measuring cup—a cup used to measure large amounts of ingredients
knife—a sharp tool used to cut food into small pieces
measuring cup—a cup used to measure ingredients
measuring spoons—tools used to measure small amounts
medium—in between; moderate
melted—very hot, soft and gooey
microwave oven—a machine used to heat food very quickly
mixing bowl—a bowl you use to mix ingredients
nostalgic—making you remember happy past times
optional—possible, but not necessary
oven—a machine used to bake or broil food
oven mitt—something you wear on your hand when you take a hot pan out of the oven
oz.—ounce
piece of cake—very easy
pizza cutter—a tool you use to cut pizzas
plate—a flat dish used to serve food on
preheat—to heat an oven to a certain temperature before putting food in it
saucepan—a small, deep metal pan used to cook food on the stove
seasoned—having flavor from herbs, spices, or salt
serving—the amount of a food that one person eats
set—to become solid
shape—to form something with your hands
spatula—a tool used to lift, turn, or flip pieces of food
spill the beans—to tell a secret
spray—to put a liquid onto something using a pressurized can
sprinkle—to scatter tiny pieces of something on something else
swirling—going around and around
tbsp.—tablespoon
tsp.—teaspoon
type—a kind
wedge—a piece of something, shaped like a triangle
whisk—a tool used to beat or whip liquids
wooden spoon—a spoon used to stir or mix food together

UNIT 7

according to—said or written by someone
assignment—a piece of schoolwork
beat the heat—to stay cool when the weather is hot
beverage—something to drink
broken—cracked in pieces
close second—a person or thing that is almost in first place
core—the center of something, like an apple
crumpled—crushed into a ball
number one—the best or most important person or thing
overdue—late being returned to the library

percent—the amount in every hundred
pick—the best thing out of a group
prefer—to like something better than something else
recess—free time during the school day
reed—a thin piece of wood attached to the mouthpiece of an instrument to help it make a sound
researcher—someone who studies a subject
rotten—going bad or decaying
series—a set of things, like books, that come one after another
source—a person or book you get information from
sugary—having a lot of sugar in it
survey—a set of question you ask other people to find out what they like or think
temperature—how hot or cold something is

UNIT 8

afraid of—frightened by something
all-star—involving only the top athletes
grave—the place where a dead body is buried
league—a group of sports teams that play against each other
legend—someone who is famous for being very good at something
ligament—one of the "bands" that hold your bones together
lose—to come in last in a game or contest
offensive guard—the person in a football game who plays guard when his or her team has the ball
sled—to ride a vehicle that slides over snow
softball—a game like baseball except that a larger, softer ball is used
surprise—a feeling you have when something happens that you don't expect
tore—the past tense of the verb *tear*, which means to rip or split apart
touchdown—the action of moving the football into the other team's end zone to score points
uniform—clothing worn by team members
win—to be first in a game or contest

UNIT 9

bay—an area of water with land around most of it (smaller than a gulf)
canyon—a deep valley with very steep sides
considered—thought to be true by most people
continental—relating to a continent
continent—one of the seven great areas of land: Africa, Antarctica, Asia, Australia, Europe, North America, and South America
feet—the plural of *foot*, a unit for measuring length (1 foot = 12 inches or 30.5 centimeters)
gulf—an area of ocean with land around most of it (larger than a bay)
mightier—stronger; bigger
mile—a unit for measuring long distances (= 5,280 feet or 1.6 kilometers)
peak—the top of a very tall mountain
peninsula—land with water on three sides
plain—a large area of very flat land
prairie—a large area of flat land with tall grasses and few trees
sea level—the height of the water in the oceans
summit—the top of a mountain
valley—a low place between two mountains

UNIT 10

action—exciting things that happen
all over—everywhere you look
allowed—having permission to do something
bat—a long wooden stick used for hitting a baseball
blue—sad
challenge—something new or difficult that requires skill
chop—a piece of meat
comfortable—at ease or relaxed
crack—a loud noise that sounds like something breaking
different—not like something or someone else
dunk—to push a basketball through the hoop at close range
embarrassed—feeling shy or ashamed in front of other people
fast-paced—having lots of action
feast—a large meal, often for many people
home run—a long hit in baseball in which the hitter is able to run around all the bases and score a point
lobster—an ocean shellfish with large claws
on the ball—able to think quickly
out of style—not in fashion or popular any more
outdoor experiences—activities like camping and fishing
pressure—a feeling that you have too much work and other things to do
skill—the ability to do something very well
still—continuing until now or until a particular time
stress—worries that keep you from relaxing
sunny—happy
thankless—unpleasant and without thankful feelings
till—until
viewpoint—what someone believes or thinks
year-round school—schools that are open all year. Students have many short vacations rather than a long summer vacation.

Common Irregular Verbs

Simple Form	Past Form	Past Participle	Simple Form	Past Form	Past Participle
be	was/were	been	lay (= put)	laid	laid
beat	beat	beaten	lead	led	led
become	became	become	leave	left	left
begin	began	begun	let	let	let
bend	bent	bent	lie (= lie down)	lay	lain
bite	bit	bitten	lose	lost	lost
break	broke	broken	make	made	made
bring	brought	brought	mean	meant	meant
build	built	built	meet	met	met
buy	bought	bought	pay	paid	paid
catch	caught	caught	put	put	put
choose	chose	chosen	quit	quit	quit
come	came	come	read	read	read
cost	cost	cost	ride	rode	ridden
cut	cut	cut	ring	rang	rung
do	did	done	rise	rose	risen
draw	drew	drawn	run	ran	run
drink	drank	drunk	say	said	said
eat	ate	eaten	see	saw	seen
fall	fell	fallen	sell	sold	sold
feed	fed	fed	send	sent	sent
feel	felt	felt	set	set	set
fight	fought	fought	show	showed	shown
find	found	found	shut	shut	shut
fly	flew	flown	sing	sang	sung
forget	forgot	forgotten	sit	sat	sat
forgive	forgave	forgiven	sleep	slept	slept
get	got	gotten	speak	spoke	spoken
give	gave	given	spend	spent	spent
go	went	gone	stand	stood	stood
grow	grew	grown	swim	swam	swum
have	had	had	take	took	taken
hear	heard	heard	teach	taught	taught
hide	hid	hidden	tear	tore	torn
hit	hit	hit	tell	told	told
hold	held	held	think	thought	thought
hurt	hurt	hurt	throw	threw	thrown
keep	kept	kept	understand	understood	understood
know	knew	known	wake	woke	woken

Listening Script

UNIT 1

A. 1. Tuning In. (page 4)

1. I like many things. I like to eat. I like pizza. What about you?
2. I like burritos. What about you?
3. I like ice cream. What about you?
4. I like French fries. What about you?
5. I also like sports. I like baseball. What about you?
6. I like soccer. What about you?
7. I like football. What about you?
8. And I *love* music! I like hip-hop. What about you?
9. I like country music. What about you?
10. I like many things. Do *you*?

UNIT 2

A. 1. Tuning In. (page 22)

Conversation one

Girl: Excuse me, I'm looking for Ms. Flores

Boy: Her office is at the end of the hall. There's a sign on her door. It says, "PRINCIPAL'S OFFICE."

Conversation two

Boy: How far is it? I'm tired!

Girl: There's a sign over there. It says "LOS ANGELES, 65 MILES."

Conversation three

Woman: I need to buy just one more thing.

Man: I'll find a place to sit and wait for you.

Woman: Where will I meet you?

Man: Near the sign that says "INFORMATION," right in front of the Toy Department.

Conversation four

Woman: We need milk.

Girl: Where do I find it?

Woman: See the sign that says "DAIRY"? It's over there.

Conversation five

Girl: Hurry up, Carlos! We can still cross...!

Boy: We'd better wait. That sign says "DON'T WALK."

UNIT 3

A. 1. Tuning In. (page 40)

Lori: What are you doing? Playing on the computer?

Maria: I'm making my own Web page. You can help me. What kind of things do I put on my Web page?

Lori: Hmm. Tell me about you ... *and* about your family, too.

Maria: Well...I have one sister and two brothers.

Lori: What do you like to do for fun?

Maria: I like to go to the mall... and watch TV.

Lori: What TV shows do you like a lot?

Maria: The Simpsons! I *love* The Simpsons.

Lori: What about food? What do you like?

Maria: Pizza.

Lori: What kind of music do you like?

Maria: Hip-hop.

Lori: What are you good at? What subject do you like best?

Maria: I like math.

Lori: This is an interesting Web page!

UNIT 4

A. 1. Tuning In. (page 58)

Diego: What street are we on?
Juan: We're on Palisade Avenue. Keep going on Palisade. When we get to New School Street, turn.
Diego: Which way?
Juan: Uh ...turn right. And then it looks like we go two more blocks ... then turn left.
Diego: On to what street?
Juan: Maple. Then we turn right again, on to Linden. The address is... *OH, NO*! I forgot to write down the address!

UNIT 5

A. 1. Tuning In. (page 76)

Eduardo: My name is Eduardo Valdez.
Brian: And my name is Brian Lee. We both travel around the world to find amazing, or interesting, animals.
Eduardo: Last year, Brian and I were in South America. We were looking for giant snakes. We study reptiles—animals like snakes, lizards, and alligators.
Brian: We were walking in a swamp—a place with a lot of water.
Eduardo: There was a dead tree in front of me, lying on the ground. And so, I stepped on it. Suddenly, it moved! It wasn't a tree at all!
Brian: It was a HUGE snake! It was about 20 feet long and as thick as my leg. I was scared! This snake was so big he could eat us both!
Eduardo: The snake twisted around my body, then my neck. Snakes like that kill you! They don't kill you with poison. They crush you to death!
Brian: That's right! Some snakes kill you by biting you. And some snakes kill you by crushing, or squeezing, you to death.
Eduardo: Brian thought fast. He pulled the snake loose.
Brian: Yes, I pulled the snake loose! Then it disappeared into the water.
Eduardo: Brian saved my life! I was really scared!
Brian: So was I! I was really scared, too!

D. 1. Word Detective (page 80)

1. A thread snake is very tiny.
2. An anaconda is huge.
3. A king snake is a very large snake.
4. A brown snake weighs less than a pound.
5. An anaconda weighs up to 100 pounds.
6. A boa constrictor can grow to over 8 feet long.
7. A brown snake is no longer than a foot.
8. A thread snake weighs only two or three ounces.

UNIT 6

A. 1. Tuning In (page 94)

Boy: Hey, Mom, let's have burritos for dinner.
Mother: OK. I'll show you how to make them. First, let's take out the ingredients. We'll need tortillas, shredded chicken, beans, and rice.
Boy: What's "shredded" chicken?
Mother: That means it's torn in tiny pieces.
Boy: What about cheese?
Mother: Right! We need cheese. OK, let's take out the large skillet.
Boy: Here it is.
Mother: Turn on the stove. We need to warm the tortillas in the skillet first, to make them soft. Here ... you can heat the first one.
Boy: Here's the first tortilla. It's really hot.
Mother: OK, now watch me. First you add the rice. Then you add the beans. After that you add the chicken...and you sprinkle the cheese on top of the chicken.... Next you wrap the tortilla around the filling.

Then you roll the burrito up really tight. Put it in the microwave oven for a few seconds to make it hot.

Boy: Yummmmm.... This is really good!
Mother: Now you know how to make a burrito.

UNIT 7

A. 1. Tuning In. (page 112)

Interviewer: Do you all like pizza?
All: Yes!
Boy #1: It's my favorite food!
Girl: I love pizza!
Boy #2: Pizza's my favorite, too!
Interviewer: What's your favorite topping—besides cheese?
Boy #2: Pepperoni. I always order pepperoni.
Boy #1: I like sausage.
Girl: My favorite topping is ham and pineapple.
Boy #1 and Boy #2: *Pineapple*!
Interviewer: What about anchovies? Does anybody like anchovies?
All: Eeeewww! Yuck!

UNIT 8

A. 1. Tuning In. (page 130)

Bernie Davis: I remember a Little League game when I was eight. I had no idea how to play baseball. I ended up hitting the ball for the winning base hit. But afterward, I had to ask the coach who won the game!

UNIT 9

A. 1. Tuning In. (page 148)

1. Girl: A mountain is higher than a hill.
2. Boy: A stream is wider than a river.
3. Girl: A pool is bigger than a lake.
4. Boy: An ocean is deeper than a lake.
5. Girl: A river is longer than a stream.

UNIT 10

A. 1 Tuning In. (page 166)

Juan: Do you want to watch TV?
Lori: You watch too much TV. It isn't good for you to watch TV.
Juan: What are you talking about? TV is good for you.
Lori: No, it isn't. If you watch TV, you don't have time for homework.
Juan: But you learn a lot from TV.
Lori: You learn more from reading books.
Juan: TV is interesting.
Lori: TV is *silly*. It's a waste of time. Kids who watch a lot of TV don't do well in school.
Juan: But I get A's and B's!
Lori: If you don't watch TV, you'll get all A's.

H. 1.5. Writer's Workshop—Getting It Out—Activity 5. (page 177)

Lori: Should kids have to take PE?
1. Boy #1: Yes! Kids need exercise.
2. Girl #1: No! Most kids hate taking showers at school.
3. Boy #2: No! You don't learn anything in PE!
4. Girl #2: Yes! PE teaches you teamwork.
5. Boy #3: No! Other classes are more important.
6. Girl #3: Yes! PE makes you feel better.

Index

Reading (Comprehension strategies, skills, text organization)

Real World Applications

Spelling and Phonics

Style

Visual Literacy

Word Analysis Skills

Writing

Text and Audio Credits

p. 19 "My Name Poem" by Ben Matsunaga. Courtesy, The DISKovery Center & Ben Matsunaga; *p. 19* "Brianna" found at http://saintmarysschools.com; *p. 19* "John" found at http://abcteach.com. Copyright © www.abcteach.com. Used by permission.; *pp. 24, 28 Signs* by Susan Canizares and Paula Chanko, Copyright © 1999 Scholastic; *p. 31* Logo design by The Logo Factory Inc. Used by permission.; *p. 37* "No" from *Falling Up* by Shel Silverstein, Copyright © 1996 by Shel Silverstein. Used by permission of HarperCollins.; *p. 42* "Welcome to Keith's Home Page" found at http://www.hollywoodchristian.org; *p. 46* Profiles of Darryl, Rachel, and Steven from "Maryland's Tomorrow" Web page at www.smcps.k12.md.us.Used by permission.; *p. 55* "Mikey" by Mikey Libbey. Used by permission of Nancy Libbey.; *pp.* 60-61, 64 From *Looking at Maps and Globes* by Carmen Bredeson. © 2001 by Children's Press®. A Division of Scholastic Inc. All rights reserved. Used by permission.; *p. 73* "Door Number Four" from *If I Had a Paka: Poems in Eleven Languages* by Charlotte Pomerantz. Reprinted by arrangement with the author and Writers House LLC, acting as agent for the author. Reproduced by arrangement with the author and Writers House LLC, acting as agent for the author.; *pp. 78, 86* "The Komodo Dragon," "The Anaconda," "The Praying Mantis," "The Great White Shark," "The Vampire Bat," "The Saltwater Crocodile," and "The Bengal Tiger" from *The Meanest: Amazing Facts about Aggressive Animals* by Mymi Doinet, Copyright © 2000, 2002 by Les Editions Play Bac. Reprinted by permission. Reproduced by permission.; *p. 82* "The Cow," "The Cat," and "The Hippopotamus" from The Laziest: Amazing Facts about Lazy Animals by Mymi Doinet, copyright © 2000, 2002 by Les Editions Play Bac. Reprinted by permission. Reproduced by permission.; *p. 91* "Wild Animals" by Kenneth Baker and Megan Abbott from Lewisporte Academy found at www.k12.nf.ca; *p. 96* "Mexican Quesadillas" from *The Everything Kids' Cookbook* Copyright ©2002, Adams Media Corporation. Used by permission of Adams Media. All rights reserved.; *p. 100* "Nostalgic Meatloaf" from *The Everything Kids' Cookbook* Copyright ©2002, Adams Media Corporation. Used by permission of Adams Media. All rights reserved.; *p. 102* "Quick Eating S'mores" from *The Everything Kids' Cookbook* Copyright ©2002, Adams Media Corporation. Used by permission of Adams Media. All rights reserved.; *p. 106* "Chunky Chocolate Peanut Butter Pudding" from *The Everything Kids' Cookbook* Copyright ©2002, Adams Media Corporation. Used by permission of Adams Media. All rights reserved.; *p. 109* "A Recipe for Weather," www.humanitiessoftware.com. Copyright Renaissance Learning, Inc. Used with permission.; *p. 114* "Top Five Ice Cream Flavors," *TIME for Kids*, Sept. 19, 2003, Vol. 9, No. 12, p. 3. Used with permission from TIME For Kids Magazine.; *p. 114* "Top Five Beverages," *TIME for Kids*, Sept. 26, 1997, Vol. 3, No. 3, p. 2. Used with permission from TIME For Kids Magazine.; *p. 118* "Top Five Favorite Subjects," *TIME for Kids*, Sept. 26, 1997, Vol. 3, No. 9, p. 2. Used with permission from TIME For Kids Magazine.; *p. 118* "Top Five Favorite Kids' Books of All Time," *TIME for Kids*, Sept 12, 2003, Vol. 9, No. 11, p. 3. Used with permission from TIME For Kids Magazine.; *p. 127* Untitled poem from *Love Me When I'm Most Unlovable* by Robert Ricken. Copyright © 1987 by The National Association of Secondary School Principals. www.principals.org. Reprinted with permission.; *pp. 132, 136* From "My First Sports Memories: Nine Star Athletes Share the Highlights of Their Early, Early, Early Careers!" *Sports Illustrated for Kids*, July 1, 2000. Courtesy of Sports Illustrated for Kids.; *p. 145* "Feelings Poem" by Mac Babb in Essential *Ingredients: Recipes for Teaching Writing* found at www.ascd.org; *pp. 150, 154* From *Hottest, Coldest, Highest, Deepest.* Copyright © 1998 by Steven Jenkins. Reprinted by permission of Houghton Mifflin Company. All rights reserved.; *p. 163* "The Earth" by Ivan found at Pizzaz! at darkwing.uoregon.edu; *p. 168* From "Is Baseball Still America's Favorite Sport?" *Sports Illustrated for Kids*, Sept. 1, 2001. Courtesy of Sports Illustrated for Kids.; *p. 172* From "Should boys be allowed to play on girls' sports teams?" *Sports Illustrated for Kids*, Mar. 1, 2001. Courtesy of Sports Illustrated for Kids.; *p. 181* "Point of View" from *Where the Sidewalk Ends* by Shel Silverstein. Copyright © 2004 by Evil Eye Music, Inc. Used by permission of HarperCollins Publishers.

Photo Credits

Cover Images: **From the Getty Images Royalty-Free Collection:** Female College Student; Railroad Crossing; Ice Cream Cone; Praying Mantis; Shark; **From the Corbis Royalty-Free Collection:** Male College Student; Lion; Guitar; **Other Images:** Volcano: Jim Sugar/CORBIS; Avalanche Area: Dave Schiefelbein/Getty Images; Outfielder: Getty Images; Goalkeeper: Chris Cole/Getty Images; Akashi Kaikyo Bridge: Kyodo News; Man with Frozen Sunglasses: Patrick Endres/Alaska Stock; Angel Falls: James Marshall/CORBIS; Globe spread: William Westheimer/CORBIS.

Interior Images: All photos in the collage on *p.* 3 are from the Getty Images Royalty-Free Collection except Justin Timberlake: JEFF J MITCHELL/Reuters/CORBIS; Beyonce Knowles: Reuters/CORBIS; Fun: Royalty-Free/CORBIS; **From the Getty Images Royalty-Free Collection:** *p.* 11, row 1, photo 1; *p.* 11, row 1, photo 2; *p.* 11, row 1, photo 4; *p.* 11, row 1, photo 5; *p.* 11, row 1, photo 6; *p.* 11, row 2, photo 1; *p.* 11, row 2, photo 2; *p.* 11, row 2, photo 3; *p.* 11, row 2, photo 4; *p.* 11, row 2, photo 6; *p.* 13, photo a; *p.* 13, photo b; *p.* 13, photo d; *p.* 13, photo f; *p.* 19; 24, row 2, left; *p.* 24, photo c; *p.* 31, top left, left half of photo; *p.* 39; *p.* 48; *p.* 60; *p.* 73, top; *p.* 76, photo a; *p.* 76, photo c; *p.* 77, photo 1; *p.* 77, photo 4; *p.* 77, photo 5; *p.* 78, bottom; *p.* 80, row 4; *p.* 82, top; *p.* 85, photo 2; *p.* 85, photo 3; *p.* 85, photo 4; *p.* 93; *p.* 109; *p.* 110; *p.* 122, photo c; *p.* 145; *p.* 134; *p.* 137, row 1, far left; *p.* 137, row 1, second from left; *p.* 137, row 2, second from left; *p.* 137, row 2, second from right; *p.* 137, row 3, second from right; *p.* 158, bottom right; *p.* 163; **From the Corbis Royalty-Free Collection:** *p.* 8; *p.* 24, photo b; *p.* 50; *p.* 51; *p.* 75; *p.* 85, photo 1; *p.* 148, photo 3; *p.* 148, photo 6; *p.* **Other Images:** *p.* 11, row 2, photo 5: Marilu Lopez-Fretts 2003 ©Syracuse Newspapers/The Image Works; *p.* 20: Richard Cummins/CORBIS; *p.* 24, row 1, left: Peter Adams/Getty Images; *p.* 24, row 1, right: D. Boone/CORBIS; *p.* 24, row 2, right: Michael Keller/CORBIS ; *p.* 24, photo a: James Leynse/CORBIS; *p.* 24, photo d: Dave Schiefelbein/Getty Images; *p.* 28, photo e: Richard Cummins/CORBIS ; *p.* 28, photo f: Brad Rickerby/Getty Images; *p.* 28, photo g: Todd A. Gipstein/CORBIS; *p.* 28, photo h: David Averbach; *p.* 28, photo i: Bryan Mullennix/Getty Images; *p.* 28, photo j: Louis K. Meisel Gallery, Inc./CORBIS; *p.* 28, photo k: Richard Cummins/CORBIS; *p.* 30, top left: D. Boone/CORBIS; *p.* 30, top right: Dave Schiefelbein/Getty Images; *p.* 30, bottom left: Bryan Mullennix/Getty Images; *p.* 30, bottom right: David Averbach; *p.* 31, top left, right half of photo: Todd A. Gipstein/CORBIS; *p.* 31, top center: Michael Keller/CORBIS; *p.* 31, top right: James Leynse/CORBIS; *p.* 31, bottom left: Bryan Mullennix/Getty Images; *p.* 31, bottom right: Richard Cummins/CORBIS; *p.* 37: Jeff Albertson/CORBIS; *p.* 38: Walter Hodges/Getty Images; *p.* : Duomo/CORBIS; *p.* 46, top: Walter Hodges/Getty Images; *p.* 46, bottom: Al Petteway III/Getty Images; *p.* 49, photo 1: Martyn Goddard/Getty Images; *p.* 49, photo 2: Bettmann/CORBIS; *p.* 73, bottom: Daniel Pomerantz; *p.* 76, photo b: Ed George/Getty Images; *p.* 76, photo d: Dennie Cody/Getty Images; *p.* 76, photo e: Anup Shah/Getty Images; *p.* 76, photo f: Bool Dan /CORBIS SYGMA; *p.* 77, photo 2: Tom Bean/Getty Images; *p.* 77, photo 3: Roy Toft/Getty Images; *p.* 77, photo 6: American Images Inc./Getty Images; *p.* 78, top: Bool Dan / CORBIS SYGMA; *p.* 78, middle: Ed George/Getty Images; *p.* 80, row 1: Michael & Patricia ©Fogden/Minden Pictures; *p.* 80, row 2: Joseph Collins/Photo Researchers, Inc.; *p.* 80, row 3: Gerold and Cindy Merker/Visuals Unlimited; *p.* 80, row 5: Ed George/Getty Images; *p.* 82, middle: Anup Shah/Getty Images; *p.* 82, bottom: Dennie Cody/Getty Images; *p.* 84, top: Bool Dan/CORBIS SYGMA; *p.* 84, bottom: Ed George/Getty Images; *p.* 85, photo 5: Gary Braasch/CORBIS; *p.* 85, photo 6: Harvey Lloyd/Getty Images; *p.* 86, row 1: Carl Roessler/Getty Images; *p.* 86, row 2: Gary Braasch/CORBIS; *p.* 86, row 3: S. J. Vincent/Getty Images; *p.* 86, row 4: U.S. Fish & Wildlife Service/Ron Singer; *p.* 90, top: Kevin Schafer/Getty Images; *p.* 90, middle: John Dunning/Photo Researchers, Inc.; *p.* 90, bottom: Gavin Hellier/Robert Harding/Getty Images; *p.* 91: IT Stock Free/Picturequest; *p.* 118, far left: *Harry Potter And The Order Of The Phoenix* used courtesy of Warner Bros. Entertainment Inc.; *p.* 118, second from right: From *The Cat In The Hat* by Dr. Seuss, (tm) & by Dr. Seuss Enterprises, L. P. 1957, renewed 1985. Used by permission of Random House Children's Books, a division of Random House, Inc.; *p.* 118, second from left: *Goosebumps: Ghost Beach* by R. L. Stine/Scholastic Books; *p.* 118, far right: *Arthur Writes a Story* by Marc Brown/Little Brown & Co.; *p.* 122, photo a: PhotoAlto/PictureQuest; *p.* 122, photo b: Digital Vision/PictureQuest; *p.* 122, photo d: Image Source/PunchStock; *p.* 122, photo e: Larry Dale Gordon/Getty Images; *p.* 122, photo f: Stock Image/PictureQuest; *p.* 129: Duomo/CORBIS; *p.* 130, top left: Zac Macaulay/Getty Images; *p.* 130, top right: Digital Vision/PictureQuest; *p.* 130, bottom left: Bob Gomel/CORBIS; *p.* 130, bottom right: Chris Jones/CORBIS; *p.* 137, row 1, second from right: Getty Images; *p.* 137, row 1, far right: Chris Cole/Getty Images; *p.* 137, row 2, far left: Brent Smith/Reuters/CORBIS; *p.* 137, row 2, far right: Mike Simons/CORBIS; *p.* 137, row 3, far left: Rebecca Cook/Reuters/CORBIS; *p.* 137, row 3, second from left: BRENT SMITH/Reuters/CORBIS; *p.* 137, row 3, far right: LUCY NICHOLSON/Reuters/CORBIS; *p.* 141: Duomo/CORBIS; *p.* 146: Tim Davis/CORBIS; *p.* 147: Steve Satushek/Getty Images; *p.* 148, photo 1: Planetary Visions Ltd./Photo Researchers, Inc.; *p.* 148, photo 2: Digital image 1996 CORBIS; *p.* Original image courtesy of NASA/CORBIS; *p.* 148, photo 4: Kyodo News; *p.* 148, photo 5: Patrick Endres/Alaska Stock; *p.* 158, top left: Sinclair Stammers/Photo Researchers, Inc.; *p.* 158, top right: Tim Davis/CORBIS; *p.* 158, bottom left: James Marshall/CORBIS; *p.* 165, left: Digital Vision/PictureQuest; *p.* 165, right: Arthur Tilley/Getty Images; *p.* 172: Digital Vision/PictureQuest; *p.* 181: Jeff Albertson/CORBIS; Globe spread (border): William Westheimer/CORBIS.

Practice Book Answer Key

UNIT 1

A. Revisit and Retell

Answers will vary. Possible answers: He is the best student. He is special. He likes hip-hop. He is popular. He is good at sports.

B. Word Work

1. c; 2. e; 3. b; 4. f; 5. a; 6. d.

C. Grammar

1: 1. are; 2. am; 3. are; 4. is; 5. is; 6. are; 7. is; 8. is; 9. is; 10. are.
2: 1. They're in the tenth grade. 2. She's lazy. 3. We're late. 4. I'm a good basketball player. 5. He's nice. 6. They're both from Mexico. 7. She's friendly and popular. 8. We're good at sports. 9. I'm quiet. 10. He's a baseball player.

D. Test-Taking Practice

Reading Vocabulary: 1. B; 2. B; 3. A; 4. C; 5. D.
Reading Comprehension: 1. C; 2. B; 3. D; 4. B; 5. D.

E. Using New Vocabulary

Pedro's part: baseball, tostadas, math; **Luisa's part:** volleyball, salads, art, science; **Overlap:** ice cream, pizza, PE.

F. Focus on Organization

What Stefan is like: smart, nice, popular; **What Stefan likes:** pizza, Sno Cones, parties, movies, music; **What Stefan likes to do:** go to school, play baseball, play guitar, take pictures.

G. Focus on Style

Answers will vary.

H. Writer's Workshop

Answers will vary.

I. Responding to Literature

Answers will vary.

UNIT 2

A. Revisit and Retell

Avalanche Area; Recycle Area; Railroad Crossing; Crocodile Crossing; Danger! Thin Ice.

B. Word Work

1. 1. e; 2. d; 3. c; 4. a; 5. b.
2. Possible answers: No talking without raising your hand. No eating in class. No running in the halls. No littering. No yelling in the halls.

C. Grammar

1. 1. open; 2. pick up; 3. write; 4. take out; 5. touch; 6. laugh; 7. look at.

D. Test-Taking Practice

Reading Vocabulary: 1. C; 2. C; 3. D; 4. A; 5. D.
Reading Comprehension: 1. B; 2. A; 3. C; 4. D; 5. B.

E. Using New Vocabulary

1. PLEASE WAIT TO BE SEATED; 2. NO TALKING; 3. WAITING ROOM; 4. DIRECTORY; 5. PLEASE CLEAN UP AFTER YOUR DOG; 6. BAGGAGE CLAIM AREA; 7. PRODUCE; 8. NO RUNNING.

F. Focus on Organization

In the City: Joe's Restaurant, Police Department; **In the Outdoors:** Watch for Bears, Danger! Falling Rocks; **On Streets and Highways:** One Way, Detour, Main Street; **At School:** Nurse's Office, Quiet Please, No Running, Principal's Office, Cafeteria.

G. Focus on Style

1. Kennedy Soccer Team; 2. No Running; 3. Jim's Diner; 4. Doctor's Office; 5. Recycle Center; 6. Sarah's Shoes.

H. Writer's Workshop

Answers will vary.

I. Responding to Literature

Answers will vary.

UNIT 3

A. Revisit and Retell

1. April 5, 1991; 2. basketball; 3. sports; 4. Rock and R&B; 5. blue; 6. Kurt; 7. Danielle; 8. Michael Jordan; 9. Sunrise; 10. 12; 11. A's; 12. Thai food.

B. Word Work

1. rock climbing; 2. softball; 3. roller skating; 4. kite flying; 5. table tennis; 6. bike racing

C. Grammar

Answers will vary. Possible answers: 1. I am fifteen years old. 2. My name is _____. 3. I am a student. 4. I go to _____. 5. I am in the _____ grade. 6. I am from _____. 7. My favorite hobby is _____. 8. My best friend is _____.

D. Test-Taking Practice

Reading Vocabulary: 1. D; 2. A; 3. A; 4. B; 5. C.
Reading Comprehension: 1. D; 2. B; 3. A; 4. B; 5. D.

E. Using New Vocabulary

Answers will vary. Possible answers: 1. baseball; 2. hiking; 3. checkers; 4. football; 5. surfboard; 6. running; 7. biking; 8. racquet, tennis balls; 9. fishing rod (pole), line, lures, worms.

F. Focus on Organization

Information about Veronica: I'm 16 years old. My hometown is Chicago. My nickname is Vero. **Friends and Family:** My mother is a teacher. I have three older brothers—Tomas, José, and Nestor. My brother Nestor is in college. **School:** I go to Central High. My grades are pretty good. I always get A's in science. **Favorite Things:** I love burritos. I like to go bowling. I like R&B music the best.

G. Focus on Style

Possible answers: 1. Veronica loves burritos. 2. Veronica's favorite hobby is dancing. 3. Her favorite activity is bowling. 4. Her favorite class is science. 5. Her best friend is Amy.

H. Writer's Workshop

Answers will vary.

I. Responding to Literature

Answers will vary.

UNIT 4

A. Revisit and Retell

1. to find different places/things are; 2. small pictures that mean different things; 3. house; 4. mountain; 5. school; 6. park; 7. airport; 8. road.

B. Word Work

1. easy; 2. old; 3. stupid; 4. short; 5. bottom; 6. rude; 7. wide; 8. slow; 9. excited; 10. east; 11. wonderful; 12. boring.

C. Grammar

1. birds; 2. buses; 3. watches; 4. bridges; 5. blocks; 6. boxes; 7. buildings; 8. symbols; 9. dishes; 10. sandwiches; 11. cups; 12. glasses.

D. Test-Taking Practice

Reading Vocabulary: 1.A; 2. C; 3. D; 4. B; 5. B.
Reading Comprehension: 1. D; 2. A; 3. C; 4. A; 5. B.

E. Using New Vocabulary

1. movie theater; 2. supermarket; 3. post office; 4. bakery; 5. library; 6. car dealership; 7. playground; 8. hotel.

F. Focus on Organization

Students trace the route and add labels to the five symbols on the map.

G. Focus on Style

1: 1. Laurel Dr.; 2. Sunrise Hwy.; 3. Rose Blvd.; 4. Fifth Ave.; 5. Ford Rd.; 6. River St.
2: 1. TX; 2. NY; 3. FL; 4. CA; 5. NM; 6. NJ; 7. HI; 8. MA; 9. MO; 10. OH.

H. Writer's Workshop

Answers will vary.

I. Responding to Literature

Answers will vary.

UNIT 5

A. Revisit and Retell

Komodo dragon: They're almost ten feet long. They weigh about 300 pounds. They like wild boar and deer. They can swallow over six pounds of meat in a minute; **Anaconda:** They live in South America. They weigh 440 to 506 pounds. They can swallow a 7-foot-long caiman whole.

B. Word Work

1. heavy; 2. long; 3. short; 4. light; 5. big/gigantic; 6. big/gigantic; 7. medium; 8. tiny; 9. length; 10. weight.

C. Grammar

1. loves; 2. weighs; 3. goes; 4. speak; 5. play; 6. finishes; 7. wear; 8. draws; 9. swim; 10. chases; 11. like; 12. walks; 13. teaches; 14. drink; 15. catches.

D. Test-Taking Practice

Reading Vocabulary: 1. C; 2. A; 3. A; 4. B; 5. C.
Reading Comprehension: 1. B; 2. B; 3. D; 4. A; 5. A.

E. Using New Vocabulary

1. giraffe; 2. rhinoceros; 3. tiger; 4. gorilla; 5. leopard; 6. dingo; 7. lion; 8. orangutan.

F. Focus on Organization

Dingos: The Dingo; Australia; 24 inches tall; 35 pounds; small desert animals, sheep. **Aardvarks:** The Aardvark; Africa, south of the Sahara desert; two feet tall and three to four feet long; up to 140 pounds; ants and other insects.

G. Focus on Style

Possible answers: A hungry aardvark can eat 50,000 tiny ants in a single day. 2. The gorilla is a huge animal. 3. Parakeets are colorful birds. 4. I'm not afraid of friendly animals like house cats, but I am afraid of ferocious lions. 5. I like my lazy cat, Larry, even though he sleeps all day. 6. I like to visit the wild animals in the zoo, especially the friendly orangutans. 7. The female praying mantis is a mean/an ugly insect. 8. The elephant has four heavy legs and a long trunk.

H. Writer's Workshop

Answers will vary.

I. Responding to Literature

1. cougars—the mountains, dingoes—Australia, elephants—the African savannah, hares—the forest floor; 2. anacondas—giant snakes, belugas—small white whales, giraffes—tallest; 3. belugas—white, cougars—beauties; frogs—blood-red eyes.
4. Answers will vary.

UNIT 6

A. Revisit and Retell

1. Put a tortilla on a plate. 2. Sprinkle the tortilla with cheese. 3. Put a second tortilla on the first tortilla. 4. Cook the tortillas and cheese in a microwave for 20 to 30 seconds. 5. Cool the quesadilla. 6. Cut the quesadilla into six wedges. 7. Dip the quesadilla into salsa and sour cream.

B. Word Work

1. hot dogs; 2. potato salad. 3. plastic wrap; 4. paper plates; 5. toaster oven; 6. orange juice; 7. paper towels; 8. salt shaker; 9. ice cream; 10. fruit salad; 11. apple pie; 12. pie plate.

C. Grammar

1. out of; 2. into; 3. on; 4. on; 5. on top of; 6. off of; 7. onto; 8. between; 9. between; 10. underneath; 11. in 12. out of.

D. Test-Taking Practice

Reading Vocabulary: 1.B; 2. C; 3. D; 4. A; 5. D.
Reading Comprehension: 1. B; 2. B; 3. C; 4. D; 5. C.

E. Using New Vocabulary

1. chicken; 2. Big Apple; 3. piece of cake; 4. eat my words; 5. baloney; 6. spilled the beans.

F. Focus on Organization

Ingredients: eggs, four slices of bread, mayonnaise, salt, and pepper. **Introduction:** There is nothing like a cold egg salad sandwich on a hot summer day. **Utensils:** a saucepan, a mixing bowl, and measuring spoons. **Difficulty:** It's easy. **Steps:** 3, 2, 6, 4, 1, 5.

G. Focus on Style

1. Tasty; 2. Creamy; 3. Tropical; 4. Fluffy; 5. Old fashioned.

H. Writer's Workshop

Answers will vary.

I. Responding to Literature

Answers will vary.

UNIT 7

A. Revisit and Retell

Answers will vary.

B. Word Work

Answers will vary. Possible answers. 1. verb, Sometimes I get paint on my clothes. 2. noun, I need to brush my hair. 3. noun, I cut it on this knife. 4. verb, I wait for the bus at the bus stop. 5. noun, I walk to school every day. 6. verb, How long was your visit with your grandparents? 7. verb, He has a great laugh. 8. noun, Please show me the correct answer.

C. Grammar

1. Who; 2. Which; 3. What; 4. Who; 5. What; 6. Which; 7. What; 8. Who; 9. Which; 10. Who; 11. What; 12. What.

D. Test-Taking Practice

Reading Vocabulary: 1. B; 2. A; 3. B; 4. B; 5. D.
Reading Comprehension: 1. C; 2. A; 3. B; 4. B; 5. B.

E. Using New Vocabulary

1. half; 2. 25%; 3. 12.5; 4. ⅙; 5. a quarter; 6. two-thirds; 7. 75%; 8. ⅓.

F. Focus on Organization

Teenagers' Top Five Favorite Snacks;
Can you guess which snack foods teenagers like best? They talked to 2,000 American youth from 14 to 18. "What is your favorite snack food?" 32% prefer pizza. 24% like burritos best. 22% like ice cream. 12% like chips best. 10% prefer chicken fingers. The American Food Association.

G. Focus on Style

Answers will vary. Possible answers: 1. What do teenagers like to do after school and on weekends? 2. Who is the most popular singer in the U.S. today? 3. Who is your favorite actor? 4. What do American kids like to do on their birthdays? 5. What are the most popular birthday gifts for American teens? 6. When teenagers have serious problems, who do they talk to?

H. Writer's Workshop

Answers will vary.

I. Responding to Literature

Answers will vary.

UNIT 8

A. Revisit and Retell

Jonny Moseley: skier, San Francisco, tore ligaments in his knee, sledded; **Terrell Davis:** San Diego, football player, scored five touchdowns in one game, Denver Broncos; **Nykesha Sales:** basketball player, played in an all-boys league, Connecticut, Orlando.

B. Word Work

1. great; 2. shocked; 3. happy; 4. mad; 5. fun; 6. alone; 7. afraid; 8. sad.

C. Grammar

1. won, lost, practiced, needed; 2. went, took, was, fell, told; 3. were, ran, missed, fell, dropped; 4. was, had, wore, looked, went, danced.

D. Test-Taking Practice

Reading Vocabulary: 1. B; 2. D; 3. B; 4. C; 5. A.
Reading Comprehension: 1. C; 2. C; 3. B; 4. D; 5. A.

E. Using New Vocabulary

Answers will vary.

F. Focus on Organization

1. Describes: One day she read. . ., Remembers: I will never forget. . . Feelings: I was really proud! 2. Describes: I worked for three hours. . . Remembers: It was a good experience. . . Feelings: I was so unhappy. 3. Describes: First I played. . . Remembers: I remember that day. . . Feelings: I was excited. . .; 4. Describes: During my first game. . . Remembers: I'm sure my love of. . . Feelings: I was really proud.

G. Focus on Style

Answers will vary. Possible answers. 1. Ramon and I went to a terrible movie last night. It was totally boring, the actors were awful, and the story was stupid. I don't know why we stayed until the end 2. I remember the first time I had Giorgio's pizza. The pizza was so terrific. The crust was crispy and the sauce was spicy. And the people at Giorgio's were friendly. 3. I had a wonderful time at Consuelo's party. The food was fabulous and the music was excellent! But her little brother was annoying. He kept turning the lights on and off.

H. Writer's Workshop

Answers will vary.

I. Responding to Literature

Answers will vary.

UNIT 9

A. Revisit and Retell

1. The Nile River is 4,145 miles long. 2. The Chiang Jiang River is in Asia. 3. The Mississippi River is in the United States. 4. The Chiang Jiang River is 3,964 miles long. 5. The Amazon River is in South America. 6. The Amazon River is 4,007 miles long. 7. The Mississippi River is 3,710 miles long. 8. The Nile River is in Africa.

B. Word Work

1. eighth; 2. third; 3. twenty-first; 4. fourteenth; 5. Forty-second, Eighth; 6. fiftieth; 7. Thirty-third, Fifth; 8. ninth; 9. second; 10. twenty-fifth.

C. Grammar

1. colder; 2. smaller; 3. the smallest; 4. the coldest; 5. colder; 6. taller; 7. the tallest; 8. shorter; 9. the shortest; 10. taller.

D. Test-Taking Practice

Reading Vocabulary: 1. D; 2. C; 3. C; 4. A; 5. B.
Reading Comprehension: 1. D; 2. B; 3. A;. 4. C; 5. A.

E. Using New Vocabulary

Everest: Mountain, Nepal, Highest mountain in the world; Angel Falls: Waterfall, Venezuela, Highest waterfall in the world; Nile: River, Egypt, Longest river in the world; Lake Baikal: Lake, Russia, World's deepest lake; Kilimanjaro: Mountain, Tanzania,

Highest mountain in Africa; Australia: Island (Continent), Southern hemisphere, Largest island in the world.

F. Focus on Organization

1. Topic: The Dead Sea is the lowest place on earth. Facts #1 and #2: The Dead Sea is 1,319 feet below sea level. The Dead Sea is between Israel and Jordan. 2. Topic: The coldest place in the world is Antarctica. Facts #1 and #2: The lowest temperature in Antarctica was −129° F. Ice covers 98% of Antarctica. 3. Topic: The hottest place in the U.S. is Death Valley, California. Facts #1 and #2: The nighttime temperature in Death Valley can reach 100° F or more. July is the hottest month in Death Valley.

G. Focus on Style

Answers will vary. Possible answers: 1. The Alakai Swamp, in Hawaii, is one of the wettest places on earth. In this large swamp there are many unusual plants and beautiful birds. 2. Death Valley, in California, is the hottest place on earth. At 282 feet below sea level, it is also the lowest place in the U.S. Death Valley National Park covers almost 3,400,000 acres and has about 800,000 visitors a year. 3. The Akashi Kaikyo Bridge, in Japan, is the longest bridge in the world. It was completed in 1998 and cost $4.5 billion. The bridge is over two miles long and connects Kobe and Awaji-shima Island. With 928-foot towers, it is the tallest bridge in the world.

H. Writer's Workshop

Answers will vary.

I. Responding to Literature

Answers will vary.

UNIT 10

A. Revisit and Retell

Answers will vary.

B. Word Work

1. help; friendly; warm; difference; beautiful; child; dangerous; wind; long; care.
2. 1. friendly; 2. beautiful; 3. wind; 4. childish; 5. helpful; 6. difference; 7. dangerous; 8. careful; 9. warm; 10. long.

C. Grammar

1. more intelligent than; 2. stronger than; 3. as strong as; 4. more interesting than; 5. better than; 6. as important as; 7. cleaner than; 8. more difficult than; 9. as old as; 10. cheaper than.

D. Test-Taking Practice

Reading Vocabulary: 1. C, 2. B, 3. C, 4. A, 5. D.
Reading Comprehension: 1. D; 2. C; 3. B; 4. A; 5. D.

E. Using New Vocabulary

1. thinks that; 2. believe that; 3. in his opinion; 4. says; 5. believes that; 6. in her opinion; 7. My opinion is.

F. Focus on Organization

1: Should the School Charge a Fine for Returning Library Books Late?
2: Answers will vary. Possible answers: **Opinion:** Students should pay for breaking a rule. **Reason:** It helps them learn the rules. **Opinion:** Students should pay a small fine. **Reason:** Students don't have much money. **Opinion:** Students should get a warning. **Reason:** They can't remember everything because they're too busy. **Opinion:** The librarian should remind students of due dates by email. **Reason:** This teaches students responsibility instead of punishing them.

G. Focus on Style

1. "Be quiet."—Mrs. Torres; 2. "Students should turn in their homework on time."—Mrs. Torres; 3. "Meet me after school."—Juan; 4. "Can you drive me to school?"—Tran; 5. "I'm tired."—Lori; 6. "Ouch! You dropped your book on my foot!"—Tomas; 7. "Please close the window."—Ms. Chang; 8. "I'm going to Mexico next summer."—Carlos.

H. Writer's Workshop

Answers will vary.

I. Responding to Literature

Answers will vary.

References

Armbruster, B.B. (1991). Content area reading instruction. In Cooper, J.D. *Literacy, helping children construct meaning*, 3rd ed. Boston, MA: Houghton Mifflin Company.

Baker, L. & Brown, A. (1984). Cognitive monitoring in reading. In J. Flood (ed.), *Understanding Reading Comprehension* (pp. 21–44). Newark, DE: International Reading Association.

Calkins, L. (1991). *Living between the lines*. Portsmouth, NH: Heinemann.

Chamot, A. & O'Malley, M. (1994). *The CALLA handbook*. New York: Longman.

Chamot, A. & O'Malley, M. (1999). *The learning strategies handbook*. New York: Longman.

Cooper, J.D. (1993). *Literacy: Helping children construct meaning*. Boston, MA: Houghton Mifflin Company.

Cummins, James (1981). The role of primary language development in promoting educational success for language minority students. In California State Department of Education (Ed.), *Schooling and language minority students: A theoretical framework* (1st Edition), pp. 3–49. Los Angeles: Evaluation, Dissemination and Assessment Center, California State University, Los Angeles.

Danielson, L.M. (2000). The improvement of student writing: What research says. *Journal of School Improvement*, 1:1.

Dole, J.A., Duffy, G.G., Roehler, L.R., and Pearson, P.D. (1991). Moving from the old to the new: Research on reading comprehension instruction. *Review of Educational Research*, 61: 239–264.

Duke, N.K. & Pearson, P.D. (2002) Effective practices for developing reading comprehension. In A.E. Farstrup & S.J. Samuels (eds.) *What the research has to say about reading comprehension*. Newark, DE: International Reading Association.

Emig, J. (1971). *The composing processes of twelfth graders*. Urbana, IL: National Council of Teachers of English.

Graesser, A.C., NcNamara, D.S., & Louwerse, M.M. (2002). What do readers need to learn in order to process coherence relations in narrative and expository text? In A.P. Sweet and C.E. Snow (eds.) *Rethinking Reading Comprehension*. New York: The Guilford Press.

Graves, D. (1983). *Writing: teachers and children at work*. Portsmouth, NH: Heinemann.

Hiebert, E. (1999). *Text matters in learning to read*. CIERA Report 1.001. Ann Arbor: University of Michigan. Center for the Improvement of Early Reading Achievement.

Hogan, K. & Pressley, M. (1997). *Scaffolding student learning: Instructional approaches and issues*. Cambridge, MA: Brookline Books.

Jimenez, R.T. (1997). The strategic abilities and potential of five low-literacy Latina/o readers in middle school. *Reading Research Quarterly*, 32, 224–243.

Johns, A. (1997). *Text, role, and context: Developing academic literacies*. New York: Cambridge University Press.

Keene, E. and Zimmermann, S. (1997). Mosaic of thought: Teaching comprehension in a reader's workshop. Portsmouth, NH: Heinemann.

Kintsch, W. (1998). *Comprehension: A paradigm for cognition*. Cambridge: Cambridge University Press.

Klinger, J.K. & Vaughn, S. (2000). The helping behaviors of fifth graders while using collaborative strategic reading during ESL content classes. *TESOL Quarterly*, 34(1), 69–98.

Krashen, S. (2004, April). The phonics debate: 2004. *Language*, 3: 8, 18–20.

National Council of Teachers of English (2004). Beliefs about the Teaching of Writing.

National Reading Panel (2000). Teaching *children to read: An evidence-based assessment of the scientific research literature on reading and it's implications for reading instruction.* Washington, DC: National Institute of Child Health and Human Development.

Padron, Y. (1992). The effect of strategy instruction on bilingual students' cognitive strategy use in reading. *Bilingual Research Journal*, 16, 35–52.

Pearson, P.D. & Fielding, L. (1991). Comprehension instruction. In R. Barr et al (eds.), *Handbook of reading research*, 2: 861–883. White Plains, NY: Longman.

RAND Reading Study Group (2002). Reading *for understanding: Toward an R&D Program in Reading Comprehension.* Santa Monica, CA: RAND Corporation.

Roehler, L. & Duffey, G. (1991). Teachers' instructional actions. In R. Barr et al (eds.), *Handbook of reading research*, 2: 861–883. White Plains, NY: Longman.

Smith, F. (1994). Understanding reading. Hillsdale, NJ: Erlbaum.

Tierney, R. (1990). Learning to connect reading and writing: Critical thinking through transactions with one's own subjectivity. In Shanahan, T. (ed.) *Reading and writing together: New perspectives for the classroom.* Norwood, MA: Christopher Gordon.

Weaver, C. (1996). Teaching grammar in context. Portsmouth, NH: Heinemann.